THE MEANING OF "RELATIONSHIP" IN INTERPERSONAL COMMUNICATION

Edited by
Richard L. Conville
L. Edna Rogers

PRAEGER

Westport, Connecticut
London

Library of Congress Cataloging-in-Publication Data

The meaning of "relationship" in interpersonal communication / edited
   by Richard L. Conville and L. Edna Rogers.
       p.   cm.
   Includes bibliographical references and index.
   ISBN 0–275–95211–8 (alk. paper)
    1. Interpersonal communication. 2. Interpersonal relations.
   3. Communication—Psychological aspects. I. Conville, Richard L.
   II. Rogers, Lilian Edna, 1933–
   BF637.C45M376   1998
   302.2—DC21   97–14472

British Library Cataloguing in Publication Data is available.

Library of Congress Catalog Card Number: 97–14472
ISBN: 0–275–95211–8

First published in 1998

Praeger Publishers, 88 Post Road West, Westport, CT 06881
An imprint of Greenwood Publishing Group, Inc.

Printed in the United States of America

∞™

The paper used in this book complies with the
Permanent Paper Standard issued by the National
Information Standards Organization (Z39.48–1984).

10 9 8 7 6 5 4 3 2 1

Copyright Acknowledgment

The editors and publisher gratefully acknowledge permission to reprint excerpts from V. N.
Volosinov (1973). *Marxism and the philosophy of language* (L. Matejka & I. R. Titunik,
Trans.). Cambridge, MA: Harvard University Press. Used with permission of Academic
Press, a division of Harcourt Brace & Co.

Every reasonable effort has been made to trace the owners of copyright materials in this
book, but in some instances this has proven impossible. The editors and publisher will be
glad to receive information leading to more complete acknowledgments in subsequent print-
ings of the book, and in the meantime extend their apologies for any omissions.

Contents

Introduction   vii

1   Ants to Elephants: A Comparative Perspective on the   1
Meaning of Relationship
Jo Liska

2   Historical Frames of Relational Perspectives   23
John Stewart

3   Relationships and Communication: A Social   47
Communication and Strongly Consequential View
Stuart J. Sigman

4   The Meaning of Relationship in Relational Communication   69
L. Edna Rogers

5   Giddens' Conception of Personal Relationships and   83
Its Relevance to Communication Theory
Robert D. McPhee

6   "But I Thought that We Were More than Error Variance":   107
Application of the Social Relations Model to Personal
Relationships
Sandra Metts

7   Narrative, Dialectic, and Relationships   133
        Richard L. Conville

8   Making Meanings with Friends   149
        William K. Rawlins

References   171
Index   191
About the Contributors   201

Introduction

In looking across the changing landscape in the field of interpersonal communication, one finds a recent resurgence of interest in the concept of relationship, an interest centered less on individual psychological constructs or the traditional sociological meaning of social roles and more on the communication grounding of the concept. The emerging interpersonal emphasis on relationship is perhaps a natural unfolding of the general, theoretical movement in communication from individual units of behavior to process-oriented concerns.

As evidence of the developmental shift toward a relational focus, one can hardly pick up a recent interpersonal text without finding "relationship" and related terms, highlighted by title or purpose (for example, Conville, 1991, *Relational Transitions: The Evolution of Personal Relationships*; Knapp and Vangelisti, 1992, *Interpersonal Communication and Human Relationships*; Birtchnell, 1993, *How Humans Relate: A New Interpersonal Theory*; Erber and Gilmour, 1994, *Theoretical Frameworks for Personal Relationships*; Wilmot, 1995, *Relational Communication*; Galvin and Cooper, 1996, *Making Connections: Readings in Relational Communication*; Baxter and Montgomery, 1996, *Relating: Dialogues and Dialectics*; Vanzetti and Duck, 1996, *A Lifetime of Relationships*). At present, the common, generalized usage of the phrase "relational communication," diffused from its original meaning within the pragmatic, relational communication perspective, is becoming practically synonymous with the term "interpersonal communication."

HISTORICAL ROOTS

"Relationship" has not always enjoyed the prominence and ubiquity it does today. The word does not even appear in Johnson's 1755 *Dictionary of the English Language*. For "relationship," Noah Webster (1828) gives: "The state of being related by kindred, affinity or other alliance," but then, in brackets and italics, he opines, "This word is generally tautological and useless" (n.p.). So, we must conclude that the currency of relationship is a rather recent phenomenon.

Etymological dictionaries are more helpful. *The Oxford English Dictionary* (Simpson & Weiner, 1989) gives, for "relation," (meaning 6.a.) "The position which one person holds with respect to another on account of some social or other connexion between them; the particular mode in which persons are mutually connected by circumstances." For the plural (6.b.) "relations," it records, "the aggregate of the connexions, or modes of connexion, by which one person is brought into touch with another or with society in general." For "relationship," the entry is "The state of being related, a condition or character based upon this; kinship . . . an affair; a sexual relationship" (pp. 550–51).

As for the history of the term's usage, the earliest date *The Oxford English Dictionary* shows for the use of relationship is 1744 in Alexander Pope's lengthy satirical poem *The Dunciad*. The sentence is so innocuous and thoroughly modern-sounding that the word seems to have entered the language fully mature ("Our author let it pass unaltered, as a trifle, that no way altered the relationship.") The sample entries in *The Oxford English Dictionary* run the gamut from Pope's modern sound to the genuinely postmodern, in C. R. Lajeunesse's *Dead Man Running* (1981) "Rowena and I had a relationship at first, which had been a no-strings-attached affair. Then . . . she became serious and I had shied away" (Simpson & Weiner, 1989, p. 551).

The Oxford Dictionary of English Etymology adds, for "relate," the verb form, "give an account of . . . bring into connexion or comparison" (Onions, 1966, p. 753). The *Barnhart Dictionary of Etymology* reports that "relate" is borrowed, through Middle French, from the Latin "*relatus*, a form serving as the past participle of *referre* to tell of, to refer." Hence, a relation becomes "a bringing back, restoring, a report, narration, association, reference" (Barnhart, 1988, p. 906).

There seem to be five implications to be gleaned from these documented usages of "relationship." First, someone, a relational partner or an observer, compares the members of the relationship ("bring into . . . comparison). Second, a difference between the members is observed (implied by the phrase "position . . . [of] one . . . with respect to another"). Third, the members enjoy an association between themselves ("some social or other connexion between them") that may vary in the number of others involved ("with another or with society in general") or in the roles of the partners ("the position which one person holds with respect to another"). Fourth, this peculiar kind of connection can have its origins in the circumstances involved ("persons are mutually connected by circumstances"). Finally, the etymological roots of *relatus* and *referre* suggest that a relationship is the kind of association that is instantiated by talk ("restoring, a report, narration") and that that talk may be of a special kind, that is, conversation that retrieves human connections from memory and restores them to the present, something akin to storytelling.

Dictionaries provide a historical record of usage. The etymological study of relationship suggests these key dimensions of the concept: comparison, difference, association, circumstance, and talk. To what extent do these dimensions provide a basis for today's students of relationship to explore the meaning and use of the term in interpersonal communication? That verdict is left to the reader. Meanwhile, an important criterion, we believe, was enunciated 25 years ago by anthropologist Neville Dyson-Hudson when he said, "the demand of our science is . . . to try to bring our analytical concepts to the point at which our experience is made sense of: not to lop off stretches of our experience in conformity with our limited analytical perceptions" (1972, p. 239).

CONCEPTUAL OVERVIEW

Despite the growing emphasis on relationship in interpersonal writings and research, serious attention to the conceptual meaning of relationship has been more limited. As with other fields of study, central, foundational terms often remain broadly conceived and conceptually illusive. Their usage is commonly invoked in an unspecified, taken-for-granted manner, under the guise that, as primary concepts, their meaning is understood; of course, they are, until we try to define them. Such is the case with the concept of relationship. Out of a concern with the underdeveloped conceptual treatment of relationship and resulting ambiguities in its use, the present effort was undertaken.

The overriding purpose of this book is to explore the meaning and use of relationship in interpersonal communication, and, in this sense, "problematize" the concept. Conceptual meanings do not stand alone; they emerge out of and, in a sense, "ride on the back" of the ontological-epistemological assumptions within which they are, knowingly or unknowingly, embedded. Just as "inquiry is never innocent" (Duck & Montgomery, 1991, p. 7), definitions are never atheoretical.

Thus, the goal of this book is to examine in depth the definitional stance and locus of the meaning of relationship within a broad range of perspectives relevant to the interpersonal area. A conceptual exploration and explication of relationship from a number of different approaches will both clarify and expand our understanding of one of the most frequently used but rarely defined concepts in the interpersonal literature.

A 1992 International Communication Association conference program on the meaning of relationship, organized by Richard Conville, set the idea and tone for this project. Four of this book's contributors, representing related but differing perspectives, outlined the definitional boundaries and conceptual implications stemming from their particular ontological or epistemological approach. With this initial thrust and an expansion of the perspectives included, the present book came into being.

However, cognizant of the many theoretical levels one could occupy for launching such a project, we take to heart Clifford Geertz's (1973) image of the theoretical formulation as soaring bird: able to rise to great heights above one's "data" in flights of "imaginative abstraction" as well as to hover so low over the immediacies of one's evidence as to be "unseverable" from it (p. 24). Thus, the reader will notice that the contributions to this book on the meaning of relationship "float" at, or represent, varying analytical levels, some hovering close to the ground and others tethered more loosely. In expanding our understanding of relationships, the perspectives offered traverse a range of conceptual and empirical concerns from Jo Liska's bioevolutionary view of cross-species, semiotic comparisons to John Stewart's review of the historical and philosophical groundings of relational thinking and speaking; from Stuart J. Sigman's social communication perspective emphasizing the consequentiality of communication to L. Edna Rogers' relational communication, process view; from Robert D. McPhee's critique of A. Giddens' structuration and modernity theories in regard to personal relationships to Sandra Metts' utilization of D. Kenny's statistical, variance-based model for depicting relationship interaction effects; and from Richard L. Conville's relationship-focused narrative analysis of the stories people tell to William K.

Rawlins' examination of the dialectical meanings of relationship uncovered in personal conversation.

OVERVIEW OF THE CHAPTERS

Lest we forget, Liska reminds us that social relationships are not the sole domain of *Homo sapiens*. In doing so, Liska takes us on an intriguing, thought-provoking "safari" into a multispecies-populated world of relationships with the goal of making cross-species, relational comparisons. Our guide for this panoramic view is a system of semiotic distinctions that form a continuum of symbolicity. Based on the degree of arbitrariness of sign relations, the continuum moves from the least arbitrary signs, referred to as "symptoms," to ritualized, and, thus, somewhat abstract, semblances to fully arbitrary symbols. A significant shift in the types of relationship possible rest on an evolutionary break from genetically inherited signs (symptoms) to the realm of ritualized abstractions (semblances). Movement from these evolutionary precursors into the creative world of symbolic sign relationships sets the scene for relational possibilities far removed from the immediate, material world. Liska argues that "the substance and manifestations of social relationships take the form of signs" with the type of relationship "intimately linked to . . . semiotic capabilities." Through a comparative analysis of sign use across species, Liska adds to our understanding by identifying basic elements of social relationships.

The historical perspective given by Stewart takes us back to the Sophists for a philosophical foregrounding of relational thinking in terms of the "twofoldness" of the human world reflected in the central construct of *dissoi logoi*. The implications of a "twofold" world view continue with a discussion of the writings of Martin Buber on the concept of the "between" and M. M. Bakhtin and V. N. Volosinov on the "translinguistics" of "living language." Buber's insistence on the "reality of the between," on the inherent "one with the other" of dialogue, is in close concert with Bakhtin and Volosinov's (1973) idea that words express "the 'one' in relation to the 'other,'" much like a "bridge thrown between" them (p. 86). For understanding the wholeness of human life, Stewart's chapter illuminates the essentialness of attending to speaking, the presentational, constitutive qualities of utterances, which bring our human beingness into being.

Stewart also points out that earlier philosophers struggled with many of the same issues that face relational scholars today in their quest of how to think about relationships relationally. Stewart's chapter extends our vision of the long history of relational thought and accompanying difficulties of breaking the tightly bound bands of traditional, onefold thinking.

Sigman expands the relational foundations outlined by Stewart as he draws on three interrelated perspectives for understanding interpersonal relationships, namely, the vantage points of social realism, consequentiality, and continuity. At the heart of all three are the emergent, constitutive qualities of communication practices. Through the communicative enactments of the participants, relationships are created, sustained, and transformed (consequential view). Yet, the dynamic unfolding of these communication activities and, thus, their relational implications are oriented toward and interpreted within the "constraints and affordances" of the enfolding sociocultural, rule-bound systems within which they abide (social realist view). Further, although engendered in communication practices, relationships as sociocultural forms have an enduring quality that bridges the temporal bounds of interaction enactments (continuity view). In line with the three views, relationships are seen as categories of meaning realized in the members' sociocultural, situated, patterned interactions. Sigman's discussion of these ideas provides a rich line of detailed clarification. His explication of the meaning of relationship offers an integrated, conceptual framework with firm research implications.

The chapter by Rogers is seen as complementing Sigman's consequential view of communication. In the development of the relational communication view of relationship, Rogers, as does Sigman, draws on a legacy of thought emphasizing the centrality of studying communicative processes in their own right as formative, constitutive processes of relationships. Taking a systemic, cybernetic perspective, Rogers outlines an interaction, communication-based conceptualization of relationship and three central, underlying dimensions of interpersonal relations — control, intimacy, and trust. In line with the ideas of G. Bateson on the "patterns that connect," Georg Simmel's emphasis on social form, and Stewart's discussion of Buber (a student of Simmel), the relational view focuses on "the between," the emergent, ecologically embedded, patterns of temporal form, based on the relational implications of the conjoint, communicative interactions of relationship members.

McPhee draws on yet another influential resource for the study and meaning of relationship — that of Giddens and his writings on structuration theory and his more recent analysis of the influence of modernity on personal relations. As McPhee points out, the concept of social agency is central in both lines of work for theorizing a coherent link between social action and the larger, social-structural system. Although Giddens' theoretical structure attends to the recurrent patterns of interaction through which social structuring is "produced and reproduced," what McPhee finds amiss in Giddens' theory is sufficient development of the constitutive nature of these relational processes. In a word, McPhee finds Giddens' treatment of relationships to be "undersocialized." Although not undermining the value of Giddens' work, McPhee, in his highly informative critique, demonstrates that, within both lines of theorizing (structuration and modernity), the classic "individual-society problematic" in sociological theory has not been fully illuded.

The chapter by McPhee provides an integrated and insightful analysis of the ideas put forth by Giddens that have particular relevance to the study of relationships. Importantly, and in line with his critique, McPhee suggests ways for enhancing the relational orientation of these ideas. His chapter brings into clearer focus the theoretical strengths of Giddens as well as some of the more illusive limitations of his work.

Metts expands the range of perspectives taken by utilizing Kenny's social relationship model for both conceptually understanding and empirically identifying the interactive properties of a relationship versus strictly individual qualities of the interacting participants. From this perspective, the meaning of relationship rests on the interdependency of the interactors, a commonly argued necessary condition for depicting relationship. The approach provides a statistical method for indexing the presence of the participants' interdependency and, thus, of relationship.

Application of the model has been limited primarily to the study of interpersonal perception but can be applied, as Metts suggests, to a variety of relational indices, including the study of interpersonal interaction. In this chapter, Metts presents an extensive and useful review of three lines of personal relationship research for which Kenny's model is relevant. For appropriately devised questions and corresponding measures, the social relationship model, as its name implies, is designed to statistically distinguish variance because of individual qualities and behaviors from variance because of the individuals' relationship. In other words, the model allows one to identify qualities unique to the relationship and those unique to the individuals involved. With this model, the concept of relationship is defined in terms of unique relational effects; when no interdependent relationship uniqueness is exhibited, by definition, no relationship exists. In the chapter title, "'But I Thought that We Were More than Error Variance': Application of the Social Relations Model to Personal Relationships," Metts aptly captures what may be problematic for some with this approach. Nevertheless, a strength of the social relationship model is a clear distinction between individual and relationship level properties, a difference that too often is ignored in relationship research.

The chapter by Conville presents a cogently crafted narrative analysis based on James Agee and Walker Evans' (1988) classic documentary *Let Us Now Praise Famous Men*. Drawing on P. Ricoeur's (1971) understanding of discourse, Conville offers a unique rendering of this work for focusing his dialectical-narrative-structural method of discourse analysis on the meaning of relationship.

The focus of analysis is the account of Agee and Evans' first encounter with the overseers and laborers who inhabited the world of Alabama cotton tenantry in the summer of 1936. Conville's hypothesis is that such discourse depicts human relationships and, thereby, sheds light on the meaning of relationship. Using his discourse analytic method, he parses their account into significant episodes (each of which exhibits Ricoeur's four basic traits of discourse), thus, capturing the relational core of the account and, following Ricoeur, delivers it up to the human sciences for study.

The upshot of Conville's study is that three dialectical dimensions marked Agee and Evans' relationships that they formed across race, class, and geographic boundaries: dominant-submissive, compelled-volunteered, and closed-open. The first two dimensions were indigenous to these relationships; the third was conventional, appearing commonly in the literature. Agee and Evans' relationships also were found to exhibit a condition in which normal dialectical oscillation was suspended in the face of relational impasse, a kind of dialectical stasis. Finally, normally independent, the dialectical dimensions marking Agee and Evans' relationships were found to share a common semantic space.

In the chapter by Rawlins, we take yet another turn in the analysis of relationships. Based on a tape-recorded conversation of two adult female friends (and a cat), Rawlins discusses the meaning-making processes of relationship. By reproducing segments of the conversation, Rawlins invites the reader along on an interpretive excursion of enacted and interacting themes and dialectic tensions of friendship engendered by the women in their talk with one another. Out of their discourse flow themes of enjoyment and support as well as hesitance and critical expressions. From Rawlins' engagement with the text and reflections on it, he depicts the two friends' relationship in terms of the dialectic of judgment and acceptance and the dialectic of freedom to be independent and freedom to be dependent.

Eschewing traditional methodologies, Rawlins approaches this dialogue between friends with a minimum of theoretical baggage as well and reports his responses to it as a thoughtful, observant, and somewhat involved onlooker. Moreover, he asks the reader to do likewise, to engage the transcript as he has, by "problematizing" their motives and experiences on their own reading of making meaning and level of involvement with the text.

Amid the mundane conversational housekeeping of a 30-year friendship, played out over an unspectacular meal, the reader will note a relational impasse that the two friends recently experienced and need to resolve. It floats beneath the surface of the conversation at first, hardly seen but clearly present, until it emerges as the dominant topic. To follow closely the friends' deft handling of the strong emotions accompanying this misunderstanding plus Rawlins' insightful commentaries will richly reward the patient reader. That ideal reader is not one looking merely for another "finding" to display, as an ancient hunter might display a prized trophy, but rather, in this case, one who remains open for a somewhat mysterious, uncharted tour of a relationship as it unfolds before one's very eyes.

With this overview as background, we now move to the heart of the text for a full discussion of the array of offerings focusing on the meaning of relationship. Each of the chapters, separately and collectively, expands our understanding and mapping of the conceptual terrain of relationship meaning in interpersonal communication.

1

Ants to Elephants:
A Comparative Perspective on the
Meaning of Relationship

Jo Liska

> And we are biologically grounded in relationships, which operate at all the different levels of our beings, as the basis of our natures as agents of creative evolutionary emergence, a property we share with all other species.
>
> — Goodwin, 1994, p. xiii

There are a number of perspectives from which we can view social relationships. As in the story of the blind men and the elephant, each image is only a piece of the overall pattern. Some perspectives provide closeups of a particular species or species characteristics, and the social sciences typically choose to focus on humans, with emphasis on presumably unique features of human behavior — language, culture, tools and technology, religion, art, and so forth — all aspects of behavior deeply interconnected with the ability to use symbols. Human dependence upon symbols in the formulation of social relationships is highly unusual, if not unique, in the animate world. However, grab a wide-angle lens, drop back a few paces, and note the panorama. Species engaging in a wide range of social relationships fill the scene. Some, like many arachnids, come together solely for procreative purposes, and mother-infant bonds end long before the young are born. Social insects such as ants and bees build organized and diversified networks of social relationships that appear remarkably similar to human social systems, but the similarity is more apparent than real, and the differences lie along a continuum of arbitrariness, which I define as the extent to which relationships are independent of genetic constraints. The behavior of the arachnids and social insects is hard-wired into their genes. For them, adaptation to changing ecological conditions necessarily occurs in genetic recombination. On the other hand, humans have come to adapt by modifying symbolic representations of their social relationships, which, in turn, have allowed for extensive modification of the social environment to suit those symbolic representations. Indeed, arbitrariness appears to be the hallmark of human behavior. Nevertheless, humans, too, are guided by their genetic history, a history that is reflected to varying degrees in other species. It is this relationship among species in terms of arbitrariness of their social relationships with which I am concerned here.

Basically, my thesis is that conceptualization of human social relationships can benefit from observations of the social relationships of other species. Indeed, we cannot know the extent to which human relationships are unique except by systematic comparison with other species. "Although human behavior is human behavior, not chimpanzee behavior nor rat behavior, an understanding of the principles that underlie the evolution and behavior of both diverse and similar species can provide valuable information with important implications for [hu]man[s]" (Gallup & Suarez, 1983, p. 23). Illustrating this thesis will include comparison of the social relationships of a variety of species, and because semiotic systems are so thoroughly intertwined with social relationships, analysis will focus on the types of signs employed in negotiating social relationships by various species, including humans. These differences in semiotic behavior rest along a continuum of semiotic arbitrariness (Liska, 1986, 1993a, 1993b, 1994a, 1994b).

HUMAN UNIQUENESS: FACT OR FANCY?

"[Sigmund] Freud claimed that all important scientific revolutions share the ironic property of deposing humans from one pedestal after another of previous self-assurances about our exalted status" (Gould, 1995, p. 8). Nicolaus Copernicus did not find earth in the center of the heavens where we thought it was; instead, earth was a minute speck in a mass of universes. Charles Darwin firmly grounded humans in a genetic history subject to the same forces of natural selection that wrought all other organisms. Nevertheless, and in spite of a growing body of evidence in support of Darwin's theory, humans persist in their quest to set themselves apart from other animals and from their own genetic history. S. J. Gould (1995, p. 8) concluded that, "although we have yet to make our peace with Darwin, the first revolution of cosmic realignment passed quickly to public acceptance."

Generally, the social sciences have yet to make their peace with Darwin by incorporating bioevolutionary descriptions and explanations into a general theory of human social behavior. "Social scientists, schooled in the idea that humans inherit only a general learning mechanism that absorbs a culture's mores (bad ones now, better ones in a reformed society), resisted the idea of an inherited complex human nature" (Pinker, 1994, p. 3). Natural selection may account for physical adaptations in response to changing environmental conditions, but social behavior is well outside the reach of genetic influence. Social relationships are human constructions — tapestries of patterns woven from symbolic threads. All relationships, from kinship through sexual liaisons to friendships, are defined, enacted, and understood symbolically. Accordingly, scholars in the social sciences trained their focus on the symbolic substance and manifestations of human social interaction. The social interactions of other animals, however, were routinely explained by biological concepts, such as instinct, innateness, and reflex. No contradiction was apparent, because human social relationships, indeed, human behavior in general, is qualitatively different from that of other species. The laws of nature applied to those other species but only in limited instances to humans. In this view, little benefit to understanding human social behavior could be derived from an examination of the behavior of other species.

However, times have changed, and "many aspects of human nature can no longer be glibly written off as products of Western enculturation now that cross-cultural surveys have shown them to be ubiquitous" (Pinker, 1994, p. 3). Moreover, cross-species observations suggest that behavior thought to be species-specific is present to varying degrees in other societies but especially in our close relatives, nonhuman primates. Nevertheless, humans are different from other species in a number of dimensions, and it is those patterns of difference with which I am most interested.

A SYSTEM FOR COMPARISON

Minimally, a social relationship occurs whenever there is interaction between two or more members of the same species. Relationships across species occur also, but they are not within the purview of this discussion. "In the study of relationships attention is directed to what are generally perceived as important functional links between individual interactions and the structure of the group as a whole" (Quiatt & Reynolds, 1993,

p. 90). D. Quiatt and V. Reynolds go on to write that "a relationship serves participants as a two-way repository of information" (p. 92). Clearly, then, sign relationships are integral to this discussion because social relationships are constructed of and understood via sign relationships; thus, sign relationships are the data on which analysis of social relationships depends. "The study of social behaviour is in many respects equivalent to the study of communication between individual organisms" (p. 93).

Elsewhere, I have described three general types of semiotic relationships that depend upon the extent to which those relationships are arbitrary — function independent of genetic constraints (Liska, 1986, 1993a, 1993b, 1994a, 1994b). Those semiotic relations are symptomatic, semblamatic, and symbolic.[1]

Symptomatic relationships, the least arbitrary, are defined by "signs that bear a natural, functional, or physiological relationship to their significates" (Liska, 1993a, p. 18). One's age, height, and bone structure are examples of signs that are symptoms. Other examples include pupil dilation in response to changing light conditions, amount of body hair, and face shape.

Semblances are signs that either resemble the symptoms on which they are based (ritual) or bear a perceptual similarity or resemblance to their significates (iconic). Ritual semblances are the result of exaggeration and transformation of behavior to serve a largely communicative function, which process is typically referred to as "ritualization" (Jolly, 1985). When one "puts on a happy face," one is using a ritual semblance. Bluffs, such as raising a fist, an outstretched hand forming a begging gesture, or pretend or play fighting, are all examples of ritual semblances.

Iconic semblances resemble their referents as in a map of a territory or the blueprint of a building. The smiley face sticker is the iconic counterpart to the ritual semblance of "putting on a happy face." The drawings on cliff faces and cave walls left by ancient peoples frequently represent easily interpreted events (for example, scenes of the coming of the Europeans painted by the San of South Africa) or allow contemporary people to know the species, many now extinct, that frequented the area. On the other hand, some of the drawings are so abstract as to make the referent undiscernible (for example, circles overlaid with dots). "The extent to which the copy matches the original is an indication of the degree of arbitrariness of the sign. Some semblances are so isomorphic with their significates (or, in the case of ritual semblances, with the behaviors on which they are based) as to present a correspondence to reality and these signs are considerably less arbitrary than those copies which are so stylized, abstract, or simplified that the original may be undiscernible" (Liska, 1994a, p. 168).[2]

Symbolic relationships, of which there are several subtypes (proper, conceptual, and syntactic), are the most arbitrary and specify relationships independent of reality. Proper symbols name objects and people, that is, they refer to a specific stimulus or stimulus complex. Their acquisition may be explained by operant or classical conditioning. Conceptual symbols have no external referents and refer to abstract constructions, which mandate explanation via postulating a schema, concept, or "internal mediating response" (Osgood, 1963). Words for such concepts as "justice," "equality," and "fairness" are abstract constructions without counterparts in material reality. Syntactic symbols specify patterns of relationship among symbols (for example, rules of grammar and expressing relationships, such as tense, possession, and function). Syntactic symbols guide us in understanding relationships among events (for example, who did what to whom and at what time). "Symbols allow for the activation of memory independent of sensory stimulation. Indeed, conceptual symbols afford the creation of symbolic realities that could be manipulated and modified in ways that freed its creators from dependence on physical and physiological reality. Moreover, 'symbols afforded the opportunity to characterize, revise, modify, manipulate, and share internal representations of reality for the benefit of self and others'" (Liska, 1990, p. 21; 1993b, p. 389).

The present approach provides a foundation of comparison that avoids pitfalls associated with other approaches, which largely described behavior in dichotomous terms. Over the protests of a few (for example, Tanner & Zihlman, 1976; Tanner, 1981), behaviors, such as tool use and manufacture, culture, language, and so forth, were conceptualized as discrete — one either engaged in them or not. Moreover, definitions and their applications lacked precision and frequently were homocentric. Language was defined in terms of human performance, thereby restricting its use by definition to humans (for example, Dance, 1977). This resulted in thwarting comparisons across species at the onset. If only humans used language, then there was no point to looking to other species' sign systems for clues about human language. Ultimately, humans, the ones doing the defining, eliminated all challenges to their sacred territory of "advancements," such as language, art, culture, civilization, and technology, by defining them in ways that precluded participation by other species. The problem was those pesky chimpanzees who made termite fishing poles and used rocks to crack nuts (tool use?), the orca and songbirds who learn dialects specific to their group (language?), and the elephants who bury their dead (conceptualizing mortality?). How were these observations to be explained?

New conceptualizations emerged to account for these new data, which conceptualizations were grounded in several tenets:

Fundamental to the comparative method is the belief that nature is conservative. A few raw materials, simple equations, and fundamental principles resulted in the plethora of species that populate the planet (for example, Dawkins, 1986, 1989; Gould, 1991). The secret apparently lies in the mixture — the amounts and ways in which those ingredients are combined, which in turn is attenuated by the specific demands of the environment. These demands change over time, thus, producing changes in the mixture that result in new species.

Humans, like all other organisms, are a by-product of evolution. Although humans may be "intellectually gifted," as G. G. Gallup and S. D. Suarez (1983) describe them, those gifts nevertheless find their roots in the intimate relationship of ecological constraints acting upon genetic reproduction over time.

All species are unique; so, humans hold no special place in this regard. The differences appear to be a matter of degree rather than kind. Thus, behavior is seen as continuous, dimensional, and patterned.

Thus far, I have argued that the substance and manifestations of social relationships take the form of signs and, furthermore, that the types of social relationships in which any species engages is intimately linked to their semiotic capabilities. Moreover, I have suggested that those semiotic abilities, and, thus, the social relationships they represent, can be fruitfully described along a continuum of arbitrariness. The succeeding analysis is offered as illustration in support of this chain of thought.[3]

SAPIENS, SIMIANS, SPIDERS, AND SNAKES: SIGNS OF RELATIONSHIP

For some species, like the ants and bees, relationships are constrained by and limited to those specified by the genetic code — they are "hard-wired" into the species. However, for many species, the signs of relationship include semblamatic and, sometimes, symbolic signs. The latter tend to occur in species with long life spans, long periods of postnatal development, and complex social interdependencies necessary to survival. Of course, their behavior, too, is constrained but is not limited to genetic determinants. I have elected to illustrate the various types of signs by reference to a wide range of social relationships, beginning with the case of a two-headed rat snake because it represents the most fundamental, as well as genetically bound, social relationship.

Signs of Kinship

One of the more interesting, and nonarbitrary (genetic), social relationships is that of a two-headed rat snake named IM, the left head named "Instinct" and the right head named "Mind." "Everyone watching IM feed or locomote readily agreed that there was often an obvious conflict occurring between what each of the two heads (that is, brains and minds) 'wanted' to do. In some respects, there was perhaps no better subject than an IM for addressing problems of intention, communication, problem solving, decision making, and the locus of control" (Burghardt, 1991, p. 57). Specifically, locomotor decision making, prey trailing, olfactory arousal, and feeding were analyzed in an attempt to understand the relationship between the two heads. Although sometimes there were differences between the heads in the timing of striking prey, both heads regularly struck simultaneously, and both heads generally tried to consume the prey, resulting in considerably more time to ingest than is typical for nonsiamese snakes. The relationship was one of competition in spite of the fact that feeding time was delayed and the food was going to end up in the same place regardless of which head did the feeding. In noncaptive circumstances, this delay could be critical, because it lengthens the time the snake is vulnerable to predation. Nevertheless, at the age of 14, Instinct and Mind were still in conflict with one another. G. M. Burghardt (1991, p. 61) concluded: "In the case of IM we may be seeing the importance of prior evolutionary history as an important constraint on altruistic and cooperative behavior — constraints holding all mental processes on leashes of varying lengths. All two-headed snakes are monsters with no evolutionary history for dealing with the problems faced by having a siamese sibling. Given the unprecedented problems facing our own species today, IM should not be too quickly dismissed as an irrelevant freak!"

Mother-infant relationships are the foundation on which other kin relations rest. Some mother-infant relationships are purely genetic, as in the case of arachnids who deposit eggs and go off, leaving their offsprings' survival to chance and the law of large numbers. Crocodiles, alligators, and caimans stay with their young until they are sufficiently developed to swim about on their own. Canids (wolves), felines, primates, and elephants tend their young for long periods, and many of those offspring remain with the group for the rest of their lives. These societies are characterized by intense social contacts, the formation of friendships and alliances, and strong mother-infant bonds that are essential to the survival of the infants. Mothers (and aunts, in the case of canids, some primates, and elephants) are the repository of knowledge necessary to survival for infants who are biologically unequipped to fend for themselves. Vervet monkeys must learn the alarm calls appropriate to a series of predators as well as the appropriate response. Tool use and modification in primates and elephants is transmitted largely by females and by mothers to their offspring. Status differences and the appropriate signs for showing respect, deference, and so forth are transmitted from mother to infant. Although status hierarchies change over time and conditions, rank to some extent is determined by the status of one's mother. Thus, awareness of kinship "emerges in the context of rank acquisition, when older monkeys will give place to younger monkeys of senior rank if their mothers are nearby, and in the context of apparent danger to an infant, when its mother is looked to by other adult females for support" (Quiatt & Reynolds, 1993, p. 220).

Bottle-nosed dolphins develop signature whistles used to identify other members of the pod. Males, who leave the natal group at maturity, develop signature whistles similar to their mothers', but females develop whistles that are distinct from their mothers' (Wells, 1991; Tyack, 1991). This male-female pattern in the development of whistles probably acts to limit inbreeding. At maturity, males form groups with others their age but pair-bond with another male with whom they maintain contact for many years. Mature females also form groups, but they leave their natal pod more gradually and later than do males. Daughters maintain close associations with their mothers throughout their lives. R. S. Wells (1991) observed that daughters rejoin their mother's band to raise their young among relatives and with calves of similar age.

The strength of mother-infant bonds in Sarasota dolphins is evident in their behavior when confronted with the death of an offspring. Wells (1991, pp. 58–59) describes one situation:

Losing an infant appears to be stressful for the mother. Numerous reports, both from oceanariums and from the wild, describe mothers supporting dead calves at the surface, sometimes for days. Saida Beth's first calf died within one day of birth. After the death, we found Saida with ten other dolphins, including three mother-calf pairs and her own mother, Melba, traveling slowly north over a seagrass meadow in the northern half of their home range. While we watched, the rest of the group continued north, but Saida and Melba remained. Saida circled in a highly agitated manner, lifting her dead son to the surface, whistling, dropping the calf, then repeating the process every few minutes. Melba fed nearby. After we had watched this behavior for nearly an hour and a half, a pair of teenage males charged into the area, perhaps attracted by the whistling, and chased Saida. After the chase, Saida made no ʳ ʳre attempts to recover the carcass.

Primates, and likely most, if not all, mammals, recognize one another as individuals, the distinctions based on visual, vocal, and probably olfactory cues. Additionally, monkeys and apes recognize the kinship relationships of others (Cheney & Seyfarth, 1982a, 1982b, 1990; Cheney, Seyfarth, & Smuts, 1986; Dasser, 1988). That monkeys and apes, close kin to humans, recognize individuals, their lineage, and their relationships with nonkin may not be particularly surprising, but the ability to recognize kin among species, such as paper wasps, sweat bees, and sea squirts, is likely to raise more than a few eyebrows (for example, Hepper, 1991). Nevertheless, this seems to be the case. Recognition appears to take two forms: discrimination of kin from nonkin on the basis of direct cues, such as physical features, or by indirect means dependent on clues of time and space (Pfenning & Sherman, 1995). For example, bank swallows (*Riparia riparia*) feed any young in the burrow nest they build. Because these chicks are flightless, the chicks stay in the burrow, and the parents appear to assume those in the burrow are their offspring. When the chicks learn to fly, they mix with other species, necessitating recognition by their parents on the basis of more direct cues. Those cues are vocal patterns, "distinct signatures," upon which parents can distinguish their own chicks from others (Pfenning & Sherman, 1995).

Primates recognize kin largely on the basis of di. ⸱t visual and vocal cues. Moreover, they recognize the relationships among members of their group on the same basis. D. L. Cheney and R. Seyfarth (1982a) have demonstrated, on the basis of playback experiments, that vervet monkeys associate the distress calls of particular youngsters with those of that youngster's mother. On the basis of those relationships, aid or assistance is provided among relatives. Moreover, others in the group appear to expect kin to come to the defense of kin. So, for example, if a youngster screams, others in the troop look to the youngster's mother expectantly (Cheney & Seyfarth, 1991). One of my favorite illustrations is provided by S. Strum's (1987) observations of free-living baboons in Kenya. She describes the following scenario: Olive was persistently harassed by Toby, Tina's son. One day, Toby was "strutting his stuff" to almost everyone in the vicinity but especially at Olive. Olive watched Toby intently; then, noticing her older brother Sean in the area, who was larger and dominant to Toby, she screamed bloody murder. Sean sized up the situation and without hesitation taught Toby a resounding lesson.

Kinship relations in humans are based on genetic relationships but overlaid with semblamatic and symbolic signs. Some signs of human genetic relationships are symptomatic and show up in physical similarities across generations. There are exceptions, of course, as in adoption and the joining of genetically unrelated families by marriage. Human lineages are marked by symbolic connections (for example, names). They also are indicated by such semblances as mother-daughter dresses or dressing same-sex children in the same outfits. In Chevy Chase's film *European Vacation*, Chevy's character identified his family connections by making everyone in his family wear identical berets.

Signs of Family Relationships

Elephant societies are matrilineal. Males move from their natal group in their mid-teens and join bachelor herds or become solitary. The females form tight bonds, with alloparenting (aunting) behavior being a significant influence on the development of individuals (Douglas-Hamilton & Douglas-Hamilton, 1975; Moss, 1988). Siblings also play an important role in tending to their younger sisters and brothers. Offspring in the throes of death are carefully tended to by their relatives, but especially by their mothers. Elephant mothers will linger long after their infants have died, and in some instances, family members will attempt to bury them (Douglas-Hamilton & Douglas-Hamilton, 1975; Chevalier-Skolnikoff & Liska, 1985, 1993). On somewhat rare occasions, an elephant family group, generally with at least one lactating female, will even adopt an orphaned elephant.

Elephants use a series of infrasound calls identified by K. B. Payne (1991) and J. H. Poole (1987). In addition to calls used by males in musth, a period of heightened sexual activity, who are looking for mates, some 30 other calls are used to coordinate social activity. Elephants also use a series of audible calls in greeting, as well as tactile engagements, such as intertwining trunks. Many of these tactile exchanges are used in greetings, dominance displays, and play. The reuniting of family groups is an impressive affair characterized by excited and loud exchanges (Chevalier-Skolnikoff & Liska, 1985, 1993).

Most primate societies are matrilineal; however, among chimpanzees (*Pan troglodytes*), it is females who move from their natal group. Chimpanzee groups do not appear to form ranked patrilines, however. Instead, the males form tight bonds, move around together, share mates (in that they are promiscuous), and form hunting parties. Their attention to the infants in the troop generally takes the form of play. Male baboons who form a close association with a particular female later will take on a somewhat nurturing and protective stance with their offspring (Smuts, 1985).

These groups I have mentioned will act as a coordinated unit in defense of their offspring. Countries that practice culling elephant herds to control their population have learned to eradicate family groups rather than types of individuals (old, male, and so on) because the rest of the herd will come to those individuals' defense (Moss, 1988; Chadwick, 1992). Moreover, elephant semiotic systems may be elaborated enough to share information about the threat (for example, men with guns) from group to group. Poachers seeking to capture gorilla and chimpanzee infants typically end up shooting others in a gorilla family or chimpanzee troop because those primates fight together in defense of the infants.

Signs of Sexual Relationships

Mating, subsequent bonding, and the semiotic displays on which mating is based vary enormously across species. Spiders, such as the black widow, enjoy brief encounters frequently ending with the male serving as a meal for the female. A similar situation occurs in insects, such as the praying mantis. Female sea horses deposit their eggs in a specially designed pouch on the male and then swim off, leaving the male to incubate the eggs. Some birds, such as toucans and macaws, are monogamous and mate for life. So too, gibbons maintain monogamous and egalitarian relationships, in that both participate in rearing their offspring and in defending an exclusive territory. Elephants are promiscuous, and adult males do not participate in rearing of the young. A single male gorilla establishes a harem of females; orangutan males maintain a large territory in which several females establish smaller home ranges. Adult male orangutans are generally intolerant of other males and associate with females only for copulation. Adult female orangutans are largely solitary but form strong bonds with their offspring until they are able to fend for themselves (four to five years). Chimpanzee males form strong bonds with one another and mate promiscuously. Females do not form strong bonds with unrelated males or females.

Bonobos (*Pan paniscus*), also known as pygmy chimpanzees, are a rather unusual case. De Waal (1988, 1995) described their social relations as characterized by strong social bonds between females and with male status dependent upon the status of his mother. Mothers and sons remain closely bonded throughout her lifetime. De Waal characterizes bonobos as "female-centered and egalitarian and as one that substitutes sex for aggression. Whereas in most other species sexual behavior is a fairly distinct category, in the bonobo it is part and parcel of social relations — and not just between males and females" (1995, p. 82). Sexual relations, except among kin, occur in just about every partner combination. Further, sexual relations occur more frequently among bonobos than any other primate with the possible exception of human. However, reproductive rates are consistent with the other apes, with offspring born five to six years apart. In terms of relationships, bonobos "share at least one very important characteristic with our own species, namely, a partial separation between sex and reproduction" (p. 82).

The separation between sex and reproduction may be important to the development of the nuclear family in human societies. Human females are sexually receptive without restriction by estrus cycles, which allowed them to exchange sex for male commitment and paternal care. Natural selection would favor this arrangement, because females could raise more offspring with the help of a male than they could on their own. Bonobos do not show evidence of long-term commitment or a nuclear family, but their sexual arrangement is otherwise similar to that of humans.

T. R. Insel and C. S. Carter (1995) conducted a series of experiments on two species of voles (rodents) with dramatically different mating and parenting patterns. The prairie vole is monogamous, with both parents participating in rearing their young. The comparison was with the montane vole, which is an asocial species. They maintain individual burrows, and the males do not participate in parenting or defending their mates. Insel and Carter were particularly interested in the effects of two hormones, oxytocin and vasopressin, produced in the hypothalamus and known to control behaviors, such as sex, aggression, and feeding. Their findings demonstrated the role of each in differentiating voles that form attachments from those that do not. They speculate that these two hormones also play a role in attachments in humans but "mediated by — and perhaps inhibited by — many other factors, especially by the complex activities of our enormous cerebral cortex" (1995, p. 14).

Specific physical characteristics and mating displays are crucial to the process of sexual selection. Many of those characteristics are genetically fixed, as in the plumage of the male peacock and the bright colors of male birds, such as bluejays and cardinals. The complexity of songs in canaries and the sedge warbler is another example. In both these species, females are attracted to those males with complex song repertoires (Krebs &

Davies, 1982). Physical strength, age, size of one's antlers, and so forth are all factors in mating and sexual selection.

Polygynous species (for example, gorilla, orangutan) evidence greater sexual dimorphism than do monogamous species (for example, gibbon). Competition among males of polygynous species is intense, and size and strength are critical factors in sexual selection. Secondary sexual characteristics are also more pronounced among polygynous species. J. Diamond notes that "males and females of the monogamous gibbons look identical at a distance, while male gorillas (befitting their polygyny) are easily recognized by their crested heads and silver-haired backs" (1992, p. 72). The observable differences between men and women suggest polygynous tendencies in humans, although those differences are not as extreme as is found among gorillas and orangutans. The most obvious and unusual sex differences in humans are male body and facial hair, unusually large penises relative to other primates, and large breasts even before a first pregnancy, which is unique among primates.

Human females have some other unusual biological attributes relative to other species: concealed ovulation, constant receptivity, and brief periods of fertility during the menstrual cycle. The reasons for this unusual set of traits are the substance of considerable controversy and seem, to some extent, to depend on the sex of the theorist. Space limits treatment of this controversy, so I direct the reader to D. Symons (1979), S. B. Hrdy (1981), I. Elia (1988), and M. Small (1995). Whereas traditional theory described sexual selection in terms of male choice, more recent conceptualizations emphasize the role that females of many species play in the process (see preceding authors, as well as Tanner, 1981).

Signs of Social Networks

Social insects live in what are probably the most genetically similar and cooperative social networks to ever inhabit this planet. Their social units are characterized by strict divisions of labor, with all involved working on the survival of the unit as a whole. Theirs is the paradigmatic example of socialism and collectivism. They are also, undeniably, one of the most successful orders on the planet. E. O. Wilson (1992, p. 6) describes an ant colony as a:

Superorganism, an assembly of workers so tightly knit around the mother queen as to act like a single, well-coordinated entity. A wasp or other solitary insect encountering a worker ant on its nest faces more than just another insect. It faces the worker and all her sisters, united by instinct to protect the queen, seize control of territory, and further the growth of the colony. Workers are little kamikazes, prepared — eager — to die in order to defend the nest or gain control of a food source. Their deaths matter no more to the colony than the loss of hair or a claw tip might to a solitary animal.

There are exceptions, however. H. Topoff (1994, p. 41) describes ants in the genus *Polyergus*, in which all species "have lost the ability to care for themselves." These ants do not tend to their nests, their queen, or their own defense and food gathering. Instead, they obtain workers — slaves — from a related genus *Formica* to do their chores for them. New colonies of *Polyergus* are rounded by a *Polyergus* queen who invades a *Formica* nest, fends off workers who attempt to attack her, and kills the *Formica* queen. Upon the death of the *Formica* queen, the *Formica* workers approach the *Polyergus* queen and begin grooming her. Based on experiments in such takeovers, Topoff describes the workers as behaving as though they were sedated. What accounts for this strange transformation in their behavior? Topoff suggests that, rather than chemical mimicry, as is found in some animals, it is a "chemical heist" in which the *Polyergus* queen acquires pheromones from the *Formica* queen during their struggle by ingesting her body fluids via bites and licking. Those pheromones make her recognizable to other *Formicas* — she becomes one of them. An ingenious series of experiments supported this explanation.

Some species of ants probably practiced agriculture, animal husbandry, and slave taking long before the rise of mammals some 60 or so million years ago, making the development of similar practices by humans some 12,000 years ago redundant. Indeed, one may speculate that the development of those practices in human cultures may have been influenced by their observations of social insects. In any event, their social systems challenge the prevailing view that "vertebrates are higher on the evolutionary tree than invertebrates, and are therefore more complex in both structure and function" (Topoff, 1994, p. 46). Topoff elaborates:

Yet the behavior of *Polyergus* queen during colony rounding offers perhaps the best illustration that the evolutionary process yields a mosaic of species — often with unique and extremely sophisticated social adaptations — and is not an escalator leading methodically and inexorably to ever greater complexity. Ant societies, with their behaviorally specialized castes, elaborate systems of chemical communication, and huge potential for adjusting to ever changing environments, have evolved levels of social organization that far exceed even those of most vertebrate species. (p. 46)

However, ants do not appear to rebel against the existing system; organize unions of workers with the purpose of obtaining day care, sick leave, and overtime; gain access to desirable resources based on their social standing (save the queen, of course); or manipulate other siblings into doing their work for them, the *Polyergus* system notwithstanding. They also do not keep records of their labors, tabulate productivity, or create systems of exchange and trade with other ant communities. Ants do not hold colony meetings, elect queens or representatives to the queen, or invent laws to regulate social interaction. The laws by which they are governed are those enacted by nature, and the ants have little choice in the execution of those laws. Their semiotic system, like their social system, is written in their genes, and adaptation to changing environmental conditions proceeds by genetic means.

SEMBLAMATIC RELATIONSHIPS:
A CRITICAL JUNCTURE

There is a critical distinction between ants — indeed, social insects in general — and organisms that exercise some voluntary control over their semiotic systems. I have written elsewhere that:

The chemical communication used to structure ant societies is an example of a semiotic system that depends on genetic memory. Ants simply do not live long enough to depend upon a semiotic system that requires extensive learning. Instead they are born to fulfill certain roles in the complex, and to respond to the chemical transmissions of other ants in genetically predictable ways. Yet, their genetically-coded system enables them to construct highly organized and complex societies with remarkable longevity. (Liska, 1993b, p. 385)

Semblances afford the construction of other types of social relationships, ones based on more arbitrary semiotic signs. Semblances suggest a certain amount of voluntary control over semiotic channels (voice, face, body, and so on) and sensory systems, which facilitates constructing and transmitting increasingly abstract, detailed, and arbitrary information. Ritual semblances facilitate social interaction: A. Jolly (1985, p. 196) defines the process of "ritualization" as "an item of social behavior [that] has been subject to selection that has increased its communicative value, in particular, that has made it less ambiguous and more easily interpreted." Play, something apparently foreign to ants, along with tool use and manufacture, are examples of ritual semblances. In both cases, reality is manipulated to suit one's needs. Tool use and manufacture among chimpanzees is a feature of mother-infant relationships in that youngsters learn to use and make tools by observation of and mimicking their mother's behavior (Reynolds, 1994). Using stones to crack nuts and fashioning termite fishing poles out of grass are common among wild-living chimpanzees.

Play, identified by some as the critical distinction between genetically derived semiotic systems and those acquired by learning and experience (Bateson, 1973; Osolsobe, 1986), facilitates social development as well as physical and cognitive development. Through play, friendships and alliances may be forged. Play may well participate in establishing dominance relationships by testing the strength and determination of participants. Play is rather arbitrary in that it is a pretense, an instance of make-believe. "Play is not real, and species who engage in play must have the capacity [at least to some degree] to alter their conceptions of reality, as well as the ability to manipulate their semiotic behavior to communicate those alternative conceptions" (Liska, 1993b, p. 387). Mammals, such as dogs, wolves, and chimpanzees, adopt the "play-face," an open-mouth, relaxed expression indicating bouts of play. Chimpanzees frequently use "finger wrestling" to initiate bouts of play (Goodall, 1986).

Threat displays, the means by which many mammals resolve status, dominance, mating, and territorial disputes, are further illustrations of signs under voluntary control of the individuals who use them. Threat displays frequently are followed, at least among chimpanzees, with conciliatory gestures such as hugging, kissing, and "presenting," additional examples of ritual semblances. Among New York street gang members, rapping, "playing the dozens" (ritual insults), and break dancing are used as means for avoiding physical violence.

The ability to engage in deception is another instance of using semblances to present a view of reality somewhat different from events. Cheney and Seyfarth (1991, p. 131) note that "signals that are not dependent on physiological attributes, but instead function as cues to probable courses of action or the possession of a resource, are at least potentially open to deceit." Semblances allow one to modify conceptualizations of reality and thereby misrepresent it. A vervet monkey involved in a dispute who utters an alarm call when no predator is present is manipulating their own communication system to misrepresent reality to their own benefit.[4]

Instances of deception occur among nonhuman primates (for example, de Waal, 1982; Strum, 1987; Whiten & Byrne, 1988; Cheney & Seyfarth, 1991; Jolly, 1991), in humans (Mitchell & Thompson, 1986), and in other animals, such as death feigning in hognose snakes and the broken wing display of plovers (for example, Burghardt, 1991; Ristau, 1991). Both of these forms of deception require considerable attention to the source of the threat, along with ability to "read" or predict the potential predator's next move. Hognose snakes' and plovers' responses to threatening situations suggest that their responses depend on their assessment of the potential predators' eye gaze direction and duration.

Symbols exponentially enhance our ability to deceive, and one of the best examples of the use of symbols to create a scenario contrary to events comes from the O. J. Simpson trial. Mark Fuhrman used language to deny that he used bigoted language ("nigger") and then used language to invoke the institutionalized privilege to avoid self-incrimination. It is hard to imagine being able to pursue this elaborated deception with a semiotic repertoire consisting of symptoms and semblances.

Deception in response to a threat to self (hognose snake) or offspring (plover) is certainly a reasonable response. However, deception among those with whom one has a long-term relationship is risky. "In close-knit groups of animals, where individuals recognise one another and interact with each other over extended periods, the long-term penalties which may arise if deceit is discovered may more than outweigh any short-term gain it makes possible" (Slater, 1983, cited in Byrne & Whiten, 1988, p. 206). Nevertheless, deception of the sort that rests on manipulation of semiotic signs suggests considerable social awareness — "at least the possibility of intentional falsification of signals and of the attribution of knowledge and motives to others" (Cheney & Seyfarth, 1991, p. 137).

The first break away from genetic constraints and lives ruled by symptoms occurred with the ritualization of those symptoms to semblances, signs that came increasingly under voluntary control, which could be used to act upon the social (and physical) environment. Semblances laid the foundation for acting out stories and for sharing the "norms and traditions of the culture [that] could be told and retold to successive generations and acted as a means for retaining and reinforcing collective memory and history" (Liska, 1994b, p. 246). Iconic semblances in the form of petroglyphs and pictographs on cliff faces and cave walls were relatively permanent records of the beliefs, expectations, activities, and traditions of those who drew them. Those semblances provide those of us living now some insight into the lives of our distant ancestors.

Symbols afforded the opportunity to *create* reality, and a reality not necessarily consistent with events. With symbols, one could consider alternative realities, imagine the future, and even reconstruct the past. Symbols made it possible to develop political and judicial systems for coordinating social relationships, for realizing social roles and expectations, and for contracting mating relationships into what we call "marriage." Cultural diversity is the manifestation of our symbolic inclinations — the manifestation of human groups coping with the vagaries of their social environment. Culture is, for humans at least, largely a symbolic construction.

SIGNS OF CULTURE

The institutionalization of relationships may be the critical difference between humans and other animals (Hinde, 1987). Conventionalization of social knowledge is essential to the evolution of culture and basic to the development of language-dependent institutionalized social relations, although conventionalization of social knowledge is not language dependent:

Language, whatever its behavioral origins, brings to full flower this trend by affording conventional names for concepts and relationships as well as for material things. For individuals striving to maintain and increase their reproductive fitness both in cooperation and, as occasion requires, in competition with their day-to-day interactional associates, precise delineation of social concepts, social relationships, social strategies, and social repositories of knowledge seems so obviously advantageous as to cause one to wonder why only in hominids has there evolved a language extensive and flexible in its capacity for categorizing information. (Quiatt & Reynolds, 1993, p. 209)

The institutionalization of social relationships is manifest in what may be referred to as "culture." This is not to suggest that there is a clear distinction between culture and nonculture and, thus, by implication, between species with and without culture. Although one could, and some have, defined culture in a way that makes it a unique property of humans, to do so here would be to defeat my attempts at discerning the roots of culture in other species, where surely they exist. Quiatt and Reynolds (1993, p. 101) define "culture" as "socially processed information, a definable subset of the environmental (as opposed to genetically encoded) information that is accessible to a given species." J. T. Bonner emphasizes the role of teaching and learning in the emergence of culture:

An animal society is a cohesive group of intercommunicating individuals of the same species. We defined culture as the transfer of information by behavioral means, most particularly by the process of teaching and learning, stressing its difference from the genetic transmission of information. This behavioral transmission is communication. . . . Since both culture and a social grouping are by definition utterly dependent upon communication, it is obvious that the evolution of the social condition will bear a close relation to the evolution of culture. But they are nevertheless quite separable phenomena. . . . A complex social organization does not necessarily mean elaborate culture. Social existence is a necessary but not sufficient basis for culture. (1980, p. 72)

This distinction is clearly illustrated among social insects. They have developed highly organized, complex, elaborated, and successful societies, but they evidence little culture, because shared information is largely transmitted genetically. They do have a rudimentary culture in that the development of castes, providing divisions of labor, progresses by behavioral (pheromone) transmission rather than by genetic means.

Bee dances are largely inherited with the exception of indications of direction and distance (for example, Wilson, 1971; Holldobler, 1977). A bee cannot tell other bees the color of the flowers, their size, or their shape, nor can she report on unexpected conditions, such as about flowers in the back of a pickup moving south on a gravel road. The communication system is largely fixed and inflexible; thus, cultural transmission of information is severely limited.

Birds, such as cuckoos and cowbirds, directly inherit their songs. On the other hand, birds, such as bullfinches, mockingbirds, and starlings, learn their songs by hearing the songs from their parents. These dialects probably help them recognize individuals, especially important in species that maintain long-term pair bonds. Some African shrikes (Thorpe, 1972) provide another interesting example. Males and females sing songs in unison or, sometimes, alternate notes so well that one would think it was a single bird. "Dueting birds are characteristically found in thick forests, and it is presumed that the double song is a way in which they can keep in touch with one another in dense foliage. These duets involve considerable learning during the initial practicing period of the development of the song" (Bonner, 1980, p. 116).

Orca and humpback whales develop dialects that are distinct to their pods. Many of the calls have distinct acoustic patterns. Some of the calls are shared with other, presumably related, pods, but many are so unusual as to discriminate among pods. Both species are matriarchal, and the songs may be ways of distinguishing different lineages for the purposes of mating.

A growing body of research on chimpanzees points up group traditions among wild populations. Tool use and manufacture to harvest and process foods is one of the clearest examples of group traditions that vary across chimpanzee groups. The Gombe chimps fish for termites (Goodall, 1986), and chimps in the Tai forest use stones and rock anvils (Boesch & Boesch, 1983) or wooden clubs (Boesch & Boesch, 1984) to open nuts. However, the Gombe chimps do not open nuts, and the Tai forest chimps do not fish for termites. Tool use and modification may be common in chimps, but group variation is significant in the particulars (Boesch & Boesch, 1990).

Provisioned Japanese macaques on the island of Cayo Santiago developed a number of behavioral innovations disseminated generally by young individuals. Potato washing, wheat rinsing, and a begging gesture developed after provisioning — none of those behaviors were observed prior to provisioning (Kawai, 1965). "Much of the significance of this work lay in the observation that behavior may be modified in the course of utilizing resources introduced into the environment, that the innovators tend to be young animals, and that transmission of innovations within the group begins with close associates" (Thompson, 1994, p. 99).

De Waal (1988) reported the development of a culturally expressed behavior among one group of captive bonobos. The behavior was clapping, which occurred during bouts of grooming by groomers, not groomees. Thompson (1994) observed the behavior in two groups, both groups containing members from the original group observed by de Waal. This behavior is not seen (or heard) among wild-living bonobos or among any other captive group. Thompson noted that those who engaged in clapping were included in grooming sessions more frequently than those who did not clap. Clapping was reinforced by the group until it became a regular feature of their communication system. "However, the remarkable issue as far as evidence for culture is concerned is that the behavior clearly has been transmitted in invariant form to other individuals" (p. 112).[5]

Rudimentary forms of culture — variation in group traditions among species transmitted behaviorally — probably exists in other group-living species with elaborated communication systems (for example, elephants) who experience long periods of youth being dependent upon kin for survival, learning based on multiple methods, and considerable plasticity in neural capacity. The data are difficult to come by, in part because of the limitations imposed by our view of other species through the species-specific lens of our humanness. Nevertheless, it now should be apparent that the roots of our own social relationships are found in the social relationships of other species. That notwithstanding, there is an important difference between humans and all those other species, and that difference is language.

IF YOU WANT TO CATCH A
FISH, THINK LIKE A FISH

In *This Simian World*, Clarence Day (1936) underscores our human proclivities, and especially our fascination with ourselves, by comparing the civilization we have constructed with speculations about what the world would be like if another organism had attained the prominence that humans currently enjoy. Day's discussion focuses on the special attributes of a variety of species and on how those attributes would contribute to the creation of a multiplicity of unique civilizations. Ants would create absolutely unselfish civilizations with intense interest in property, but cat civilization would be "rich in hermits and solitary thinkers" (p. 17). Elephants would create a kind and gentle civilization. Simian civilization is characterized by talk and by inventions that facilitate talk. "So precious to a simian is the privilege of making sounds with his tongue, that when he wishes to punish severely those men he calls criminals, he forbids them to chatter, and forces them by threats to be silent" (p. 23).

Like Day, I have attempted to put perspective on human civilization by comparison with the civilizations found among other species. Also like Day, and others, of course, I must conclude that human social relationships differ dramatically from those of other species in one important way — symbolicity. Based on the data gathered thus far, it would appear that no other species challenges humans' place on the semiotic arbitrariness continuum. However, systematic observations and descriptions of nonhuman behavior are still in infancy, and our place is, therefore, best held with some tentativeness. It may be that the very qualities that characterize us as human limit our ability to understand the lives of other species. Crossing the lines of human languages and cultures may be trivial when compared with the difficulties in understanding the social and communication lives of other species. Nevertheless, the effort expended in trying to bridge the chasm that separates humans from other species is undoubtedly worthwhile, if only for obtaining a more reasonable and humble perspective on our own lives.

Quiatt and Reynolds (1993, p. 119) provide an apt closing: "To be a language-using human being is to think in terms of role expression and of communication as revelatory social discourse. This does not mean that internal or external representation of an objectively realized self cannot be achieved without something like human language; it does mean that human beings must have a hard time thinking about how such representation might be accomplished."

NOTES

1.   Differences among species are real, and a comparative review of the data on nonhuman social and semiotic behavior suggests a number of dimensions on which such behavior appears to differ (for example, cognitive-perceptual, methods of learning, dependence on contextual constraints). Arbitrariness appears to be one of the more fundamental dimensions in that those other characteristics appear to rest on varying degrees of arbitrariness, which is defined as the extent to which a relationship is independent of genetic constraints.

2.   I am aware that the nature of or what constitutes "reality" is the subject of some serious philosophical discussion. In my view, there are multiple realities — biogenetic, cognitive, linguistic or symbolic, and so forth. I have tried to be specific about the kind of reality to which I refer and ask the reader sophisticated in the literature on differing views of reality to indulge my sometimes singular use of the term.

3.   The case for evolutionary foundations of social behavior is more easily made using data gleaned from our close evolutionary relatives, the primates. However, comparison with a broad array of species makes the argument more pointed in that more distantly related species provide an especially good test of conservativeness in the evolutionary process.

4.   A. Whiten and R. W. Byrne (1988) have collated data on what they term "tactical deception" in primates in order to explore patterns and examine functional consequences of deceptive behavior. Based on this analysis, they provide a typology of deception consisting of five major functional classes: concealment, distraction, creating an image, manipulation of target using social tool, and deflection of target to fall guy. The extent to which each type of deception is suggestive of social perception abilities is considered.

5.   A parallel to this case is found in the development of pidgin languages that emerge where two or more distinct languages (and peoples) converge. D. Bickerton (1990), for example, observes that children are the progenitors of the pidgin language.

2

Historical Frames of Relational Perspectives

John Stewart

Among interpersonal communication scholars, the term "relationship" often simply labels the association or involvement between persons that is of research interest. This involvement may be by reason of blood, affection, marriage, employment, ethnicity, or group membership, which means that the scholar may study family relationships, dating relationships, superior-subordinate relationships, intercultural relationships, or some other association. In other cases, however, the term "relationship" carries ontological freight in that it identifies something distinctive about the basic nature of the phenomenon focused on. Here, the term foregrounds the point that the object of study cannot be reduced to any individual party, because the scholar is interested in the association — or, often more pointedly, the associating — itself. In these cases, relationship is understood to be a systemic, irreducibly multiple, polysemous, situated, co-constructed event or phenomenon identifiable separate from the parties who constitute it. When the term "relationship" is used in the former sense, definitional issues may arise about, for example, what constitutes a family, couple, or interracial work group. However, the most difficult and, I believe, the most consequential questions about the meaning of relationship in interpersonal communication are raised when the construct is understood ontologically.

Increasing numbers of communication theorists and researchers are attempting to explicate and apply this ontological focus, often because they are interested in studying precisely that which is common or communal in communication. The fascination with this topic has persisted at least since David Berlo (1960) underscored the importance of understanding communication as "process" in the late 1950s. Berlo's emphasis helped initiate the move by communication scholars away from previously dominant linear, causal, and telementational models (Ogden & Richards, 1923; Reddy, 1979) and toward understandings of communicating first as interactional (Berlo, 1960; Watzlawick, Beavin, & Jackson, 1967) and later as social, dialogic, or relational. Today, this interest in relationship as an ontologically identifiable phenomenon in its own right is evident in such influential books as *Conversational Realities: Constructing Life Through Languages* (Shotter, 1993), *The Dialogical Alternative: Towards a Theory of Language and Mind* (Wold, 1992), and *Social Approaches to Communication* (Leeds-Hurwitz, 1995) and in the presence in the communication theory and philosophy literature of such neologisms as "co-construction" (Jacoby & Ochs, 1995), "transversality" (Schrag, 1992), "translinguistics" (Bakhtin, 1986; Volosinov, 1973), "identity negotiation" (Shotter & Gergen, 1989), and "worlding in talk" (Stewart, 1995).

These odd- and awkward-sounding terms often reflect their creators' and users' convictions that their attempts to think, theorize, research, and write relationally require a radical break from many of the traditions they have inherited. Barnett Pearce and Karen Foss (1987) use the term "new paradigm" to label a version of this orientation, and Wendy Leeds-Hurwitz (1992) characterizes another version as "revolutionary." Partly because these ways of thinking are novel, they sometimes can be confused or confusing. For example, although relational perspectives generally adopt some version of the "social construction of reality" (Leeds-Hurwitz, 1992, 1995), this metaphor can be understood in both "old paradigm" and "new paradigm" ways. From the old paradigm standpoint, to say that reality is socially constructed is to say that individuals informally and formally form dyads and groups in order to instrumentally develop construals of salient elements of the objective world into what counts for the individual or group as "reality." This understanding of the way reality seems to be "socially constructed" maintains the Enlightenment distinction between subjects and objects in that it features Cartesian subjects ("individuals") who operate on objective reality and create interpretations ("social constructions"), the accuracy of which can be tested by correspondence with the reality from which they are constructed. However, from a post-Enlightenment, relational perspective, the social construction of reality metaphor foregrounds the understanding that what counts as real emerges in or is an accomplishment of the group's or culture's verbal-nonverbal articulate contact (Schegloff, 1995; Stewart, 1995; Stewart & Philipsen, 1984). On this view, conversational interaction is considered to be "sociological bedrock" (Schegloff, 1995, p. 187); there are no brute data more primary than language (Taylor, 1985); and the crucial construct "language" is taken to mean speech communicating (Volosinov, 1973; Stewart, 1995), rather than a semiotic system existing separate from its users (de Saussure, 1986). Moreover, this ontological perspective avoids claims that conscious subjects instrumentally operate on ("construct") objective realities.

Inherent ambiguities like these underscore the need for conceptual clarification of relationship, and one particular literature can be an important resource for this conceptual clarification. Although I do not believe that philosophy is the queen of the sciences or that history is our only teacher, I do find in the history of philosophy three narratives that can further inform communication scholars' understanding of what it means to study relationships relationally. The oldest chronicles the struggle between Plato and the sophists. Two others are framed by Michael Theunissen's (1984) influential study of "social ontology." One focuses on Martin Buber's understanding of what he called "the between" and the other on the "translinguistics" of Mikhail Bakhtin and Valintin Volosinov. In all three cases, distinguished philosophers struggled with precisely the problem that faces communication scholars today: how to give a coherent account of the theory and praxis of relational understanding.

RELATIONSHIP IN THE SOPHISTS' *DISSOI LOGOI*

Without Plato and Aristotle, Western humanity's self-understanding would be radically different from what it is, and, without the sophists, there would be no works of Plato and Aristotle as they now exist. In other words, many of the most influential classic Hellenic writings can be fruitfully understood as responsive (Volosinov, 1973) to the sophistic teachers who were their authors' intellectual and academic competitors. Aristotle's *Sophistical Refutations*, *Topics*, and *Rhetoric* grew directly out of his encounters with sophistic thinking, and his views of sophistic writings also surface often in the *Nicomachean Ethics* and *Metaphysics*. This influence is even more marked in Plato's works; as John Poulakos (1995) puts it, "If there is only one preoccupation in the Platonic corpus, it is the sophists and their rhetoric" (p. 74). This is to say that Plato and, to a lesser degree, Aristotle can usefully be read *in relation to* the teachings of Protagoras, Antisthenes, Alcidamas, Gorgias, Prodicus, Thrasymachus, and their sophistic colleagues.

Even more importantly, one primary reason why sophistic thinking has been so strongly resisted, not only by Plato and Aristotle but also by a tradition of prominent authors that can be traced from the fifth century B.C. to the present, is that, in the language of poststructural and postmodern philosophy, the sophists favored difference over identity, while the most influential Hellenic thinkers attempted to develop identity philosophies. As M. Lane Bruner (1996)[1] puts it, "Western metaphysics from Plato on displays an overfocus on identity that leads to an excessive bracketing of difference" (p. 1). Thus, one way to understand the current clash between relational and "psychological," "mechanistic," or "scientific" approaches to communication is as a continuation of this dispute between difference and identity ontologies.

The difference-identity dispute may be understood as an extension of the clash between the Heraclitean view that reality manifests in the phenomenal world, which is in flux and filled with contradictions, and the Parmenidean conviction that, although *appearance* may support Heraclitus' view, *reality* — to be found in the noumenal world — does not. Philosophies of difference focus on the context-dependent, incomplete, often-contradictory nature of the world revealed in human knowledge and discourse, whereas philosophies of identity attempt to construct routes to absolute knowledge and truth and to design strategies and tactics for making language accurately mirror reality. In the fifth century B.C., sophistic thinkers responded to the Parmenidean focus on identity in part by arguing, as did Michel Foucault in the 1970s, that, even when successive utterances or texts speak of "reality," "truth," or "Being," no identities are achieved; rather, as Foucault put it, each "enunciation is an unrepeatable event; it has a situated and dated uniqueness that is irreducible" (1972, p. 101). This belief in the irreducibility of difference brought the sophists in direct conflict with Plato's and Aristotle's insistence on identities that ultimately may produce certainty and closure, or, to shift vocabularies to the one elaborated by Richard Bernstein (1985), the sophists got caught in recorded history's first battle between "objectivism" and "relativism," were misleadingly labeled "relativist," and then were savaged as "skeptics" and "nihilists" by their objectivist critics.

Some recent criticisms of relational approaches to interpersonal communication are marked by arguments heavily indebted to Parmenides, Plato, and Aristotle. These arguments surface, for example, in the claims by self-styled "empiricists" that researchers who view communication relationally represent "a kind of intellectual nihilism in which the possibility of theory construction, let alone reasoned action, is impossible" (Bostrom & Donohew, 1992, p. 109). These are some of the same criteria that Plato and Aristotle used to reject sophistic thinking, and their attitudes toward this thinking dominated Western intellectual history until at least the mid-twentieth century. Partly because of the successes of efforts to rehabilitate the sophists (Havelock, 1982; Guthrie, 1971; Vickers, 1988), Plato's condemnation of them now is taken with a liberal grain of salt. It now is possible to appreciate more of what is of continuing value in sophistic thinking. One feature, I believe, is its relational ontology. In short, I think a case can be made that contemporary relational thinking echoes some of the ontological assumptions of the sophists and that this is one important reason why it is viewed as radically different from, and as a serious threat to, the objectivist, identity-based perspective it purports to critique and, ultimately, to replace. A brief review of sophistic ontology can highlight these commonalities and thereby contribute to an understanding of the contemporary meaning of relationship considered ontologically.

In the second half of the fifth century B.C., a loosely-related group of itinerant teachers became well-known for the ways they helped the political leaders of emerging Greek democracies exploit the importance of persuasion in the coordination of sociopolitical action and the resolution of conflicts. The teachings of the sophists emphasized, as Poulakos (1995) puts it, "the primacy of logos as the medium circulating between human beings and constituting both human beings and the world. In this sense, they can be said to have instituted a new regime whose sympathies and character were neither aristocratic nor democratic but logocratic" (p. 15). The Greek term *logos* is notoriously ambiguous, but to say that the sophistic regime was logocratic is to foreground its focus on linguisticality, meaning, and the negotiation or construction of linguistic worlds or discursive sense in oral-aural articulate contact (Stewart, 1995). Protagoras' insistence that the human is "the measure of" all things was not a claim that reality exists only in human minds but, rather, that "world" or "reality" is a human construct and, thus, an interpretive, that is, a linguistically-negotiated, one. This is not the claim of a solipsist, in other words, but of a thinker who affirms that perception of reality is necessarily perspectival and that humans live in a world not of objects or things but of meanings or, preferably, one of meaning making.

The sophistic understanding and articulation of this ontological claim emerged centrally in "the most characteristic feature of the thought of the whole sophistic period" (Kerferd, 1981, p. 85), the *dissoi logoi*. This term labels both an anonymous text found at the end of manuscripts of Sextus Empirieus and the sophistic teaching that opposing arguments on a given topic can be expressed by a single speaker, "as it were *within* a single complex argument" (p. 84). The construct is attributed to Protagoras by, among others, Diogenes Laertius, but examples of such discourses also appear in Euripides' play *Antiope* and in Aristophanes' *The Clouds*.

Some interpreters of sophistic thinking view treatments of *dissoi logoi* as only pedagogical or narrowly instrumental. From this perspective, sophistic writers were simply acknowledging that any speech coach who wanted to be maximally employable would have to be ready to help a speaker build a case on either side of any important topic. However, an author as serious as Plato hardly would have focused the primary intellectual energy of virtually his entire corpus on a pedagogical technique. This is why more thorough interpreters acknowledge that the *dissoi logoi* construct embodied an important, if not definitive, feature of sophistic ontology. Poulakos (1995) argues, for example, that Protagoras' insight reflects the sophistic conviction that the human world is twofold. Poulakos also connects this notion with Protagoras' claim that the human is "the measure of all things." As Poulakos explains, "In a univocal world, very single utterance would have its place unquestionably, and there would be no need for debate or persuasion — everyone would be listening to and speaking the same logos. But in *the polyvocal world we inhabit*, the status of all things is questionable; and this is why people often find themselves at odds with one another, disagreeing, differing, and seeking to resolve their differences" (p. 58, emphasis added). Poulakos explains that the notion of *dissoi logoi* is central to the sophistic view of competition, a view that emerged from the opposition between the stronger and the weaker, an opposition best managed through playfulness. Similarly, the sophistic view of circumstances emerged from the opposition between the proper and the improper, which can best be managed by focusing on opportunity (p. 57). As these examples show, the notion of *dissoi logoi* turns the practitioner not toward one alternative (stronger, proper) or the other (weaker, improper) but to an understanding of what emerges when the alternatives are considered in tension (playfulness or opportunity).

Poulakos argues that the sophistic notion of *dissoi logoi* is most important because of the status it afforded rhetoric; it provided, he writes, "a worldview with rhetoric at its center" (1995, p. 58). I would emphasize instead the significance of the ontological claim itself. The *dissoi logoi* construct is a primary feature of sophistic ontology. This means that, from a considerable part of the sophistic perspective, "the real" is objectively indeterminable, because the human world is inherently and irreducibly tensional. As M. Heidegger (1959) put it, Heraclitus linked *logos* to *physis* and, "by uniting the opposites maintain[ed] the full sharpness of their tension" (p. 134). As was noted, this perspective emphasizes that the basic human reality is not things but the meanings of things, not object but world. World is always world-of- and world-for-humans, which means that it is inherently perspectival. Because perspectives differ and vary, absolutes obfuscate, and a tensional or relational view is the closest one humans can get to perceiving "the way things actually are."

By all indications, Plato simply could not abide this kind of thinking and speaking. Throughout his "all consuming literary campaign of dismissal and vilification, Plato portrays the sophists as formidable adversaries whom he opposes with all the might that his own ideational project affords" (Poulakos, 1995, p. 74). Plato cast the contest between the sophists' tensional and his own absolute world-view as a battle between rhetoric and philosophy and, in the process, defined each in terms that still dominate much of Western thinking. He offered dialectic, which promised privileged access to certainty (identity), as a replacement for sophistic rhetoric by caricaturing the sophistic ontological claim as a commitment to appearance rather than reality. Plato developed a new set of oppositions completely devoid of the tensionality inherent in the *dissoi logoi*: "One idea rather than myriads of linguistic representations already in circulation; one knowledgeable specialist rather than all the opinionated generalists in the society and one truth above all the deceptions of the world. This was Plato's philosophical stance, a stance suggesting a compensatory project designed to return to order a disorderly world" (Poulakos, 1995, pp. 100–101). As the interpersonal dynamics of Plato's dialogues aptly demonstrate, his thinking was oligarchical if not despotic. One of his goals was to dissuade thinkers from relativist projects and to urge at least an elite to the achievement of closure and certainty.

Aristotle's treatment of the sophists was considerably less vituperative than Plato's, but, at many points, he echoed his teacher's preferences. In *Metaphysics*, for example, he applied the appearance-reality doublet to distinguish between the concerns of sophists and philosophers: "Dialectic is merely critical where philosophy claims to know," Aristotle wrote, "and sophistic is what appears to be philosophy but is not" (1004b.25–26). He also may have been ridiculing the application of *dissoi logoi* when in the *Rhetoric* he advised the speaker to use interrogation when one's opponent "answers 'True, and yet not true', or 'Partly true and partly not true', or 'True in one sense but not in another'," because "the audience thinks [such a speaker] is in difficulties, and applauds his discomfiture" (1419a.14–15). As Poulakos (1995) points out, however, Aristotle relied on exactly this polyvocal form of expression in *Physics* when discussing the ontologically difficult topic of the nature of the "now." There, Aristotle wrote, "The 'now' in one sense is the same, in another it is not the same. In so far as it is in succession, it is different (which is just what its being now was supposed to mean), but its substratum is an identity: for motion, as was said, goes with magnitude, and time, as we maintain, with motion" (219b.13–16). In short, it appears that Aristotle sometimes questioned and sometimes embraced Plato's version of the appearance-reality doublet.

Focused as he is on discourse and rhetoric, Poulakos (1995) concludes his account of Plato's, Isocrates', and Aristotle's responses to the sophists by arguing in part that "the philosophers drive to, push for, or invite closure, completion, and culmination. By contrast, with the sophists there is no truth, no unity, no *telos* [that is, no identities]. When presented with a given proposition, the sophists respond with challenges. For them, rhetorical contests are never finished. In a word, the distinction we have made holds because the philosophers articulated positions [identities] while the sophists provided only *op*-positions [differences]" (p. 189).

Other contemporary writers extend Poulakos' keen insight by emphasizing that the dispute over the efficacy of perspectives that privileges either "the one" or "the many" is about more than discourse or "mere rhetoric" typically conceived. It is an ontological dispute about the nature of being and about the human world, and this means that it is a dispute both about linguisticality and carried out in language. In other words, the theories of language that divided the sophists from Plato and Aristotle are ontologies with profound consequences. This is why so many thinkers — including Plato and Aristotle — are so impassioned about their choices between them.

Literary theorist Wlad Godzich (1994) is one contemporary analyst who notes the ontological content of this dispute. He tells part of the story this way: From the fifth century B.C. until at least the modern era,

There operated a set of identity equations, first drawn up by Parmenides, between being, the world, and language, so that the truth of the world was statable in language and was thus knowable; practical activity (ethical and political) was [thus] properly grounded. These identity equations failed to survive the onset of the moment that Heidegger has called "The Epoch of Worldviews" . . . which operates by means of "images of the world," that is, representations. These representations are discursive in nature and self-consciously provisional since they are legitimated not by the Parmenidean equations but by increasingly more elaborate procedures of verification. This process . . . shatters the stability assured . . . by the identity equations and makes legitimation a constant preoccupation . . . that must be addressed locally and specifically in each instance rather than globally as was the case in earlier times. (p. 138)

Because identity equations now are considered untenable and legitimation is, thus, "a constant preoccupation," Godzich believes that one main challenge faced by contemporary humanity is the necessity of coping with the recognition that "to speak is to construct, to falsify, and therefore to lie, and to tell the truth" (p. 139). In other words, Godzich and other post-Heidegger thinkers argue that all discourse both reveals and conceals, that contradiction and paradox are present everywhere, and that identities are illusory. The sophists hardly could have said it better.

As Godzich implies, the distinctive features of this part of the sophist world view are that human reality is a world of meaning, not a realm of objects and that meaning is negotiated in discourse, and, as a result, not only is human reality tensional, relational, or emergent-and-receding (Heidegger, 1972) but also humans cannot get beyond or behind discourse to some stable, certain realm of "objects" or "absolute reality." I suspect that this basic clash between difference and identity narratives could, indeed, be traced through the history of Western philosophy, just as Godzich claims. However, in order to stay focused on the concerns of communication scholars and to respect the limits of a single chapter, I hope it will be enough to review only two more historical stories, each of which illustrates additional distinctive features of relational thinking.

RELATIONSHIP AND BUBER'S "BETWEEN"

Theunissen's (1984) study *The Other: Studies in the Social Ontology of Husserl, Heidegger, Sartre, and Buber* is considerably less historically inclusive than either Poulakos' or Godzich's accounts. Theunissen argues that the version of relational thinking he labels "social ontology" was independently developed by several influential thinkers between 1916 and 1922, including philosopher Ludwig Feuerbach, Jewish thinkers Hermann Cohen and Franz Rosenzweig, and Catholic philosophers Ferdinand Ebner and Gabriel Marcel (p. 266). Although Theunissen's historical view is much too narrow, he does sharply define several distinctive features of relational thinking, especially as he discusses Buber's writings as "the model text[s]" (p. 266) of relational philosophy construed as social ontology.

Two central features mark this shared line of thinking, Theunissen argues, and both manifest as oppositions to the neo-Kantian philosophy of the universal subject and to Edmund Husserl's account of transcendental subjectivity. The first is that dialogical ontology opposes to the philosophy of the "universal" subject or of "consciousness in general" a beginning in "my factical I, which, in its view, is always at the same time also a human I" (1984, p. 258). Protagoras made the same point when he reminded his readers that the human is the measure of all things.

Theunissen argues that the second claim that dialogicalism opposes is the Cartesian-Kantian argument that reason constitutes reality. As he puts it, dialogic thinkers highlighted the prereflective (prior to reason) feature of human being-in-the-world and substituted correlation for constitution. They argued that "reason itself discovers its 'contingency'; that is, that it, the one who posits everything, is, without its compliance, always already instated in a positing. In this way it discovers the illusion of its own self-foundation. . . . Instead of proceeding from the facticity of the constituter to thematize its relation to the constituted, [the constituter], by sinking into facticity, comes to terms with the 'correlation' that is ontologically presupposed by the former relation" (1984, p. 263). The so-called constituting being, in other words, is not an isolated Cartesian *cogito* relating to objects in the world but a dialogical or "correlational" being-in-relation. In Buber's writings, this insight is most directly developed through the construct of "the between."

Buber's basic insight about the ontological priority of the between was expressed first in the initial words of his classic work *I and Thou* (1970), which he completed in the spring of 1922. Moreover, as he later explained, most of Buber's voluminous writings between 1924 and his death in 1965 unpack and elaborate the ontology sketched in the first eight sentences of *I and Thou*. These first sentences read,

1. The world is twofold for humans in accordance with our twofold orientation.

2. The human orientation is twofold in accordance with the twofold nature of the primary words humans speak.

3. The primary words are not single words, but combined words (word-pairs).

4. One primary word is the combination I-Thou.

5. The other primary word is the combination I-It; but this primary word is not changed when He or She takes the place of It.

6. Thus the I of the human is also twofold.

7. For the I of the primary word I-Thou is different from that of the primary word I-It.

8. Primary words do not signify things that might exist outside them; by being spoken they establish a mode of existence.[2]

A claim that was revolutionary in 1922 is embedded in the first sentence. There, Buber asserted that a large group of historically prominent thinkers had overlooked a profoundly important fact about human beings. Specifically, all those who, especially since Descartes, had been wedded to subject-object analyses of the human being had mistakenly maintained that, for humans, the world is "onefold." According to these thinkers' subject-object perspective, the only way humans orient-to, or come into relation with, their world is as subjects-connecting-with-objects. However, Buber insisted that this perspective overlooked another mode of human being, the second "fold" of the human's "twofold orientation." Not only do humans orient to their world in subject-object ways, but, "alongside and in tension with this subject-to-object directed consciousness of something, [Buber] discovered a primal capacity of [the human] for a consciousness-*with* another that is in its pure form objectless" (Clark, 1976, p. 6). Thus, Buber's elementary-sounding, apparently straightforward first sentence makes a radical ontological claim. Interestingly, according to some recent commentators, this argument that subject-object analyses overlook an important feature of human being suggests that this part of Buber's philosophy could be termed "postmodern" (McCarthy, 1987; Silverman, 1990).

A second, much less widely recognized but equally important claim appears in the second sentence of *I and Thou*. Here, Buber asserted that both "folds" of this twofold orientation are embodied or manifested in speech. Those who would understand human life in its wholeness, he argued, need to focus not on Max Weber's "society," Sigmund Freud's "unconscious," B. F. Skinner's "behavior," or even Gregory Bateson's "interaction" but on the "word pairs" the speaking of which manifests the human's distinctive way-of-being, or, more accurately, the speaking-and-hearing that does this. As Buber (1965a) clarified at the end of the monograph laying out his philosophical anthropology, his program was different from those proposed by Immanuel Kant, Georg Hegel, Karl Marx, Feuerbach, Friedrich Nietzsche, Heidegger, Søren Kierkegaard, and Max Scheler in that he focused not on the "individual" or on the globally "social" but on "the between" (p. 203), the realm he later called the "interhuman" (1965b, pp. 72–88). Buber acknowledged that this realm or sphere was "conceptually still uncomprehended" (1965a, p. 203), but he also argued that it was "a primal category of human reality" and the place where his "genuine third alternative"[3] to prior accounts of the human condition "must begin" (p. 203). One primary feature of Buber's "between," then, is that it is concretely communicative; for him, "the between" occurs paradigmatically as address-and-response, oral-aural articulate contact, speaking-and-hearing.

A third important claim embedded in these first eight sentences of *I and Thou* was that this primal speaking-and-hearing does not point to or represent some external reality; rather, the speaking-and-hearing itself brings this reality into being. As Buber put it in sentence eight, "by being spoken [these words] establish a mode of existence." This assertion reflects Buber's commitment to what I have called a constitutive rather than representational view of the nature of language (Stewart, 1995). This view of language, which has been developed by, among others, Heidegger (1971) and Hans-Georg Gadamer (1989), begins from the claim that language is more than a system of signs and symbols that somehow represent referents, concepts, meanings, or ideas. Language is presentational or constitutive; it is the way humans co-construct the worlds we inhabit. This view treats language as event rather than system and emphasizes how human worlds are brought into being in conversation or dialogue. In other words, like the sophists' original insight articulated as the notion of *dissoi logoi*, this view of language effaces the distinction between "language" and "communication" and highlights the world-defining and world-modifying function of conversation or dialogue.

To summarize, the first eight sentences of *I and Thou* articulated in a very compact way three important contributions Buber made to a philosophical understanding of the construct, relationship. The first is that, at least in the twentieth century, this construct can be grasped only when one escapes the limitations of Cartesian-Kantian subject-object thinking. Relationship cannot be understood simply as an association that a *cogito* or subject intentionally establishes with some separate feature (thing or person) of its external world. Second, relationships occur paradigmatically as speech communicating. Of course, humans can and do also relate silently (Buber, 1965a, pp. 24–28), but for humans, oral-aural address-and-response is the paradigmatic site of relating or the most characteristic way of accomplishing relationship. Third, this address-and-response functions constitutively, that is, in talk (conversation, dialogue), humans build (rebuild, raze, modify) worlds. This claim is echoed by contemporary communication theorist Lee Thayer (1989) when he writes, "We literally 'say' our worlds into existence. . . . A way of talking about the world is a way of *being*" (p. x).

Shortly before he died, Buber wrote "Replies to My Critics" for *The Library of Living Philosophers* volume dedicated to his work and collected 18 brief stories or "fragments" in response to the editors' request for an intellectual autobiography (Buber, 1967). Because each story tells an event of contact, the fragments subsequently were published as a book entitled *Meetings* (Buber, 1973). Fragment nine is called "Vienna," and it, along with a portion of the "Replies to My Critics" essay, contains some of Buber's most direct elaborations of his construct "the between."

In "Replies to My Critics," Buber (1967) acknowledged the legitimacy of questions raised about "the between" by literary critic Philip Wheelwright and philosopher Marcel. The construct is vague, the critics asserted. Marcel complained that it could not be defined in an "arithmetical or geometric" language, and that, as a result, it seemed "mysterious" (p. 707). Without disagreeing about the difficulty of clarifying the construct, Buber explained how he discovered the necessity of the construct, "the between" if one is accurately to describe one of the most commonplace of events. "I proceed from a simple situation," he wrote.

Two [people] are engrossed in a genuine dialogue. I want to appraise the facts of this situation. It turns out that the customary categories do not suffice for it. I mark: first the "physical" phenomenon of the two speaking and gesturing [people], second the "psychic" phenomena of it, what goes on "in them." But the meaningful dialogue itself that proceeds between the two [people] and into which the acoustic and optical events fit . . . this remains unregistered. What is its nature, what is its place? My appraisal of the facts of the case cannot be managed without the category that I call "the between." (p. 707)

It is difficult to determine how to think or talk about a phenomenon that has neither psychic nor physical existence. However, it may be possible to indicate something of what Buber appeared to notice about dialogue by closely examining what happens in serious conversation.[4] When two persons talk, there seem at first to be just two locations for the relevant phenomena of which each is aware. Each speaker more or less fully notices what seems to be "in" him or her, as well as what seems to be there where the other is. However, perhaps there is more.

If one attends as a participant to the understanding that often develops in such conversations, it becomes apparent that this understanding is not simply one's own but is open to the other's active shaping. So long as I listen closely to the other, as one who is not-me, my interpretation and developing understanding meet the other's verbal and nonverbal talk in fruitful interplay. A critic could insist, does all this not occur simply "in" my mind? Buber would respond that there seems to be more to the event than this. The understanding is certainly very different from my own thought, in that it is mine-as-guided- or mine-as-led-by-the-other. The position of the listening-responding event is neither wholly "in" me nor "in" the other but "between."

At least two components of any actual speech situation underscore the presence and significance of this between. First, the words that are spoken are meaningful to a substantial degree because of the inheritance from generations of previous speakers who spoke and heard them. Genuine listening and speaking permit the language itself, which the partners do not simply possess as words and rules but inhabit as a living autonomous whole, to contribute to the sphere in which speaker's words and listener's responses meet. Second, the conversation is always in relation to something being talked about, and the meeting is always itself situated in time, place, and circumstance. Gadamer (1989) speaks of these aspects of the facticity of speaking as "tradition," "play," and "*die Sache*" or the subject matter. They all enter into the communication event, and not just on one side or the other as physical or psychic events but concretely in the verbal-nonverbal exchange, as contributors to the speaking-listening-responding event between the interlocutors.

Moreover, speech addressed to a listener finds its meaning not in any dictionary but in the living understanding that is aroused between speaker and listener in situation. Further, the listener experiences the meaning of speech as unfinished, so long as he or she continues to listen to the interlocutor. The speaking seems alive between the partners; it is not a set, fixed thing but a pointer to something in reality that the listener has not yet recognized or acknowledged. This sense persists as the careful conversation continues.

In the Vienna fragment, Buber belabored the potentiality and world-constituting sense of the between by describing three settings in which he experienced it: some seminars in which he participated at the University of Vienna, performances of the Burgtheater in the same city, and a garden conversation between "two market wives taking a rest" (1973, p. 32). Space permits a discussion of only his experience in the theater.

Buber described the crucial events there in this way: Seated in the student section in the highest gallery, he was most moved by the "rightly" spoken human word, which in the play consisted of dialogue among the characters spoken as if they actually inhabited the world of the play. "It was only a matter of time, however, until — as always happened — someone fell for a while into recitation, a 'noble' recitation. Then, along with the genuine spokenness of speech, dialogical speech . . . this whole world, mysteriously built out of surprise and law, was shattered for me — until after some moments it arose anew with the return of the over-against" (1973, p. 31).

Buber seems to be reporting that, in the dramatic tension between characters in the play, he experienced the potency of the rightly spoken word to create something quite specific between two persons: a "whole" world. As I noted earlier, this observation was highlighted in the eighth sentence of *I and Thou.* Many years before writing that book, Buber discovered in the Burgtheater that speech can be adequate to the task of constituting a human world. In the play, it is obviously a world of fiction that the viewer sees as fiction, but if it is not *the* real world, it is, nonetheless, really a world. In it move and play all the human forces of value and emotion, necessity and meaning.

The form of Buber's experience of the world-constituting word in the theater is significant. When the curtain went up and he could attend to the events on the stage, he noticed from that "world of fiction as fiction" below, the rightly spoken word. Furthermore, that world depended on the "spokenness" of the word, that is, on the word that is really addressed to and meant for a present partner. The world of the play, "mysteriously built out of surprise and law" through the spoken word, was shattered for him when the word spoken on the stage was not meant for another character but was performed or recited as something in itself or as a self-aggrandizing performance ("recitation"). In another essay, Buber (1965a) clarified this difference between world-building and world-shattering speech when he distinguished "turning toward" from "reflexion." Turning-toward the other, he wrote there, is "the basic movement of the life of dialogue," and its opposite is not "turning away" but "reflexion." Reflexion is a subject-object event; it occurs when one is captivated within one's own consciousness and withdraws from the contact with otherness. In reflexion, one "lets the other exist only as [one's] own experience, only as a 'part of myself'" (p. 24). On the stage, speech that was genuinely addressed, speech that manifested turning-toward, built the world of the play, whereas speech uttered out of reflexion shattered it.

Buber evidently believed that, in the act of perceiving the play in the Burgtheater, he had perceived the essence or nature of speech in the human world. This human world, the real-for-us world, is present as such just through our oral-aural articulate contact. The knowledge we have in common of the world we have in common may be communicated as the ordinary function of speech. However, each such speaking, if we really address another person, reveals another aspect of "world." Therefore, each real speech event constitutes an "agon," a situational tension between what I mean and what you mean. For Buber, human or anthropological reality is to be found where the world of one's immediately given experience endures in tension with the world of his or her partner in speech (cf. *dissoi logoi*), for the moment of the I-Thou relation. The human reality upon which language is built is my-world-meeting-your-world. This reality becomes a common possession, with all its tensions recognized and unresolved. Buber sensed that speech directly addressed to and meant for a particular present person invites and makes possible a response in which the language abilities of both persons coalesce in the re-creation of the word spoken so that its meaning includes the horizons, the potentialities, and the limitations of both its speakers (cf. Gadamer's [1989] "fusion of horizons"). Buber calls this happening "the true actual-ity of the *Geist*, as a 'between.'"

The insight that pervaded much of Buber's thought was that, whatever human being is, it proceeds from a primal sound-meant-for-another. This conviction deepened in his later years and was continuously refined and tested in his writings about psychotherapy, Arab-Israeli relations, adult education, Jewish studies, and philosophical anthropology, but it always retained its experiential base. He could point to its happening in such events as a seminar, play, or casual conversation, but it never became a fixed concept. The co-construction of the between is the movement in which both the coming-to-be of language and the coming-to-be of the human are latent. Its place of happening remains also incompletely conceptualized. It happens between humans, in the sphere of the spoken-ness by which one person means another as his or her immediate partner.

THE RELATIONALITY OF LANGUAGE IN VOLOSINOV'S *MARXISM AND THE PHILOSOPHY OF LANGUAGE*

Had Theunissen been writing a decade later, he might well have added Bakhtin (1986) and Volosinov (1973) to his list of early twentieth-century thinkers centrally concerned with social ontology or the phenomenon relationship. Bakhtin's "translinguistics" and Volosinov's account of language as "response," both of which appeared less than ten years after Buber's *I and Thou*, can be read as complementary versions of a similarly relational understanding of language and communication. The text attributed to Volosinov and published in Leningrad in 1929 as *Marxism and the Philosophy of Language* contains a particularly well-developed and relatively compact expression of this relational orientation.[5] Both the dialectical structure of the argument and the metaphors and italicized phrases that mark the book's content embody Volosinov's understanding of relationship. In recognition of this work's fecundity, I conclude this chapter with a brief close reading of *Marxism and the Philosophy of Language* as a third historical narrative that can contribute to the current meaning of relationship.

This book consists of three parts, the first of which, according to the author's introduction, is designed "to substantiate the significance of the philosophy of language for Marxism as a whole" and *"to bring out the position that the philosophy of language occupies in the Marxist world-view"* (Volosinov, 1973, pp. xiv–xv). Part II is an "attempt to resolve the basic problem of the philosophy of language, that of the *actual mode of existence of linguistic phenomena"* (p. xv). These chapters contain Volosinov's most explicit account of the relational nature of language. Part III continues the book's progression from general to particular by focusing on one specialized issue, the problem of "reported utterance" or "speech about speech," such as that which occurs in a novel when the narrator reports what a character has said. Although this topic initially might appear marginally important to all but those interested in literary theory, Volosinov explained that he chose it precisely because it embodies the central feature articulated in Part II: reported utterance "interorients" two persons' speech and is, thus, a concrete instance of the relational or dialogic nature of language. Thus, the book as a whole is a tightly orga-nized discussion that moves from a general perspective on political philosophy[6] to an explicitly relational account of the nature of language and then to an application of this account to one issue in literary practice. I focus here on the philosophy of language and quote liberally in order to underscore the similarities between this narrative and the ones by the sophists and Buber.

Volosinov began this discussion with a straightforward identification of its ontological significance: "What, in fact is the subject matter of the philosophy of language? Where are we to find it? What is its concrete, material existence like? By what method or methods can we come to grips with its mode of existence?" (1973, p. 45). He responded to these ques-tions by working dialectically to contrast his relational view with *"indi-vidualistic subjectivism"* and *"abstract objectivism."* He acknowledged that he would not provide any "conclusive definition" of language but would proceed empirically, not led so much by "the intellectual faculty for making formulas" but rather by "the eyes and hands attempting to get the feel of the actual presence of the subject matter" (p. 45). He rejected, however, the *"superficial phonetic empiricism"* that dominated most of the language sciences, partly because this approach missed "the very essence of the thing we are studying" (p. 46). Living language is much more complex than phonetics acknowledges, he argued, and the primary features of its complexity are that it is context dependent and social.

Individualistic subjectivism, Volosinov claimed, was epitomized in Wilhelm Humboldt's works in which the basis of language is considered to be "the individual creative act of speech. The source of language is the individual psyche" (1973, p. 48). From this perspective, language is an unceasing creative activity (*energeia*), governed by laws of individual psychology. Proponents of this view believed that accounts of the language system only capture "the hardened lava of language creativity" (p. 48). Although this critique was apt, the individualistic subjectivism they embraced as an alternative was problematic.

The second trend of thought, abstract objectivism, treated language as a system of phonetic, grammatical, and lexical forms. "If, for the first trend, language is an ever-flowing stream of speech acts in which nothing remains fixed and identical to itself, then, for the second trend, language is the stationary rainbow arched over that stream" (Volosinov, 1973, p. 52). From this second perspective, individual creative features of speech were "totally unimportant. What was important was precisely the *normative identity*" of language forms (p. 53).

Abstract objectivism was rooted, wrote Volosinov, in Cartesianism and in Gottfried Leibniz' conception of universal grammar. As he put it, "In somewhat simplified form, the idea of language as a system of conventional, arbitrary signs of a fundamentally rational nature was propounded by representatives of the Age of the Enlightenment in the 18th century" (1973, p. 58), and the most influential proponent of this view in the 1920s was Ferdinand de Saussure.

In the next chapter, Volosinov asked to what degree the kind of language system that de Saussure studied could be considered a "real entity?" Because such a system may be said to exist only from the point of view of the subjective consciousness of an individual speaker, this system could not be the essential mode of existence of language. *"What is important for the speaker about a linguistic form,"* Volosinov argued, *"is not that it is a stable and always self-equivalent signal, but that it is an always changeable and adaptable sign"* (1973, p. 68). In other words, the author's italicized argument contends that understanding language is not a matter of recognizing its acontextual identity but acknowledging its polysemous and, ultimately, context-dependent novelty.

Like both the sophists and the philosophers Theunissen calls "dialogical," Volosinov focused on the basic reality of language-as-it-is-lived in the utterance. At one point, he described his primary interest as the "linguistic consciousness of the speaker and of the listener-understander, in the practical business of living speech" (1973, p. 70). Later, he characterized his object of study as "language in the process of its practical implementation" (p. 70), which on the next page is paraphrased as "real-life practice in social intercourse" (p. 71) and "living speech as actually and continuously generated" (p. 71). As can be heard in these descriptions, Volosinov's focus is consistent with what Theunissen (1984) calls dialogical philosophers' interest in the "factical, human" person.

As Volosinov moved away from system and toward utterance, he clarified that the real-life, practical phenomenon on which he wanted to concentrate was, like Buber's, dialogic, not monologic. As Volosinov put it, the idea of monologic utterance, which was the favored object of inquiry in most Indo-European linguistic thought, is an abstraction, for one crucially important reason: it overlooks the discursive context to which utterance is a response. This feature of responsiveness emerged as pivotal. As Volosinov explained, "Any monologic utterance, the written monument included, is an inseverable element of verbal communication. Any utterance — the finished, written utterance not excepted — makes response to something and is calculated to be responded to in turn. It is but one link in a continuous chain of speech performances" (1973, p. 72).

These sentences argue that the central weakness of most language study is that it effaces the inherently relational or dialogic quality of every utterance. Volosinov highlighted the empirically obvious point that no utterance is purely and simply generated *ab initio*. Each is responsive to something the utterer has heard, read, or remembered. He concluded his criticism of philological analyses with these words: "The result of all this is a fundamentally erroneous theory of understanding that underlies not only the methods of linguistic interpretation of texts but also the whole of European semasiology. Its entire position on word meaning and theme is permeated through and through with the false notion of passive understanding, the kind of understanding of a word that excludes active response in advance and on principle" (1973, p. 73). This claim about the inherent centrality of response is the heart of Volosinov's dialogic or "translinguistic" perspective.

Marxism influenced Volosinov's concern with the material conditions of each utterance, the most important of which, Volosinov argued, was its addressee. The existence of an addressee is what renders utterance as a phenomenon "constructed between two socially organized persons" (1973, p. 85), that is, co-constructed. Volosinov emphasized this point in language, which further underscores his relational focus:

Orientation of the word toward the addressee has an extremely high significance. In point of fact, *word is a two-sided act*. It is determined equally by *whose* word it is and *for whom* it is meant. As word, it is precisely *the product of the reciprocal relationship between speaker and listener, addresser and addressee*. Each and every word expresses the "one" in relation to the "other." I give myself verbal shape from another's point of view, ultimately, from the point of view of the community to which I belong. A word is a bridge thrown between myself and another. If one end of the bridge depends on me, then the other depends on my addressee. A word is territory shared by both addresser and addressee, by the speaker and his interlocutor. (p. 86)

Almost as if to remove any vestige of remaining doubt, Volosinov summarized his understanding of the nature of language in these words: *"The actual reality of language-speech is not the abstract system of linguistic forms, not the isolated monologic utterance, and not the psycho-physiological act of its implementation, but the social event of verbal interaction implemented in an utterance or utterances.* Thus, verbal inter-action is the basic reality of language" (1973, p. 94).

As with each of the previous narratives, this emphatic claim substan-tially effaced a distinction that had been central to semiotics, linguistics, philology, language philosophy, and even much of rhetoric since those disciplines were invented: the distinction between language and speech communication (for the latter, Volosinov's translators sometimes write "verbal interaction" or "language-speech"). Students of language in what became several different academic disciplines had focused for centuries primarily on the abstract system or objective residue of human meaning making that is generally labeled language. However, the actual reality of language, argued Volosinov, is the event of aural-oral articulate contact (in his words, "verbal interaction implemented in an utterance or utter-ances"). Language, in other words, consists most basically of events of speech communicating.

Volosinov emphasized that the concrete form of this actual reality is dialogue. By dialogue he meant "not only direct, face-to-face vocalized verbal communication between persons, but also verbal communication of any type whatsoever," including the reading of a book (1973, p. 95). The essential feature of each instance of dialogue is response. *"Any utter-ance . . . is only a moment in the continuous process of verbal communi-cation,"* which, in turn, is "only a moment in the continuous, all-inclusive, generative process of a given social collective" (p. 95).

CONCLUSION

The project undertaken by the contributors to this volume continues a tradition of thinking about human communication that can be traced at least to the fifth century B.C.E. This is not to say that we are simply rein-venting the wheel. The meaning of relationship in the year 2000 cannot simply echo what Protagoras meant by *dissoi logoi*, Buber meant by the between, or Bakhtin and Volosinov meant by translinguistics, but the meaning options available to contemporary communication scholars are historically influenced. As a result, it would be well for those of us who want to study relationships relationally or to focus on that which is common or communal in communication to consider the degree to which our work might be guided by this history.

The three narratives reviewed here echo several common themes. The first is that the phenomenon called language functions ontologically, not simply epistemologically. The sophists, Buber, and Bakhtin and Volosinov agreed that humans co-construct worlds discursively and paradigmatically in oral-aural address and response. They concurred that the apparently uniquely human activity of meaning making occurs in speaking-and-listening. Those who describe this definitively human process as simply an epistemological one in which humans instrumentally use language to symbolize or in some other way to represent material objects that have been constituted otherwise or elsewhere cover over the world-constructing function of address and response.

A second theme is tensionality or plurivocity. Relational phenomena cannot be described in identity equations. Because they are collaboratively[7] accomplished, they are inherently context dependent and emergent, different now from their status even an utterance ago. Relating or a relationship can certainly be characterized and described, but not exhaustively or as a static fact.

A third theme is praxicality. The sophists attended to talking as it was actually happening in Greek society; Buber noticed the concrete reality of the between at the university, the theatre, and the public square; and Volosinov strove to describe living language rather than its residue. In the terms of one vocabulary, these three narratives affirm that relationality is a material fact of human living. Although conceptually still uncomprehended (see the second theme), the between is still necessary if one is to give a full account of any concrete instance of human articulate contact.

With an eye and an ear attuned to the three narratives reviewed here, communication scholars might ask ourselves, our colleagues, and our students the following questions:

1. Do we understand ourselves to be studying a world of meaning or a realm of objects? Is the ultimate focus of inquiry some aspect of a detachable, impersonal realm or of a socially constructed world? Is the basic reality potentially discoverable or irreducibly interpreted?

2. If it is socially, dialogically, or interpersonally constructed, then is it also necessarily communicational? Is discourse, conversation, or what Gadamer (1989) calls language the bedrock of the human world?

3. If it is, then is one primary feature of all discourse or communicating its ontological dynamic, its function as world defining or identity negotiating?

4. Moreover, if the human world is co-constructed discursively, is tensionality one of its primary characteristics? Was Heidegger (1972) right that Being is always both emerging-and-receding? Are human realities, as Buber might have put it, fundamentally between, affected by the other's active shaping? Is all utterance, as Volosinov argued, response? Might we, therefore, conclude, as Godzich (1994) argues (following Nietzsche), that "to speak is to construct, to falsify, and therefore to lie, and to tell the truth" (p. 139)?

5. What implications emerge from this tensional, communicative ontology? Are all understandings of communication (theories, research findings) incomplete, and does each conceal even as it reveals? If so, does this constitute a profound justification for critical theorizing and for what some critical theorists call deconstruction (Derrida, 1978; Lyotard, 1988)?

6. Less radically, must students of relationships-understood-ontologically acknowledge in their thinking, research designs, and theorizing that relationship cannot be adequately comprehended from within a subject-object paradigm and that hypostatizing this phenomenon distorts it, because it is event more than structure or object? Are communication studies most appropriately studies of this event?

Readers may derive additional questions from these narratives. Minimally, however, it should be clear that many of the intellectual forebears of both those who contributed to and those who will read this volume have attempted to study relationships relationally and that we can be informed by their efforts.

NOTES

1. Although he is only cited once, M. Lane Bruner has contributed substantially to this chapter. I have drawn important insights from our conversations and his writing.

2. My translation. Both translators of *I and Thou*, Ronald Gregor Smith and Walter Kaufmann, render *das Man* as "man" and *Verhalten* as "attitude" rather than the less-psychologistic "orientation." Smith's translation also obscures the constitutive claim about speaking in sentence eight.

3. Buber argues that the two prior alternatives, broadly speaking, are individuality (Freud) and sociality (Marx).

4. This analysis draws liberally from Allen L. Clark (1976). Clark was a doctoral candidate at the University of Washington when he died suddenly in 1975. His dissertation in progress included an analysis of Buber's account of the

between in the Vienna fragment. Allen's writing partner, Helen Martin Felton, and I edited his work into the manuscript cited as Clark (1976).

5.   The translators' preface to the 1986 edition of *Marxism and the Philosophy of Language* and related scholarship explain that this work is one of a group of more than a dozen interconnected articles and books published in the Soviet Union between 1925 and 1934 whose authorship is disputed. The works emerged from a loosely structured literary circle whose membership included Pavel N. Medvedev, Volosinov, and, by far the best known of the circle, Bakhtin. Volosinov is identified as the author of the Harvard edition of *Marxism and the Philosophy of Language*, despite the fact that several scholars believe Bakhtin was primarily responsible for this work. There are enough similarities between the positions developed in this work and those articulated in works signed by Bakhtin that it is probably most accurate — although awkward — to consider the author to be Volosinov and Bakhtin. The relationality of this identification would probably delight Bakhtin.

Many scholars accept V. V. Ivanov's 1973 claim that the work was written by Bakhtin. Bakhtin's U.S. biographers, Katerina Clark and Michael Holquist, agree with Ivanov that Bakhtin was responsible for "ninety percent of the text of the three books in question" (*Marxism and the Philosophy of Language*; *Freudianism: A Marxist Critique*, also published under Volosinov's name; and *The Formal Method in Literary Scholarship*, attributed to Medvedev). There are reports of private conversations in which Bakhtin's authorship was corroborated by Bakhtin himself, his wife, and Volosinov's wife. Clark and Holquist (1984) also note that, at least up until the breakup of the Soviet Union, the official Soviet publishing agency (VAAP) required that Bakhtin's name appear on any new edition of the disputed volumes, and they argue that these instances of "reverse plagiarism" may be attributed to Bakhtin's love of conversation, his conviction that "meaning is always a function of at least two consciousnesses," and that "texts are always shared" (p. 151).

Although Bakhtin was still alive at the time of Ivanov's original assertion, he never made a public statement accepting or denying it. In addition, when the VAAP urged Bakhtin shortly before his death to sign an affidavit concerning the authorship of these works, he refused. Tzvetan Todorov (1984) concludes that Bakhtin probably did not write all the works in question. I. R. Titunik (1984) concurs and argues that there are textual data to refute the argument for Bakhtin's authorship of several works, including a distinct lack of cross-references and important terminological differences among key concepts in the writings attributed to each of the three authors. Following translators Matejka and Titunik (Volosinov, 1973), I will generally refer to the author as Volosinov.

6.   This was both a politically necessary move to make in order to publish work during the Stalinist era and a conceptually integrated philosophical move.

7.   Collaboration simply means co-laboring. This is obviously different from agreement. Prizefighters collaborate on many matters, as do plaintiff and

defendant, labor and management, and nation-states at war. Every utterance, without exception, is collaborative in the sense, as Volosinov noted, that it is responsive, framed by its addressee(s) and that which preceded it.

3

Relationships and Communication: A Social Communication and Strongly Consequential View

Stuart J. Sigman

This chapter draws on "social communication theory" (Sigman, 1987; see also Birdwhistell, 1970; Leeds-Hurwitz, 1989; Fogle, 1992; Winkin, 1981) as the conceptual basis for the study of interpersonal relationships. Social communication theory represents an informed alternative to psychological theorizing about communication processes — informed in the sense that it is acknowledged to be deliberate and an alternative in the sense that it is "incommensurable" (cf. Garfinkel & Wieder, 1992; Pearce, 1989) with more traditional communication theories that emphasize the cognitive and affective characteristics of individuals as these impact on or are impacted by communicative behavior. Social communication theory focuses on both the social-cultural communities that form the bases of behavior (cf. Hymes, 1974) and the multiparticipant, interactive character of communication (Sigman, 1995a, b). Its basic unit of analysis is not "senders" and "receivers" who communicate about internal states, out of which relationships develop, but the social collectivity and, so, views interpersonal relationships as social and cultural episodes that "draw in" community members for their performance and instantiation.

Three understandings about relationships are offered in this chapter. The first and the third concepts derive from social communication theory as articulated in S. J. Sigman (1987, 1991; also see Kendon & Sigman, 1996). The second represents a complement to social communication theory and is described in Sigman (1992a, 1995a, b) as the theory of communication consequentiality. The three understandings are as follows:

1. The social realist view. Relationships are said to exist in a community's semantic and syntactic space; they are categories of meaning derived from an ongoing social-cultural repertoire. This repertoire provides the underlying logic for the production and interpretation of behavior and, thus, for the relationships that emerge from (exist within) communication.

2. The consequential view. Communication activities are derived from, but are not neutral adherents to, the aforementioned social-cultural repertoire. Communication activities have a dynamic of their own that is not strictly explained by the community's rule system. There is an emergent quality to each communication interaction. Persons, whose behavior is both constrained and permitted by the community's rule system, produce behavior that accomplishes, negotiates, and orients to the social-cultural categories of their relationships and that is responsive to the here-and-now contingencies of interaction. Relationships exist within a dialectical tension between the community's standard repertoire for behavior and each moment of interaction.

3. The view toward continuity. As suggested, social-cultural forms, such as relationships and institutions, are the embodiment of a community's behavioral repertoire (as per the social realist position above) and activity invoking that repertoire (as per the consequential view). Nevertheless, social-cultural forms are not ephemeral but are sustained across discrete communication episodes. Communication researchers must consider how the limits of face-to-face interaction are transcended, that is, how the scope of particular relationships is predicated on the past and projected onto the future and, in this way, is not confined to any one interactional moment.

The chapter is oriented to developing these three insights into relationships as communicative constructs. First, the social communication and consequential views are discussed as part of a general framework for the study of communication. This discussion lays the groundwork for the second and third sections, which apply the two views to the specific study of interpersonal relationships. The second section considers the social foundations of relationships, specifically the components of the social-cultural repertoire that define various types of relationships. The third section acknowledges the real-time conditions in which relationships exist and, so, considers the creative or consequential role of communicative behavior in shaping these conditions and the emergent relationships. Finally, the fourth section raises a question about the longevity of inter-personal relationships: how is relationship continuity built from the behavior invoking the social-cultural repertoire?

A GENERAL APPROACH TO THE STUDY OF COMMUNICATION

The discussion begins with a brief overview of selected tenets of social communication theory (Birdwhistell, 1970; Sigman, 1987) and the theory of communication consequentiality (Sanders, 1995; Sigman, 1995a, b). Three primary ones that are foundational for a subsequent consideration of relationship as an analytic concept follow.

Communication, as an academic discipline, involves the study of the characteristics and consequences of messages, not the characteristics of people.

People and their relationships are constituted and engendered by messages.

Communication, as an actual in-the-world activity, is decisive in the creation of social-cultural institutions; it is, thus, strongly consequential.

The first principle argues that the academic discipline of Communication[1] must take the nature of "meaning," "message," or "information" as its analytic starting point. This suggests that social structure, personality, cognition, and culture are not the phenomena to be studied by Communication scholars — except as they are construed to be categories or phenomena of meaning. The basic unit of Communication analysis is meaning, what G. Bateson describes as a "difference which makes a difference" (1972, p. 453), and the root problematic of a Communication discipline concerns how it is that meaning comes to be. As Jo Liska and Gary Cronkhite (1995) write: "In the proceedings of the New Orleans Conference . . . the basic description of the heart of the discipline of [C]ommunication was a focus on messages. We believe that at that time they should have included the word 'should'; that is messages SHOULD be the focal point of the discipline" (p. 61).

This starting point for Communication analysis recognizes the autonomy of the communication system, that is, its nonreducibility to the actions of a single individual and especially to an individual's cognitive or affective states. Although meaning is subject to community-specific grammatical constraints and affordances, it is produced in and during moments of situated behaving. It is, thus, a feature of conjoint action, that is, the coordinating behavior of multiple participants. Referential and subjective approaches to meaning are replaced by a Communicational view, which sees meaning as located in people's publicly displayed and coordinated behavior with each other. The "endogenous organization of [communication] activities replaces meaning as reference and/or subjective experience, an analytic maneuver strongly influenced by and reminiscent of the later Wittgenstein" (Matoesian, 1993, p. 47). In this view, meaning is produced in and through ongoing interaction and resides in the interactional rather than psychological arena.

The second principle of social communication theory derives inexorably from the first. This principle states that the same meaning orientation that defines the discipline as a whole must be used to explain personhood. It explicitly rejects an "essentialist" position that a person is composed of self-contained features like personality in favor of one that sees a person as the embodiment of semantic and syntactic features derived from and related to community membership. This principle, thus, reverses the traditional association said to hold between people (communicators) and communication, in which communication is conceived as the output of an already existing and freestanding person. From the social communication view, in contrast, human beings are independent neither of the behavioral resources (communication channels and grammars) made available to them by their communities nor of the interactive, meaning-generating processes that make use of these resources. Indeed, from this view, persons are organized clusters of meaning, continuously produced in and through a community's behavioral processes. As R. E. Pittenger, C. F. Hockett, and J. J. Danehy offer: "It is treacherously misleading to think of language and other communication systems as cloaks donned by the ego when it ventures into the interpersonal world: rather, we think of ego (or 'mind') as arising from the internalization of interpersonal communication processes" (1960, p. 223). In this view, persons are the products, not producers, of communication.

One significant contribution of social communication theory derives from its dual concern for the historically given behavioral resources that permit meaning to emerge in interaction and for the actual moment-by-moment processes that produce meaning (see Leeds-Hurwitz & Sigman with Sullivan, 1995). Classical social communication theory, although recognizing that persons and their identities are interactively constructed, places the social-cultural repertoire (with all its constraints, prohibitions, and entailments) that establishes the categories toward which these interactive or constructive processes are oriented at the center of its analyses. I have previously stated this position thus: "An individual member of society is . . . a *moment* in that society, a moment that has a recognizable (patterned) location in the group's process and structure" (Sigman, 1987, p. 101). This does not deny the possible role of biology, individual psychology, or cognitive or affective functioning in the lives of people, but it, nevertheless, highlights the role of communication and a transsituational social-cultural repertoire in constituting and sustaining personhood.

However, the role of ongoing communication processes in human affairs can be pursued further, leading to consideration of the third principle. In extending and modifying traditional social communication theory, Sigman (1995a) proposes that Communication scholars focus their attention on the consequentiality of communication. This is defined as the study of those dynamic features that enable communication to play a decisive role in social-cultural life. Further, "*consequentiality of communication* means that *what* transpires during, within, and as part of persons' interactive dealings with each other has consequences for those persons. Those consequences come from the communication process, not the structure of language or the mediation of particular personality characteristics or social structure" (1995a, p. 2; see also Sigman, 1995b). Although the first two principles above emphasize rules and their processual implementation, the third principle suggests that communication episodes pose emergent interactional and coordination problems for the participants to resolve. Communication does not merely involve the participants' adherence to social-cultural rule systems but also constitutes a process with its own dynamic and structure on each occasion.

In other words, the communication process is considered to be robustly consequential to the constitution of social and cultural institutions. Such institutions do not exist "prior to" or "outside" communication but, rather, are products of ongoing meaning-making processes (cf. Pearce, 1989). These meaning-making processes themselves influence and are a powerful generative force in social and cultural life. The communication process is not a neutral conveyance mechanism for social-cultural rules and structures but itself actively organizes and locates these structures.

Directly contributing to this notion of consequentiality is a distinction drawn by R. E. Sanders (1995) that has wide application to concerns about identity and relatedness. Sanders differentiates "weak" and "strong" views of communication consequentiality. In the weak version, communication is considered the vehicle for conveying information to others about persons' identities and relationships. "[C]ommunicative acts that provide information about such qualities are said to play an important, but not an essential and certainly not a formative, part in the creation of social arrangements among people" (p. 115). In contrast, the strong version of consequentiality attends to the formative character of communication: "[C]ommunicative acts do more than convey information . . . ; the enactment of role-identities depends on aspects of communicative acts that lie below the surface: the relevance relations between them and their presuppositions" (p. 115). Especially relevant is the idea that identities and relationships, because they are interactionally produced and situated, cannot exist prior to or separate from communication (nor from, in Sanders' view, the interpretive foundation that continually emerges during conversation).

In brief, social-cultural rules are necessary, but not sufficient, features of communication. The communication process exerts its own influence on the meaning that is cogenerated by participants in interaction.

A SOCIAL COMMUNICATION
VIEW OF RELATIONSHIP

A definition of relationship that is consistent with the above social communication and consequentiality frameworks would propose it as a category of meaning that requires patterned behavioral construction (communication) on the part of community members. This category of meaning is derived from the social-cultural heritage; it identifies people (that is, defines identities for them), the associations between and among the defined people, and the rights and responsibilities of these people across space and time. A relationship is, thus, not an entity from which communication emanates but a location in the ongoing behavioral stream (cf. Birdwhistell, 1970). It is communication that produces and sustains a relationship.[2]

With persons derived from communication, rather than being the initiators or sources of communication (see above; Thomas, 1980; Sigman, 1987), it is then also the case that the relationships shared by persons are to be viewed as themselves created, constituted, and sustained (or dissolved) in and through communication. This position does not deny the role of affect or intrapersonal psychology in the lives of people, but it, nevertheless, places in the forefront of Communication consideration that relationships are ongoing behavioral processes shaped by community expectations and conduct rather than being fixed entities or states (cf. Hopper & Drummond's [1991] review of "message-extrinsic" and "message-intrinsic" studies of relationships). Relationships and relationship labels are shorthand descriptions for particular, community-specific patterns of behavior; they are not independent of such behavior or of the communication process more generally. Consistent with the above discussion, a Communication approach views relationships as derived from a behavioral repertoire of behaviors and situated communication activities. As K. L. Fitch and Sanders (1994) suggest, the negotiation of relationships takes place within an existing framework of cultural and social constraints about persons, power, and relationships.

It is important to recognize that, with identities and relationships viewed as categories of meaning, there is no clear one-to-one correspondence between biophysiological entities, on the one hand, and the social-culturally significant entities that are said to enter into and form relationships, on the other hand. The temptation to see each living body as the potential anchor ("end," according to Goffman, 1972) for one or more relationships with others must give way to emic studies of those situated behaviors that define people as appropriate members of particular relationships. A priori theorizing about the nature of relationships must be replaced by empirical consideration of who, in particular communities, may form relationships and how. Questions about the constitution and membership of relationships inevitably depend upon an emic, community-based understanding of the identities of those who may enter into sanctioned associations with others. For example, in certain traditional Chinese families, when a young lady dies before marriage, her family may try to arrange a betrothal with a local male (Yang, 1945). The survivors act so as to turn the deceased female into a bride by leaving her picture, a silk scarf she may have worn, or some other artifact near a roadside shrine. In this fashion, they act as good relations who are concerned with the marital welfare of female family members. The young man who happens upon the artifacts and who subsequently agrees to the arranged marriage is eventually allowed to marry another woman but must also remain respectful of the first wife, for example, by commemorating the anniversary of her death. (See also Kligman, 1988, for a comparable illustration.) In other words, each community establishes criteria for the assumption of relationship status by biological entities.[3] In the Chinese example, then, even a deceased female may form part of a relationship.

The Chinese example points to a further aspect of relationships, specifically, their multiparticipant organization. Birdwhistell (1970, 1977) is credited with suggesting that the dyad is an unstable arrangement for social groups. In part, because communities benefit from and hold a stake in particular relationships, their members (that is, the community's membership as a whole) may play a role not only in establishing categories of relationships but also in becoming involved actively in relationship construction and maintenance (cf. Slater, 1963). There is, thus, an organization to the "partials" (behavior units) contributed by different persons to the overall integrity of each relationship. For example, marital pairs are sustained by the husband and wife as well as by friends, family members, representatives of religious and governmental institutions, and so on.

In brief, then, a relationship can be thought of as a "communicative achievement" (Rawlins & Holl, 1987; see also Hopper & Drummond, 1991). A relationship represents a particular category of meaning, distinguishable from other such categories within some target community's repertoire, and is behaviorally or processually constituted by the conduct of multiple members of the community.

Three Orders of Human Communication

Despite the assertion that relationships exist in behavior, the above discussion is not intended to equate relationships with (face-to-face) interaction. Social communication theory rejects the view that "talk," "conversation," and "discourse" represent the building blocks of relationships (cf. Owen, 1987). Although it is true that talk, conversation, and discourse — when viewed as behavioral genres — are partially the media through which relationships are formed and maintained (or transformed and terminated), it is also the case that the behavioral units and their structural arrangements that engender face-to-face interaction are not the same as those that engender relationships. Different "orders" or organizing rule systems are proposed by social communication theory for interaction and relationship (Sigman, 1987, 1991).

Human communication can profitably be seen to be composed of three behavioral domains: the interaction, social, and semiotic orders. Each order consists of rule sets for particular aspects of behavior: "The interaction order provides a structure for face-to-face discourse; the social order for the social division of labor and responsibility; and the semiotic order, the grammar of particular channels of communication — indeed . . . what constitutes a channel for a particular community" (Sigman, 1987, p. 61). The interaction order consists of those codes that enable communicators to enter, maintain, and exit both focused and unfocused interaction (Goffman, 1963, 1972). The social order is composed of those rules for the use of behavior to construct, maintain, and modify identities, relational groupings, and institutional affiliations. The semiotic order covers the structure of each communication channel, that is, the codes that establish grammatical and ungrammatical utterances or performances of a particular channel. Although the three orders partially overlap (that is, a unit of real-time behavior may be shared by rules from two or more orders), they are not hierarchically or otherwise related. Each defines its own relevant behavior and the structuring principles for that behavior.

From this perspective, the behavior of face-to-face interaction and the behavior of social relationships are governed by different rules — those deriving from the interaction and social orders, respectively.[4] The components of interaction and their arrangements are incapable of building up to a relationship between two or more people. Take greeting as a category of behavior. Although it is certainly the case that relationship comembers may greet each other, the rule for it qua greeting ritual involves such considerations as how persons coordinate access to face-to-face interaction with each other (Goffman, 1972). A greeting is "larger" than any single relationship type, and, at the same time, the work it accomplishes is more "focused." People in a wide variety of relationships engage in greeting behavior, and there are rules for producing a recognizable greeting that are distinct from those rules for communicating the relationship status of the participants. Although formality of relationship may be constituted by syntactic and lexical choices made during the greeting (Ervin-Tripp, 1972), these choices are not definitional of greeting.

Instead of considering interactional behavior as constitutive of relationships, it is preferable to consider the "multifunctionality" of real-time behavior units (cf. Sigman, 1987). A single unit of behavior (for example, the slot for an address term) may be shared across orders and, thus, serve multiple functions. The behavior is multifunctional in that it is organized by, and derives its meaning from, rules from more than one of the orders. In this sense, the performance of a greeting may convey both relational and interactional messages because various subunits derive from different orders.[5] Again, however, it must be noted that only some of the "shared" subunits may be definitional of the greeting itself.

A clear illustration of the difference between face-to-face interaction (the interaction order) and relationships (the social order) can be found through an exploration of the concept of "continuity" (Sigman, 1991). Face-to-face interaction moments comprise relatively apparent initiation and termination points (colloquially referred to as "greeting" and "leave-taking" behaviors, respectively; cf. Kendon & Ferber, 1973) and markers for the integrity of each constitutive moment (especially the topic-related and proxemic behaviors that sustain attentiveness to the interaction and one's fellow interactants; cf. Goffman, 1972; Kendon, 1977, 1978). Social relationships have different initiation and termination points: the beginning of a new conversation may not represent the beginning of a new relationship, and, similarly, saying good-bye to a relationship comember (for example, one's colleagues at the end of the work day) does not terminate that relationship, just the time period in which copresent accessibility (being "at work") existed.[6]

Sigman (1991) offers a category scheme involving three behavioral functions that permit relationship members to construct the ongoing character of their relationship in the face of various physical (interactional) separations: "1. prospective behavior occurs among relationship members in anticipation of an interactional hiatus; 2. introspective behavior occurs within the period of an interactional hiatus, during which the relationship members act in consideration of the relationship as an ongoing and intact entity; and 3. retrospective behavior is produced subsequent to an interactional hiatus" (p. 124). All three behavioral functions recognize relationship members' orientation to an ongoing relationship despite a projected, current, or previous physical separation and, thus, clearly demonstrate the independence of the interaction and social orders.

Thus, the segmentations of interactional episodes and social relationships are not parallel or contiguous. First, relationships make use of different aspects of behavior from face-to-face interaction for marking their ongoing integrity. For example, topic sequencing and proxemic face-formation do not keep a relationship going, because they do not yield the strategic moments or definitions that sustain or transform the relationship; rather, they are features of interaction. In this regard, W. F. Owen (1987) suggests there is a distinction between "conversational influence attempts" and "relational influence attempts." What accounts for this difference is not a particular utterance itself (its surface linguistic features) but, rather, which rule system structures an utterance; the two communication orders are internally constituted by, and generate, functionally contrasting behavior units. Second, relationships generally continue beyond, and are not bound by, any one interactional moment. Interactional separation does not necessarily yield relational cessation or hiatus. Thus, different explanatory structures are needed to account for the organization of face-to-face interaction and interpersonal relationships.

As human beings symbolically (communicationally) connected to others, we engage in two types of relationship with people (cf. Goffman, 1983). The first type of relationship is the one that social scientists traditionally study: the interpersonal or societal relationships we have with others (for example, friend, colleague, spouse, therapist). This is the primary focus of this chapter. The second type derives from a person's face-to-face interactional dealings with others, the aforementioned interaction order. Speaker-hearer, questioner-answerer, lecturer-audience, and so on are relationships of the second type. For ease of distinguishing the two types, I refer to the first as an "interpersonal" or "social relationship" and to the second as an "interactional relationship."[7]

To summarize the discussion to this point, this chapter proposes that, as a Communication concept, relationships are to be seen as patterns of behavioral enactment that are community specific and that depend upon a logic of development separate from that for face-to-face interaction. Alternatively put, the interaction and social orders generate different types of relationships. Social communication theory contrasts with both a psychological framework that places emphasis on individual goals and affect as they are held to determine people's attachments to each other and a sociological framework that views relationships as categories or locations within a social structure to which people respond with their actions. Relationships are seen as categories of meaning that establish identities and associations for persons and that define intercalated behavioral production. As E. Goffman (1967) writes, "I assume that the proper study of interaction is not the individual and his psychology, but rather the syntactical relations among the acts of different persons mutually present to one another" (p. 2). This syntax appears as lived behavior through the actions of the participants in upholding rules of the social-cultural repertoire and serves as the basis for the participants' relationships with each other.

Semantic and Syntactic Features of Relationships

Relationships are neither idiosyncratic nor unpatterned. As distinct categories of meaning, each relationship is defined by a community as comprising some unit of significance (its semantic dimension) and some organization to the behavior itself (its syntactic dimension). The combined semantic-syntactic features of social relationships, as defined by each community's repertoire, are the subject of the discussion in this section.

Six features of relationships are described in this section. The features do not define any particular relationship type but, rather, represent categories that are operationalized in contrasting ways for each relationship within a community.[8]

Projected Time Duration

Relationships are defined by the amount of time the comembers are expected to commit to them and to each other and by the patterning of expected activity within the proposed temporal framework. Each relationship type within a community projects its own time duration. For example, although certainly subject to negotiation and alteration, husband-wife relationships usually are thought of as permanent, enduring until "death do us part." Extramarital relationships, however, such as "affairs" and "one-night stands," are assumed to be of relatively brief duration. However, both these social relationships last longer than many casual face-to-face encounters (for example, a quick greetings-and-good-bye sequence on the street) and, moreover, extend across more than one interactional episode (although, in the case of a *Fatal Attraction*–type affair, a limited number).

Degree of On-Callness

Social relationships may make use of face-to-face interaction, but the degree to which they are dependent upon the partners' copresence is varied. The Chinese example illustrates that no copresence may be demanded (or possible) for some relationships. Relationships with one's mail carrier only minimally rely on both parties being in each other's interactional presence; in contrast, U.S. husbands and wives are expected to spend periods of copresent time with each other, and, in the case of healthcare relationships, doctors are expected to be "on call" and accessible for face-to-face dealings with their patients on an "as needed" basis. (See S. A. Ames [1993] for a discussion of the steps medical institutions may take to build such continuity of coverage.) In contrast, interactional relationships are exclusively defined by sensory copresence.

Interruptability

Related to the copresence or on-callness demanded by a relationship is the degree to which interruptions in copresence may alter the relationship definition. Death, taking out the trash, and going to work or school all extract different prices from different social relationships. In certain traditions, women are not permitted to remarry after their husbands die; in fact, they are expected to don black mourning attire for the remainder of their (biological) lives and to remain committed to (be in relationship with) their deceased spouse. This all contrasts with side engagements and related attentional shifts in face-to-face conversation, which involve temporary interruptions within an interactional episode, leaving the original participants still in each other's presence as one momentarily refocuses on another participant (Goffman, 1963; Kendon, 1977). This distinction between interruptions of social and interactional relationships leads to the next relationship feature.

Exclusivity

In how many relationships like the target one is a person allowed to engage? Some relationship categories do not permit more than one instantiation at a time (again, husband-wife pairings in nonpolygamous societies may be used as an example); others permit multiples but are, nonetheless, limited (the number of new annual pledges to a fraternity or sorority); still others have no apparent numerical restrictions (university alumni). A related component of the exclusivity feature is the degree to which constraints are placed on the number and type of other relationships one is permitted to have, given participation in some target relationship. Interactional engagements are also subject to membership restrictions, but these are more likely to be handled on each local occasion than through some set of transsituational rules defining identity and association.

Nature of On-Behalfness

The interruptability of a relationship and its exclusivity presuppose that relationship members may be allowed to interact and engage in (certain) relationships apart from the target one. In some of these "external" dealings, the relationship member may be asked to serve as a representative to outsiders on behalf of the relationship comember(s). In what ways are the relationship members empowered to represent the relationship to others or commit the relationship to certain courses of action? Although this question may be asked of social relationships, it generally is not applicable to transient interactional engagements.

Stages

The ongoing communication stream is punctuated into discrete units or episodes of meaning (Birdwhistell, 1970; Watzlawick, 1977). Consistent with this, there is a set of folk beliefs and social-cultural expectations regarding relationship progression. These include ideas and rules concerning the initiation and termination of particular relationships (appropriate contexts, personnel, and behavioral strategies), the logical progression of stages, and the behavior associated with each stage once a relationship has been established. For example, P. Watzlawick (1977) discusses the complications that resulted from the contrasting relationship stages oriented to by U.S. soldiers and British women during World War II. For each participant, there were distinct rules for sequenced behavior, and although many of the behavior units (for example, kissing or holding hands) were identical, their place within the overall sequence was not.[9] Such developmental stages, which are likely to occur across several

encounters and may result in different labels being applied to a relationship at each stage, contrast with the segmentations of a single interactional
event into activities (greetings, questions-and-answers, leave taking),
which may be labeled or even recognized only in highly ritualized
encounters.

In brief, social communication theory urges us to see relationships not
as states but as "statements," that is, communication acts extended across
space and time. They are, thus, not simply categories of meaning but are
acts of meaning. The above list suggests some of the distinguishing
features of the relationships that may be sustained within a given community. Finally, it is important to reiterate the distinction between interpersonal or social relationships that may have rights and obligations attached
to them across multiple interactional events and interactional relationships
that are largely defined by moments of physical copresence.

COMMUNICATION AS CONSEQUENTIAL
TO RELATIONSHIPS

Although the discussion so far has considered what a relationship is, I
have not as yet fully explained the relevance of communication processes
to relationships or the relevance of Communication analysis to relationship analysis. Although relationships, indeed, can be profitably seen as
categories of meaning, rather than derivatives of, say, social structure or
intraindividual affect, a Communication analysis cannot rest with describing such categories. This derives from the argument above that
Communication, as an academic discipline, must concentrate on the
processual dynamics of meaning construction (see Sigman, 1992a, 1995a,
b). Although placed under the rubric of a meaning-centered approach to
communication, what I described in the second section has largely been
about the "logics" of relationships, that is, the expectations for and products of behavior, the background understandings and rules of relationship
categories, and the semantic-syntactic dimensions that are said to be
achieved by adherence to these rules and categories. However, if we have
learned anything from ethnomethodology (Garfinkel, 1984; Heritage,
1984), it is that people are not rule-bound automatons. They are active,
indeed proactive (strategic) behavers (see also Sanders, 1995). People
perform conduct as adjustments to an ongoing behavioral flow, and this
behavioral flow is not totally predictable prior to its unfolding production
(Leeds-Hurwitz & Sigman with Sullivan, 1995). These adjustments in
multiparticipant behavior take account of relationship logics (the a priori
categories of meanings), but they are not restricted to them.

Persons act so that the meaning of their behavior is, in part, derived from the rules, the morally binding logic that is the social-cultural repertoire, and in part from its being performed in real time. For example, when a husband acts in a certain way toward his wife, he is doing so not because he is the latter's husband (that is, fulfilling the obligations of that role) and not simply because there are rules that impose themselves on him; rather, he acts the way he does because he is structuring and producing messages whose meanings at the moment of production are interpretable as the behavior of a husband (or, of that "kind" of husband). He acts to be a husband in this situation, and a particular husband at that. Thus, the man acts "out of" rules-based knowledge and "into" the ongoing behavioral stream contributed by himself and others (cf. Cronen, 1995). In general, it is this ongoing behavioral stream, with all its contingencies and its opportunities for the building of a semantically consistent message over time (see the fourth section, below) that communicationally constructs each participant's identity and the participants' relationship.

In a sense, there are two models for thinking of relationships and communication. The one sees relationships as deriving exclusively from the members' affect or sociological categorization. Communication in this view plays an informative rather than creative role in relationships. This model parallels Sanders' (1995) notion of weak consequentiality, because it largely suggests that behavior emanates from a relationship and its individual members. The relationship itself emanates from the desires, goals, and emotions that the individuals convey to each other or to a sociological status that they have achieved (for example, through marriage) that demands adherence to certain norms. Individuals adhere to those rules that permit them to communicate about their respective positions on the formation, stability, or dissolution of the relationship; this communication is directed to their relationship partner and to various others and is designed to be informative to these others about relational status.

In contrast, in the second model, persons and their relationships are in a continual process of behavior production. Although recognizing the existence of a social-cultural repertoire defining appropriate and inappropriate relationship types and features, this strongly consequential view (Sanders, 1995) examines the dynamics of each interaction moment and how these dynamics yield to or transcend the social-cultural repertoire as the communicators set about responding to each new interactional contingency and building a relationship from that. The communicators' behaviors establish commitments for certain next behavior, and it is the combination of behaviors and commitments over time that yields each person's sense of having achieved a certain relational state and others labeling the person and the relationship accordingly. In the strongly consequential view, in other words, less analytic attention is paid to the social-cultural repertoire and more to ideographic interactional occurrences. Communication does not merely inform about where in the social-cultural repertoire a particular relationship can be located; rather, it provides for participants' ongoing behavioral coordination with each other, inferences and implications for relationship arising from that behavior, and demands for further behavioral adjustments — all of which generate the relationship as it dynamically exists at any point in time.

The two models for characterizing communication and relationship can be summarized thus:

1. husband → rule → behavior (that is, a person who is a husband and knows the relevant rules behaves according to these)
2. behavior → commitments → husband (that is, behavior is produced by a person, and this behavior finds the person committed to producing other behavior [the commitment deriving from the application of a variety of relevance and coherence rules]; this behavior-through-time is what being a husband means)

This issue returns us to the discussion of the first and third tenets of a combined social communication-consequentiality framework. Specifically, it was suggested there that in-the-moment processes of communication are *sui generis*, not fully dependent upon a priori social and cultural grammars for conduct. There is a consequential character to person's conduct such that "communication is not a neutral vehicle by which an external reality is communicated about, and by which factors of psychology, social structure, cultural norms, and the like are transmitted or are influential" (Sigman, 1995a, p. 2). Rather, "communication is consequential both in the sense that it is the primary process engendering and constituting sociocultural reality, and in the sense that, as it transpires, constraints on and affordances to people's behavior momentarily emerge" (p. 2). Community-specific interactional and social relationships (qua categories of meaning) emerge through such communication practices as invocation, revision, alignment, and so on, which create situated meaning (see Leeds-Hurwitz & Sigman with Sullivan, 1995). These practices are not themselves rules, but they are activities engaged in by communicators as they go about orienting to particular social-cultural categories of meaning (and the communication orders associated with this) and negotiating the applicability and relevance of the rules and categories to the identities and relationships entailed by their actually produced behavior.

Community-specific categories of meaning are oriented to in actual moments of behaving, but from a Communication analyst's point of view, describing the a priori categories and expectations is not equivalent to accounting for the conduct that produces in-the-moment relationships and alliances. Relationships, although they are categories of meaning defined by their communities, are lived as behavioral productions, adjustments in actual conduct that take account not only of the community-prescribed categories but also of the multiparticipant behavior simultaneously being performed. In other words, communication is not merely re-creative of a priori social-cultural rules and categories, a living conduit for these structures as it were, but a decisively creative enterprise. (See Sanders [1995] and Leeds-Hurwitz and Sigman with Sullivan [1995] for examples of the behavioral contingencies that relationship members produce, confront, and resolve and how these contingencies are the consequential basis for relationship construction.)

RELATIONSHIPS ACROSS TIME

The question that leads from such a view of communication concerns why and how it is that people act in consistent ways toward each other over time, that is, that social relationships (as opposed to interactional ones) are not ephemeral and, despite their foundation in consequential communication, do not exist in the moment only. A partial answer was adumbrated in the discussion on behavioral commitments, and it is the one to be developed here.

One approach to the issue of relationship continuity would return us to consideration of those features of the social-cultural repertoire that establish the parameters of each relationship type within the community. The discussion of projected time duration, interruptability, and stages (see the second section, above), for example, might be used to explain the participants' expectations for relationship continuity. Indeed, although such repertoire components might reasonably address expectations for relationship continuity, they fail to address how such continuity is behaviorally constituted in any actual relationship. This observation is consistent with the view elsewhere in the chapter that relationships sit at the intersection of a suprasituational set of codes and in-the-moment productions of behavior. Thus, an explanation for relationship continuity must be rooted in actual implementations of codes by relationship participants.

This approach is also consistent with social communication theory's general position that appeals to stable personality traits and relationship structural characteristics, psychological and sociological explanations

respectively, should be avoided. We will not seek an explanation for relationship continuity in the makeup or traits of the individuals within a relationship, just as we will not seek an explanation in relationship rules.
Rather, social communication encourages a consistent focus on relationship behavior. More specifically, I suggest that we maintain our focus on
meaning and meaning construction and, in this way, continue to offer
communicational explanations. In particular, we must turn attention to the
nature of the meaning relations and the obligations that are placed on
persons as a consequence of their behaving. These questions must be
asked. What is the projected "life history" of a particular meaningful act?
What entailments across space and time derive from behavior?

When persons behave, they do so not only by orienting to the a priori
behavioral logics representing who they "are" (identity) and who they are
supposed to be with others (relationship) but also by orienting to how their
behavior is coherent with and predictable from other behavior they have
coenacted with those others. Stated differently, they fit their behavior so
as to be semantically aligned with the ongoing stream of behavior, that is,
the particular stream of behavior that has actually (rather than ideally)
been produced and coproduced. Furthermore, their individual and collective behaviors as they are being produced obligate them to subsequent
courses of action. This does not mean that all such commitments are
always fulfilled, only that each instance of behaving generates some set of
obligations for the participants and that any next occasion of behaving is
likely to demand some orientation to prior established commitments. The
stability, coherence, and consistency of relationships across time result
from actually produced commitments. (See Davies and Harré [1992] for a
discussion of how contradictory narratives about the self may be reconciled or renegotiated.) The longevity of relationships stems from features
of the communication system, in which courses of action are ongoing,
responsive to constraints established by broad social-cultural rules and to
the moment-by-moment unfolding of behavior, and consequential in the
establishment of subsequent behavioral commitments. Each communication act projects a next one, and a next one after that. It is the continuous
projection of behavioral commitments that gives shape and depth to relationship continuity.

This leads to recognition of a curious irony that communicators find
themselves confronting and Communication analysts find themselves
obliged to study. Communicationally constructed social-cultural categories do not transpire in an ahistorical vacuum; rather, the seeds of any
construction can be found in prior sequences of behavior and transcendent
grammars, and any construction can, further, be seen to lay the semantic

groundwork for subsequent sequences of behavior. The irony is that the social-cultural world appears stable, almost thing-like — both external to us and externally encumbering — yet it is a world totally dependent on our behavioral contributions, our active constructions, our communicational commitments (cf. Berger & Luckmann, 1966). Societal institutions are like this, and so are social relationships.

In brief, an explanation for relationship continuity can be found in the commitments that each act of behavior establishes; subsequent courses of action are constrained not merely by the rules system but also by the interpretive ground formulated by prior action. We are accountable to what we have already done and to what others have coenacted with us. In addition, we project likely future courses of action and relationship trajectories with each behavioral contribution, and temporal continuity is built from these projections and relationship members' adherence to them.

SUMMARY

Relationships from the Communication viewpoint might be studied profitably as categories of meaning regarding the associations between and among persons, but they must be studied as behaviorally or processually engendered and sustained categories of meaning, rather than as fixed states. They may depend upon, but are analytically distinct from, face-to-face interaction (interaction relationships), and they involve an accretion of meanings across space and time.

A social communication analysis of relationship, thus, provides for a three-part investigation: the social-cultural repertoire permitting and constraining behavior and defining each relationship category; the communication activities that accomplish, negotiate, and orient to these resources; and the character, composition, and continuity of the relationships across selected episodes and time frames that are built from the meaning commitments of these communication activities.

NOTES

This chapter is dedicated to the late Ray L. Birdwhistell. As I reread and edited earlier drafts, it was clear that much of what I understand to be a social communication approach to relationships already was provided for by Birdwhistell's writings and teachings at the University of Pennsylvania throughout the 1970s and early 1980s. I also am grateful for conversations with Harold Garfinkel in fall 1990 on matters related to consequentiality. An earlier version of this chapter appears in Wendy Leeds-Hurwitz (1995) with permission of Guilford Publications.

1.   When capitalized, "Communication" refers to the discipline that studies the observable process of (lower case) communication.

2.   Linear, causal language is somewhat limiting here. The discussion is not meant to imply that communication causes a relationship into being. All there really is (for us as humans to experience and for us as researchers to study) is communication behavior. A relationship is a particular logical category or patterning of behavior. Relationship and communication are different facets of the "same" behavior.

3.   A number of years back, I read about two teenagers, one male and one female, living in rural Pennsylvania, who were killed in a car accident on prom night. The community had always assumed that these high-school sweethearts would one day marry. They were buried together, and a graveside marriage cere-mony was performed.

4.   Because it plays only an indirect role in relationship formation, the semiotic order is not discussed at length here. See Sigman (1987) for a fuller treatment of this third order and its contribution to ongoing communication.

5.   "Hey, John, how's it going" is a perfectly acceptable greeting but may not be relationally appropriate in all contexts. Although this utterance may always fit the bill as a salutation, it may not be appropriate for sustaining the formality or respect owed one's minister. Thus, a given communication act may prove "grammatical" for one order and "ungrammatical" for another. In this particular case, the utterance is acceptable in terms of the semiotic order (it adheres to the rules of English) and the interaction order (it is used at the begin-ning of an interaction) but not in terms of the social order (it violates address terminology for status unequals). The canonical greeting <ATTENTION GRAB-BER + (TERM OF ADDRESS) + INQUIRY> contains a slot (the optional TERM OF ADDRESS) whose filler is defined not by the rules for greeting (the interaction order) but by those for relationship composition (the social order).

6.   It is also interesting to note with this example that a termination ritual may require the initiation of an encounter (for example, a catching-up on the day's events at the coat rack or elevator, followed by a good-bye sequence) by people who previously had been physically separated and with no immediately prior interactional contact, in order to be accomplished.

7.   Goffman (1983), Sigman (1987), and Sanders (1995) all provide contrasting analyses of how interaction order-based and social order-based rela-tionships are linked to each other.

8.   This list is not exhaustive, and the features are described primarily with regard to social relationships. Future research must consider how the two rela-tionship types — social and interactional — differ with regard to each feature.

9.   Margaret Mead is generally credited with these observations, which are used by Watzlawick (1977) to explain the communication concept of "punctuation":

In both cultures, courtship behavior from the first eye contact to the ultimate consummation went through approximately thirty steps, but the sequence of these steps was different. Kissing, for instance, comes relatively early in the North American pattern (occupying, let us say, step 5) and relatively late in the English pattern (at step 25, let us assume). . . . So when the U.S. soldier somehow felt that the time was right for a harmless kiss, not only did the girl feel cheated out of twenty steps . . . , she also felt she had to make a quick decision: break off the relationship and run, or get ready for intercourse. (pp. 63–64)

See A. Kendon and S. J. Sigman (1996) for a discussion of the impact of Mead's insights on Birdwhistell's (1970) formulation of social communication theory.

4

The Meaning of Relationship in Relational Communication

L. Edna Rogers

Viewing social processes in terms of the influence that one set of intraindividual variables has on similar variables in another individual has led to a relative neglect of the process of communication, which constitutes the ongoing interrelationship between individuals.
— Danziger, 1976, pp. xiii–xiv

Better it would be to say that the relationship *is* the exchange of these messages: or that the relationship is immanent in these messages.
— Bateson, 1972, p. 275

In a very fundamental sense it can be said that one converses one's way through life.
— Berger & Kellner, 1964, p. 53

Over the past several decades, there appears to be a growing consensus among interpersonal scholars of the intimate link between communication and social relationships. This once radical idea of viewing relationships as "ongoing conversations" (Berger & Kellner, 1964, p. 52) has gained wider acceptance, with contemporary studies being centered more frequently on the formative nature of communication; yet, the question of how to grasp the multiple aspects of this interactive process remains a formidable challenge. In response, different conceptual and analytical modes have been developed, with the relational communication approach being only one of many.

From its beginning, the relational view has attempted to take seriously the "heart" of our discipline, the communication process. Relational communication represents an interaction-based communication approach to the study of interpersonal relationships. With this perspective, relationships are viewed as moving, "living art" forms, creatively shaped by the interactive behaviors of the participants. The ongoing movement of the communicative "dance" between relational members gives character and definition to their relationship. Emergent patterns of relational form are given life, rest on, and circle around the very processes from which they arise. Such is the recursive, ecological nature of the communication process out of which relationships are formed and sculpted.

When we speak of relationships, we speak a language of connectedness — of acting in conjunction with others, of interrelating, acting in awareness of other, of mutual influence. The concept of relationship implies some form of connection between or among different sets of events or entities; in essence, relationship refers to an interconnectedness of differences.

Relationships refer to a coming together, a common thread existing or developing between people, with members being tied to one another in some manner such that each constrains the other. We speak of being involved, of being socially bound to one another, of being *in* a relationship.

In spinning out these relatively common ways of speaking about relationships, the various phrases imply a degree of mutual dependency that underscores the jointly created nature of social relationships, as well as an interconnectedness between and among relational members such that a social unity or wholeness is formed that lies beyond the individual members. The active, "-ing" verb form of speaking emphasizes movement and the potential malleability of the members' unfolding lines of action to take this or that shape for fleeting or extended periods of time. The potential for change is a constant of human relations. Continuing enactments of the present fuse into patterned combinations that fuse into more encompassing contextualizing patterns, all of which influence future enactments as well as remembered pasts. These modes of speaking about relationships are all in keeping with the relational communication view, with its emphases on process, pattern, and relational form.

Utilizing the concept of temporal form, J. M. Gottman (1982a) suggests that, analogous to an improvisational jazz group, "a relationship consists of the forms that people build when they are together" (p. 951).

As a musical composition results from the combined temporal forms of sound, social relationships emerge from the combined temporal forms of behavior. The relational perspective, grounded in an epistemology of form, locates the meaning of social relationships within the organizing principles of connectedness and interdependency, principles displayed in the jointly produced communicative practices and patterns of the interactants.

Similar to members of a jazz group, who, by performing their individual parts, are "instrumental" in the production of the full musical rendition, the relational approach views individual participants as active, choosing agents, performing their lines of action in the production of their everyday social dramas; yet, the socialness of the drama resides not in the individual participants but in the collective, patterned forms of interrelating. Thus, from the relational point of view, the importance of the individual in the creation of relationships is not trivialized but, at the same time, not privileged. Each member is a necessary part of the whole but not singularly sufficient for constructing mutually defined patterns of relationship.

Correspondingly, the study of relational patterns represents a different level of analysis than the study of individuals; different analytical levels offer different types of insight and understanding, each with its strength but nonsubstitutable for the other. This distinction is likened by J. B. Bavelas and L. Segal (1982) to a figure-ground reversal in which the relationship, rather than the individual members, becomes figure, with the individuals fading into the background. With the relational communication focus on the between, the momentarily visible interconnectiveness of the members becomes the focus of study.

What is considered figure and what is ground rest on different assumptive frames. If, from a different frame, the study of relational form appears less "grounded" or less "real," Gottman's (1982a) reply is that these forms are both "as real and ephemeral as the music" (p. 951) generated by the moment-to-moment improvisations of a jazz group.

Although our relations with others form the bedrock of our social existence, these relational realities are not based on hard, immutable substances but on the shifting sands of improvised "working agreements," the negotiated management of difference (McCall & Simmons, 1978, p. 127). Much earlier, yet in a similar vein, E. Sapir (1949) noted that, although our everyday social realities appear to be a series of stable structures, in "reality," they consist of "a vast array of partial and complete understandings, which are sustained and creatively reaffirmed from day to day in a number of particular acts of a communicative nature" (p. 104).

The common observation of the tenuous, mutable nature of social existence underscores the temporal quality of our relational world, a quality that represents both the beauty and the burden of being a social-symbolic being and living within such a world.

The purpose of this chapter is to illuminate the meaning of relationship within the relational communication perspective. In doing so, an overview of selected relationship definitions is given before turning to an expanded discussion of the relational view. This latter section presents a brief developmental backdrop to the relational approach, the conceptual foundation of the relational meaning of relationship, and a proposed communication-based, dimensional model of relationships.

OVERVIEW OF RELATIONSHIP DEFINITIONS

To broaden the context within which to situate the relational communication perspective, an overview of different definitional approaches to the concept of relationships is provided. The following review is selective in two senses. It draws from central research writings in the area of relational studies and is limited to those that offer specifically stated definitions of the relationship concept. In surveying these contemporary definitions, I find a common set of conceptual features that harken back to the earlier writing of M. Weber (1947) and G. Simmel (1950) on the meaning of relationship. In particular, whether their work is cited or not, Weber's focus on the mutual orientation of social action and Simmel's concern with the social form of interaction are evident in current conceptualizations of relationship.

Turning first to Weber's explication, he outlines the following basic elements of a social relationship: "The term social relationship will be used to denote the behavior of a plurality of actors in so far as, in meaningful content, the action of each takes account of that of the others and is oriented in these terms. The social relationship thus consists entirely and exclusively in the existence of a probability that there will be, in some meaningfully understandable sense, a course of social action" (1947, p. 118).

Weber (1947) posits two defining criteria for the existence of a social relationship. First, there must be "at least a minimum of mutual orientation of the action of each to that of the other" (p. 118) that "can and usually will have consequences for the course of action and the form of the relationship" (p. 119), and second, there must be a probability of continuing social interaction, "which constitutes the 'existence' of the social relationship" (p. 119).

With direct reference to Weber, G. McCall (1970) states that "a relationship is at base, the existence of a substantial probability of interaction between two persons" (p. 4). Within this basic definition, McCall views social relationships as forms of social organizations with the type of social bonds uniting the members, influencing "the form the interaction will likely assume" (p. 4), which, in turn, propagates and "exhibits a unique, emergent culture" (p. 15). The work by McCall (1987, 1988) and McCall and J. L. Simmons (1978, 1991) fosters an integrative analysis of levels of social organization that complements and contextualizes communication-based approaches to understanding interpersonal relationships. The inclusion of both interpretive and behavioral dimensions in their relational models draws together a combination of ideas from symbolic interaction, social exchange, and, in particular, Simmel's analysis of different social types of relationships.

The writings of Simmel, although described as "tantalizingly elusive" (Hamilton, 1984), have, nevertheless, provided lasting insights into the nature and dynamics of social relationships. Simmel's influence is seen in the ideas of the early members of the "Chicago School," for instance, R. E. Park's (1927) conception of human conduct and reputation, E. W. Burgess' (1926) view of the family as a "unity of interacting personalities," likewise in the dramaturgical perspective and E. Goffman's (1959, 1967) studies of interaction order.

For Simmel (1950), social phenomena are rooted in what he termed "forms of sociation," the emergent structuring of everyday social interaction, whether taking the form of social play or of more institutionalized ritual. Simmel saw interaction as the basis of social order and the legitimate arena for the study of different orders of social relations. Society, in his view, was another name for the interweaving of the multiple array of relationships constituted in the members' forms of interaction with one another.

In much of his work, Simmel advocated and grappled with the study of the less obvious, yet readily visible interaction forms that constitute the principles of social unity (Featherstone, 1991). Further, he argued the point "cybernetically," stressing the importance of focusing on the synchronic connection of interaction events. Simmel (1950) spoke of the circularity of social life in his description of the simultaneous interdependency of the visible and invisible threads that are woven between persons in the interaction process, such that relationships "develop upon the basis of reciprocal knowledge, and this knowledge upon the basis of the actual relations. Here we have one of the deep-lying circuits of intellectual life, where an element presupposes a second element which yet, in turn, presupposed the first," with interaction constituting the arena "where being and conceiving make their mysterious unity empirically felt" (p. 309). Simmel's conceptual and epistemological approach to relationship forms a foundation for more current approaches, including relational communication. The description of temporal form, discussed earlier, clearly fits with Simmel's basic notion of forms of sociation. Again, in Gottman's words, "a relationship consists of the temporal forms that are created when two people are together" (1982a, p. 943).

A central interaction component underlies R. A. Hinde's (1979) meaning of the nature of social relationships. No doubt influenced by a background in biology and primatology, Hinde states that a relationship implies "some sort of intermittent interaction between two people," "some degree of mutuality," and "some degree of continuity" (1979, p. 14); a relationship "is not a static entity but a process in continuous creation through time" (1987, p. 38).

In reference to relational continuity, S. Metts and W. R. Cupach (1995) make an interesting point in their study of postdivorce relationships. Although the concept of divorce is commonly used to refer to the ending of a relationship, they find in actuality that this is rarely the case. If, as these authors suggest, continuing interaction "at some level minimally defines a relationship" (p. 235), then, most frequently, divorce does not terminate the relationship but, rather, redefines and alters the relationship. As an aside, divorce illustrates the "life after death" character of relationships. Even when terminated, past relationships, in a sense, "live" in the present in that they are now part of one's accumulated social definitions — making little difference in some contexts and more in others.

Turning back to Hinde, he makes a distinction, as do others (for example, Weber, McCall, Goffman), between a singular interaction, or fleeting encounter, and a relationship that is based on a series of interactions. Further, he distinguishes levels of complexity (for example, individuals, relationship social structure) with a clear statement that "each of these levels has properties that are simply not relevant to the levels below" (1987, p. 25).

For a more complete understanding of relationships, Hinde advocates the inclusion of affective and cognitive descriptions along with those based on interaction. In his earlier work (1979), he delineated eight dimensions for describing relationships, with content, diversity, quality, relative frequency and patterning, and reciprocity-complementarity as discussions of interaction, and intimacy, interpersonal perception-understanding, and commitment representing dimensions of subjectivity. In his latest writing (1995), two additional subjective categories are included, power and autonomy, and satisfaction. Hinde outlines a broadly based "science of relationships" including both interactional and experiential dimensions but cautions that, because relationships involve at least two individuals, properties of relationships are not predicted from the characteristics of either participant alone. He notes, "Studies of how individuals perceive others, make attributions, resolve dissonance, and so on within relationships, however important and relevant they may be are not studies of relationships" (1995, p. 3).

In the study of close relationships, H. Kelley and colleagues (1983) base their definition on four basic interaction variables. They view interdependency as the essential feature of a relationship and that this feature can be indexed by describing the quantity and quality of the interaction over time. Close relationships are defined as the interconnections between two peoples' interaction "chains" that are "strong, frequent and diverse interdependence that lasts over a considerable period of time" (1983, p. 38). In contrast, weakly connected, infrequent, limited, and fleeting interaction would characterize distant relationships.

The dimension of interaction frequency, a fundamental of any relationship, reminds one of E. D. Chapple's (1940) earlier proposal of viewing and delineating relationships in terms of the frequency and duration of the participants' action-inaction sequences. The chronographic mappings and comparisons of the temporal rhythms of different types of social interaction, although limited, were innovative in approach. To be sure, the studies of Kelley and colleagues go far beyond Chapple's pioneering efforts by interlinking the actions, affect, and thoughts of each participant in each of the ongoing interactional exchanges between them.

The work of A. Kendon (1982, 1990) on the organization of interactional events focuses on behavior patterns and their interrelationship in the performance and production of social occasions. In close alignment with A. E. Schefflen (1973), Kendon's emphasis is on how behaviors, particularly nonverbal, function in concert with one another. Behavior by itself has no set meaning but takes on meaning in relation to, and within the configuration and context of, other acts. Correspondingly, social relationships are viewed as the "emergent products of the process of interaction" (Kendon, 1982, p. 445).

From this, albeit limited, overview, common elements found to arise in defining social relationships include two or more individuals, each mutually influencing the other, in the process of interacting with one another such that a form of interconnection exists between them. At the research level, these definitional features have been played out with considerable variability, depending on which aspects of the interaction process are attended to, in what manner, and at what level of analysis. With these definitions as background, we turn to an explication of the relational communication view of the relationship concept.

RELATIONAL COMMUNICATION PERSPECTIVE: DEVELOPMENTAL BACKDROP

McCall, in his 1970 volume on relationships, reflected on the limited explicit attention given to social relationships in modern sociology. N. Wiley (1988), although not speaking directly about relationships but about conceptual levels of analysis (individual, interaction, social structure, and culture), noted that the interaction level often is missing in social theory. He credits family therapy research as having the firmer grasp of this level. Hinde (1995) echoes his view by stating that, in the mid-1960s, "nearly all the data available about relationships came from clinicians" (p. 1). Hinde notes that, until recently, "the psychological sciences simply bypassed" the study of interpersonal relationships.

Likewise, during the earlier years in communication, with most models borrowed from psychology, few studies focused on relationships. In the area of interpersonal communication, research was clearly more "personal" than "inter." In the late 1960s, with the advent of system theory and cybernetics, this situation began to change. However, as M. L. Knapp and G. R. Miller (1985) comment, "Surprisingly, the widespread concern for studying behavior manifested in interpersonal transactions is of relative recent origin" (p. 11). Also, as indicated above, this influence came largely through the writings of family therapists; in particular, the publication of P. Watzlawick, J. H. Beavin, and D. D. Jackson's 1967 text, *The Pragmatics of Human Communication*, played a pivotal role in bringing system-related concepts and the earlier work of G. Bateson into the mainstream of interpersonal communication study.

System thinking presented a world-view that emphasized wholistic and ecological thinking, a way of looking "at the world in terms of relationships and integrations" (Capra, 1982, p. 266). Grounded within these ideas, the possibilities of an alternative view to more traditional models ushered in "heady" times in the field of communication and, especially, in the area of interpersonal communication. (See Wilder [1982] for a developmental description.) Within the context of these emerging epistemological influences, the development of the relational communication approach, also known as the pragmatic perspective (Fisher, 1978), took place.

CONCEPTUAL FOUNDATION:
THE MEANING OF RELATIONSHIP

Traditionally, research practices in communication were couched predominately within an epistemology of objects, which accorded primary importance to singular events or individual entities. In contrast, the relational approach is founded on an epistemology of form, an interwoven set of principles that give prominence to patterns of interaction over individual acts and interrelationships over unilateral cause (Ellis, 1982). P. Dell (1983) notes that, in shifting attention to "shapes, forms and relations" (p. 251), objects become inseparable from the pattern within which they are embedded and, thus, of secondary interest, while pattern becomes primary. As such, the implementation of the relational view necessitated not just a modification but a restructuring of traditional modes of thought.

The writings of Bateson (1972), which are foundational to the relational perspective, criticized the majority of social science for concentrating far too long on the "wrong half" of the substance-form dichotomy. Bateson argued that a reversal in thinking was necessary for a "new order of communication" (1951, p. 209) to emerge. By focusing on form, this new order placed emphasis on the centrality of communication behavior, connective processes, emergent pattern, and evolving multileveled orders of pattern. An ecology of form based on the "patterns that connect" was fundamental to what Bateson termed "ecological wisdom," "knowledge of the larger interactive system" (1972, p. 433).

Within this epistemological frame, a relationship is, in the most fundamental sense, "a connective principle" (Ellis, 1982, p. 220), based on the interrelatedness of difference. Differences come into being by drawing distinctions (Spencer-Brown, 1973); relationships come into being by drawing distinctions together. As Bateson (1979) so aptly puts it, "distinctions that remain undrawn are not" (p. 103); only through the dual process of differentiation, the bounding off of one phenomena from another, and integration, drawing them together in terms of how they stand "in relation" to one another, can we speak of relationship. The relationship lies in the connection, not in one or the other but in the between. The interrelatedness of acts of demarcation (punctuation) allow comparisons, categorizations, logical types, patterned orders of interactional form, and such.

Thus, systemic or holistic thinking that underlies an epistemology of form is "premised upon the differentiation and interaction of parts" (Bateson, 1979, p. 100). The duality of the interconnecting principle is an essential feature of the relational perspective and meaning of relationship.

By drawing ongoing communicative enactments together in more encompassing patterns, more of the holistic quality of the relationship comes
into being.

The interconnection of difference, what Bateson calls "double description," is necessary for seeing relational pattern. "Relationship is always a
product of double description" (1979, p. 142). By analogy, Bateson exemplifies this process: "It is correct (and a great improvement) to begin to
think of the two parties to the interaction as two eyes, each giving a
monocular view of what goes on and, together giving a binocular view in
depth. This double view is the relationship" (p. 142).

As two eyes in combination generate a binocular view, combined
actions generate pattern and relationship. With the interweaving of
successive levels of double description, actions are fused into patterns of
interaction, which, in turn, are fused into more global patterns, with each
level being contextualized by broader descriptions of relational form. In
this manner, recursively ordered levels of pattern are created out of the
ascending descriptions of process and form.

In describing the formative nature of the communication process out of
which relational forms emerge, the relational perspective is based on
Bateson's conceptualization of the duality of the message meaning.
Bateson (1951) proposed that messages simultaneously offer two levels of
meaning, a referential (report) meaning that is contextualized by a relational (command) meaning. The report or content level provides representational information, and the relational level provides presentational
information. At the relational level, offered definitions of self and other,
vis-à-vis one another and, thus, of their relationship, are given off.
Through the ongoing mutually influencing negotiation of implied relational meaning, codefined patterns of interrelatedness can be identified.
The interchange of relational level message meaning offers an interactive
description of the jointly constructed patterns that, over time and in
combination, characterize the nature of the relationship.

The evolving patterns evident in the communication process allow the
identification of relational form, as represented in Bateson's formulation
of symmetry and complementarity. These concepts, based on the similarity or difference of enacted relational definitions, serve as prototypes for
describing patterns of social relationship. Complementarity refers to
patterned sequences of interaction in which the participants' behaviors are
different but mutually fit together, such as question and answer, giving
and receiving, trusting and trustworthy, assertion and submission.
Symmetry refers to patterns of similar behaviors, in which one behavior

mirrors the other, such as question and question, blaming and blaming, disclosing and disclosing, assertion and assertion.

These two patterns, complementarity and symmetry, can fuse to form what has been referred to as a "parallel" pattern of patterns (Lederer & Jackson, 1968), or a combination of the two subtypes of complementarity produces what Bateson (1935) called a "pattern of reciprocal complementarity." From the enfolding of patterns within pattern, "higher" order concepts, such as rigidity, redundancy, chaos, and escalation, are formed. In a similar but more general manner, E. Tobach and G. Greenberg (1984) describe this process in terms of the embedded nature of relationship levels as "one in which lower levels are subsumed in higher levels so that any particular level is an integration of preceding levels . . . in the process of integration or fusion, new levels with their own characteristics result" (p. 2).

It is within this conceptual context that the relational communication definition of relationship takes on meaning. Relationships are defined as emergent, social structurings conjointly created by the members in the mutually influencing, interrelating process of communication. The central defining themes of this perspective emphasize the temporal patterned, jointly constructed, ecological nature of relationships.

The relational perspective underscores the socialness of relationships. Relationships are socially performed, constructed, maintained, and altered in the reciprocal actions of the relational members. Once again, this emphasis does not negate the members' perceptions, interpretations, narratives, emotions, reflections, or remembrances but, rather, draws a distinction between individual members and relationship; they are not of the same making. Relationships do not have feelings, make imputations, engage in sense making, and the like; only the members have these capacities. Relationships do not act, only members act, but out of their combined actions, an essential defining quality of relationship is evident — its social nature.

RELATIONAL COMMUNICATION
MODEL OF RELATIONSHIP

Based on the relational communication meaning of relationship and the assumption that relationships are constituted in the process of communication, a three-dimensional, communication-based model was developed to provide a conceptual framework by which interpersonal relationships can be described, differentiated, and compared in theoretically meaningful ways (see Millar and Rogers [1976, 1987] for a full description). In keeping with the relational perspective, the model is grounded within the communication patterns that form the central interactive connections between the relational members.

Obviously, multiple dimensions could be identified in describing the complexities of relationships. In the present model, control, intimacy, and trust are proposed as three generic dimensions that represent basic social structuring processes that underlie all relationships. In combination, the resulting matrix provides a way of mapping relationships within a three-dimensional social space.

The formulation of the relational model rests on the spatial metaphor of interpersonal distance that is "played out" along all three dimensions, in terms of the members' interactional behaviors with one another. In this process, relational level information is "given off" that indicates, within a given context, how close or how far members are invited or allowed to be in the "distancing dance" that is being performed. The continual, temporal structuring and rhythm of this dance is, of course, a co-negotiated affair.

The relational communication model has been shaped by multiple sources (for example, Simmel, 1950; Hess & Handel, 1959; McCall & Simmons, 1978), but in particular by D. Kantor and W. Lehr (1975) and their work on developing a family process model. Drawing on system and cybernetic concepts, they proposed that interpersonal systems are basically information-processing systems and that the central information processed is of a "distance regulation" nature (p. 222). In line with these ideas, the three dimensions for modeling interpersonal relationships are each seen as indexing important, core differences for characterizing forms of relational connectedness and separateness. The three dimensions index patterns of constraint (control), patterns of sentiment (intimacy), and patterns of predictability (trust).

Control is based on the interpersonal negotiation of the members' definitional rights. Within the conceptual matrix, this dimension represents the vertical distance between the members. Control refers to the process of establishing the right to define, direct, and delimit the actions of the system within or across different topics and contexts. It indexes the interactive structuring of the regulative function of message behavior.

The trust dimension taps the inherent uncertainty of relationships and rests on the mutual predictability of other relative to self. It forms the horizontal dimension of the matrix. Trust rests on the level of trusting behavior evident within a relationship and the degree to which trusting behavior is complemented with trustworthy behaviors. Patterns of predictability function to produce a sense of certainty about future actions, level of commitment, and investment of self in the relationship.

Intimacy, represented by the depth dimension, indicates the degree of emotional closeness or separateness. Patterns of sentiment and emotional closeness can be expressed in many forms and different modes of behavior. The "heart" of the intimacy dimension rests on the degree to which each is known by the other and the extent to which the other has become part of one's own self-definition, such that there is a potential relational irreplaceability and exclusivity.

The proposed combination of the control, intimacy, and trust dimensions offers a potentially useful approach for mapping the interactive complexities of interpersonal relationships. The model provides a conceptual frame for identifying relationships in comparable ways and integrating research efforts. Further, it allows a visualization of the interwoven movements of the members as they move in and around and away from one another in the performance and construction of their relationship. When relationships are conceptualized as a mutually defined, emergent relational form, emphasis is placed on the interactive cycles produced and reproduced through the members' distance-regulating, communicative behaviors.

CONCLUSION

The study of social relationships and the underlying communicative processes out of which they emerge and take shape is neither a trivial concern nor a small undertaking. Different approaches are open to us that offer different forms of insight and, thus, if appropriately integrated, a more comprehensive view of relationships. However, a clear challenge for interpersonal communication study is how to conceptualize and investigate the process of interrelating so that the human, social, and formative qualities inherent within this process are not lost. Such has been the goal of the relational communication perspective.

Relational communication is an interaction-based approach to the study of interpersonal relationships. Grounded within a systemic, cybernetic perspective, this approach gives primary attention to the jointly produced patterns of interrelating with one another. The emergent social structurings created in the ongoing communication process between relational members give life and form to their relationships. Through communication, we offer definitions of self in relation to other and simultaneously shape the nature of our relationship. Definitions can be accepted, resisted, or modified; the process of defining relationships is, by its nature, a process of negotiation.

The basic premises of the relational view can be visualized through the use of the metaphor of dance. Different relational dances emerge from the combination of different dance steps. How we move in relation to one another through our communication behavior forms the patterns that underlie and identify our social relationships. Analogous to dance steps, message behaviors combine into sequences of pattern, recurring interactions, that characterize our different relationships. With the relational approach, individual movements (message behaviors) are necessary parts, but the dance (relational pattern) is of central interest.

A quote from A. Lindbergh (1955) reemphasizes the image of viewing relationships as creatively performed, living, moving art forms.

A good relationship has a pattern like a dance and is built on some of the same rules. The partners do not need to hold on tightly, because they move confidently in the same pattern, intricate but gay and swift and free . . . to touch heavily would be to arrest the pattern and freeze the movement, to check the endlessly changing beauty of its unfolding. There is no place here for the possessive clutch, the clinging arm, the heavy hand; only the barest touch in passing. Now arm in arm, now face to face, now back to back — it does not matter which. Because they know they are partners moving to the same rhythm, creating a pattern together, and being invisibly nourished by it. (p. 104)

5

Giddens' Conception of Personal Relationships and Its Relevance to Communication Theory

Robert D. McPhee

Anthony Giddens' sociological writings are widely respected for many reasons, not least their utility as an assumptive frame for the study of interactional dynamics. Giddens has created a metatheory explicating basic assumptions and concepts crucial for valid social theorizing and research (mainly 1976, 1979, 1984) and a substantive social theory analyzing the unique and constitutive features of the modern era (mainly 1990, 1991, 1992, 1994; cf. 1981, 1985). In both lines of work, Giddens aims to elaborate a concept of social agency that is complex enough to cohere with theories of complex social dynamics and to demonstrate the continuity between explanations of social interactive processes and of broad social structural characteristics.

Their broad and foundational intent implies that Giddens' theories should be valuable resources for theorists dealing with interpersonal relationships, and Giddens himself has devoted a good deal of recent attention to the subject of personal relations (especially 1992). My aim here is to summarize some of Giddens' ideas that are most relevant to the study of relationships and, especially, to examine some of the limitations of his approach to relationships and to suggest revisions in Giddens' conceptual substructure.

A continuing theme of my analysis will be that Giddens' treatment of relationships is undersocialized. By this, I mean that Giddens approaches relationships as outcome-oriented repetitive interchanges between generally autonomous individuals, accomplished by drawing on broad social-structural rules and resources. His conception does not proscribe, but also does not give sufficient emphasis to, ways in which others and interaction with them make important and even constitutive contributions to the identities and relational networks of agents.

To pursue the aims of my analysis, I have divided it into five parts. First is a summary of Giddens' problematic: the horizon of tradition, assumptions, and intellectual objectives that gives his work its bearings. Second, I selectively summarize his metatheory, spending time on the parts that are most relevant to relationships and his treatment of them. Included here is a detailed review of the flow of argument that he uses to connect the interactive constitution of the agent with the involvement of the individual in social systemic organization. Third is an equally selective review of Giddens' theory of modernity. This primarily sets up the fourth section, an analysis of Giddens' specific theory of intimate relationships. The last section includes some provisional suggestions for change in Giddens' conceptual substructure.

GIDDENS' PROBLEMATIC

Giddens sees himself as a social and sociological theorist, an heir to the tradition of work established by Karl Marx, Max Weber, Émile Durkheim, Alfred Schutz, and Talcott Parsons. He argues that this distinctive tradition of sociological theorizing works from a central general problem: the nature of the novel social modes that have emerged in the transition to modernity. "The lurching juggernaut of change is still careering [sic] erratically over the surface of the earth. Sociology was born of the attempt to track its path" (1987a, pp. 15–16). One result of his focus on this problem has been Giddens' orientation to the more general issue of the individual's relation to society — a two-term, individual-society model. He has argued that this is an especially appropriate model for the analysis of modernity, because, in modern times, "Changes in aspects of personal life . . . are directly tied to the establishment of social connections of very wide scope. I do not mean to deny the existence of many kinds of more intermediate connection. . . . But the level of time-space distanciation introduced by high modernity is so extensive that, for the first time in human history, 'self' and 'society' are interrelated in a global milieu" (1991, p. 32). I have argued elsewhere (McPhee, 1989) that the discipline of communication is oriented to a different model of interagent symbolic praxis in a social context; the individual-society model may be one source of the undersocialized development (as noted later) that Giddens gives to relationships.

The tradition of sociological theory in which Giddens works has given rise to two classic problems, awareness of which colors his work. One is the problem of agency versus structure seen as causal constraint — how can the image of people as interpreting and self-directing beings be reconciled with the image of people as predictably conforming to social norms and roles? Giddens focuses his theory of structuration on answering this question. However, his emphasis on agency does not allow viewing theory as a series of mechanical causal propositions. Instead, he aims to articulate a system of concepts that can explicate the main powers and patterns that people have developed for constituting social life. He succeeds to the extent that his theory identifies the most characteristic trajectories of social development in any social system and time and gives deep insight into how such patterns are possible and probable.

More recently, the individual-society relation has generated a narrower but classic second problem, the "macro-micro problem." Giddens has discussed this subproblem influentially and revealingly, so that some background discussion is needed. Basically, this is the problem of how individual action is linked to social-systemic processes. Consider an individual's decision to get a divorce and its relation to family structure as a characteristic of U.S. society. It is tempting to say that every married person makes a decision about divorce, and the decisions simply "add up" to a divorce rate that describes (still in a pretty micro way) U.S. family structure. However, of course, things are much more complex than that — individual decisions are influenced by earlier decisions by other individuals as well as by changes developing in response to those earlier decisions. Divorce becomes more "normal," a social problem, the target of research, governmental action, and cultural discussion, yielding demographic and social network changes and so on. All of these changes would have effects that may be described more aptly as changes in divorce rate or in the family as an institution rather than as changes in individual decision situations. So, individual decisions "help" explain U.S. family structure, and vice versa, in an inadequately conceptualized way. Other relational and communicative decisions are equally liable to this problem. The macro-micro problem is the search for a system of explanatory structures to deal with this sort of situation.

One way of characterizing theoretic solutions to the macro-micro problem is suggested by Norbert Wiley in an influential article (1988). He posited some dimensions of increasing "macroness" that may be involved in the problem and solutions to it; I have added to his array of dimensions, arriving at five.

1. (a combination of Wiley's first and fourth dimensions) the dimension of abstractness, ranging from knowledge and norms related only to a specific group of people and situations to knowledge and norms (for example, of mathematics) that have meaning independent of the social positions and roles of people involved;

2. (Wiley's third dimension) the dimension(s) of time-space, with more macrophenomena involving interdependence across longer distances;

3. social differentiation, in the straightforward sense of "differences"; more macrophenomena involve people and mixed groups whose backgrounds, resource bases, and so on, are more diverse and unequal;

4. reticular or network size and complexity, ranging from one (or more) isolated individuals or relationships to increasing network extent and interconnectedness;

5. (a generalization of Wiley's second dimension) systemic-functional complexity, with macrosystems being ones with more diverse tasks that are more complexly interdependent with one another.

Seemingly, a macrophenomenon could differ from a micro one on any of these dimensions, and any of them might be chosen as central in a theory. The first three dimensions are not essentially social — they can characterize sets of people who are almost completely oblivious to one another. In contrast, the fourth and, especially, the fifth dimensions imply social interrelatedness. Giddens does, in fact, argue for preferring one or two of the earlier dimensions; I will note how neglect of the others undermines his treatment of relationships.

In order to address the problem of modernity rigorously, Giddens has explicitly written at two interconnected but distinct levels. At the most abstract level, he produced the general social theoretic position that he labels "the theory of structuration," which includes concepts and principles intended to apply across social scientific disciplines. He and varied commentators have called this theory an "ontology of potentials," but I will use the term "metatheory" for it.[1] The second level involves substantive theoretical work on various topics, centrally, the nature of modernity itself. Neglect of "relationship" in the metatheory is not necessarily a flaw; it could be merely a matter of emphasis, and Giddens surely does not eliminate the possibility of relationships.

GIDDENS' METATHEORY

Giddens' theory of structuration has been summarized many times (cf. Poole, Seibold, & McPhee, 1985; Cohen, 1989). In this section, I want to mention briefly the main concepts and claims of his theory and then highlight their relevance for the study of interpersonal relationship.

The central concept of the theory is the duality of structuration: humans both draw on the rules and resources that constitute social structure (an aspect of interaction called production) and manifest structural rules and resources that perdure as consequences of the interaction (an aspect called reproduction). This formulation is meant to guide us toward accounts that simultaneously explain interactive abilities (as access to and skill with structural rules and resources) and social order (as the result of people's dependence on the rules and resources). For instance, we might maintain relationships simply because we know of no polite or pleasant way to break them off or avoid them — no rules enabling the right kind of breakup are available. Giddens generally writes as though this approach applies only to quite general social structural regularities, but I can see no reason why the same approach cannot be taken to a specific partner's treatment of another relational partner — this issue is relevant to the macro-micro problem.

As I. Cohen (1989) has most forcefully argued, the duality of structuration, and structuration theory in general, assume an ontology of interactive praxis. "Praxis" is a term of Aristotelian origin, widely used in Marxist and European philosophy, that frames human behavior as socially meaningful purpose and value oriented, relevant to social order, and, often, socially situated, interactive, and constitutive (MacIntyre, 1984, but see Giddens' commentary on such concepts in, for example, 1976). However, although Giddens does seem committed to a concept of this form of human activity, his theory rarely directly concerns it, instead focusing on its conditions and parameters.

An important part of Giddens' metatheory is his distinction among three "dimensions" or "elements" analyzable in praxis: I will call them communication, norms, and power.[2] Giddens argues that all three dimensions, with varying combinations and emphases, are vital to every social activity and institution. This scheme is important for three reasons. First, it is one of his main ways of reacting to the monistic arguments of theories, such as interpretive and structural sociology, functionalism, and Marxism, each of which has, at times, reductionistically stressed one of the three dimensions. Second, the distinction gives Giddens a way to recognize the institutional differentiation of society without hypostatizing it. Certain systemic complexes involve interaction in which one of the three dimensions is emphasized; such complexes become the economic and political (for power), legal (for norms), and symbolic (for communication) institutions of society, although all institutions must depend to some extent on all three dimensions. Finally and most important, Giddens emphasizes that these dimensions intersect in various ways. For example, he notes that the applicability of norms depends on the interpretation of the norm and the situation, both of which often are negotiated in communication. As a second example, Giddens' definition of ideology is the use of symbols to legitimate power distributions — an intersection of all three dimensions. Giddens does not systematically follow up this insight; he also leaves no clearly allotted space for such institutionalized systems as familial, kinship, and friendship relations; on the other hand, the idea of intersections among the dimensions reminds us of the complex effects achieved in relational interaction.

Giddens sees past social theories as founded on conceptions of people that are wildly unrealistic — either robotlike in following social rules or unconstrainedly creative in constituting social reality. His main theoretic strategy to give substance to the duality of structuration is his "stratification model of agency" — which I will hereafter call the stratified model. This model is fairly complex, and only certain parts are relevant to this chapter. Giddens posits that unconscious motivations and cognitions exist, separated from (practical and discursive) consciousness through repression mainly of basic insecurities. Among the more conscious powers of agents are their capacities for reflexive monitoring and for rationalization. The former involves ongoing sensitivity to the unexpected in agents' activity patterns and contexts; the latter is agents' maintenance of a sense of where they are and what they are doing, useful in routine action and planning but also reportable to others. A summary theme for Giddens has the label "knowledgeability" — agents are able to engage in production and reproduction because they are knowledgeable about their immediate environs in the social system and their own action contexts. I would claim that the overall purpose of this model of agency is to explain the conditions under which agents can engage in structuration in the production and reproduction of the conditions of social life. One other point deserves mention: Giddens points to routineness of praxis as a foundation for the stratification of the powers of the agent; he does not give similar emphasis to concepts like membership or social support or capacities that especially depend on or support relational commitment.

A theme in structuration theory that has grown to be one of the most powerful is that time and space must be included more centrally in social theory. Giddens sees the extension of institutions in time and space and the patterning of everyday lives in time and space as the main attributes distinguishing types of societies. One main source of routineness is the establishment of time-space patterns and bounded territories, called locales or regions, which are bases of familiarity and felt control. Giddens places great emphasis on the fact that agents move in routine, ordered ways through space and time to conduct the social interaction of everyday life. He also distinguishes between social integration and system integration as two sorts of reciprocity: social integration is reciprocal face-to-face interaction of individuals, and system integration is reciprocity among actors or groups across extended space or time, mediated by writing or in various ways. Thus, in ancient empires, contact between a garrison commander and a village mayor was social interaction, and use of military sanctions to control the countryside was system integration. Technological development has led to less and less overlap between processes of social and system integration. Obviously, social integration is the terrain of real human relationships, but Giddens' analysis does not stress that fact: he emphasizes the impersonal relation of reciprocity and the tactics that allow for it, in a way that includes role-relations as well as personal ones. However, his analysis does raise an interesting question: to what extent does the unity of modern society depend on copresent interaction of the type that could foster personal relations? Giddens later argues that interpersonal interaction is vital to foster trust in abstract systems, but is that its only contribution?

Giddens characterizes societies and institutions by their spatial and temporal spread; given his conception of social structure as rules and resources, it is interesting to note how he approaches theory construction about the level of social institutions and societies. His strategy is two-pronged: on the one hand, he creates a conceptual structure for discussing rule and resource complexes at higher levels of abstraction; on the other hand, he characterizes common formations in social systems (such as cities and corporations) in terms of the generalized processes of social and system interaction that they enable, constrain, and depend on. Giddens distinguishes, for instance, two sorts of abstract features that characterize social systems: structural principles are general "principles of organization," while structural sets describe "mutual convertibility" among structural rules and resources, and such convertibility relations solidify the organizational differences spelled out as structural principles. For instance, in middle-class households of the 1950s United States, a structural set might have described the fact that (male) involvement in corporate employment implied daytime absence from the home, which implied absence from childcare duties, which implied noninvolvement in school activities; these implications helped solidify a role difference between husbands and wives. Giddens might use such structural features to describe the systemic relations of home and workplace. One of his most useful reconceptualizations is that of "contradiction." He defines it as a situation where a system operates (its members draw on its structure) in a way that contravenes itself. A couple who loved each other with such enthusiasm that they became worn out and bored with each other would have lived through the effects of this sort of contradiction — though Giddens notes that contradictions in complex systems may lead to compensating or diffuse effects.

The ideas in the previous two paragraphs illustrate Giddens' reading of the macro-micro problem. He argues most fundamentally that it is based on a misleading distinction, because it implies that microphenomena and macrophenomena have different parameters and properties, an implication that Giddens denies. He argues that the most important problems and explanatory concepts apply at multiple levels and that the levels themselves shade off into one another. When he characterizes institutions and societal systems, he uses concepts of extension in time and space, but he analyzes the day-to-day life of individuals, and even situated interaction, in ways that highlight temporal and spatial concerns (as the next section demonstrates). A narrower example is the process of reflexive monitoring, which can be carried out by individuals, groups, or governments; at the higher levels of analysis, it can involve surveillance and information storage and contributes to the concentration of power in modern societies. However, at all levels, it is part of the modern tendency to take systematic knowledge as instrumental and to act on it. In terms of our five dimensions surveyed above, Giddens emphasizes the first two — abstraction and time-space. He tries to represent the macro-micro distinction in spatiotemporal terms but also tries to demonstrate that time-space and other features supposedly separating the macro and the micro can be reconceptualized in ways that embody continuity and coherence. However, in subordinating the other three dimensions of macro-micro analysis, he may decrease the adaptedness of his metatheory to the study of relationships.

INTERACTION AND RELATIONSHIPS IN THE METATHEORY

It is standard for theories working at multiple system levels to include the level of relationships or relational systems as a mediating level between the microlevel of agency or isolated interaction and the macrolevel (Miller, 1978; Parsons, 1954). What Giddens does instead is build a chain of argument that circumvents the relational level. I think it is important, in assessing the relevance of his metatheory to relational analysis, to look closely at how he argues the tie between agency and the larger social system. An important and symptomatic presentation appears in the second and third chapters of *The Constitution of Society* (1984), the richest and most influential source.

Giddens starts the second chapter, entitled "Consciousness, Self, and Social Encounters," with a discussion of Sigmund Freud and the unconscious. His main criticism of Freud's distinction among id, ego, and superego is that its parts have explanatory power mainly as anthropomorphic or mechanistic — they are not formulated to help explain agentive process. Thus, Giddens recasts Freud's discussion of ego ("the I") in terms of reflexive monitoring and discursive articulateness, of memory in terms of knowledgeability and sensed contextual continuity, and of the unconscious in terms of the bar constituting the basic security system whereby anxiety is controlled — all of these rephrasings pointing to necessary requirements for action. The main idea occupying the rest of the chapter is anxiety and its control through the development and sustenance of basic trust. Giddens next follows Erik Erikson in distinguishing "three successive polarities associated with the transformation of the body into an instrument of acting-in-the-world," (1984, p. 53). These three phases of coping — with trust versus mistrust, autonomy versus shame and doubt, and initiative versus guilt — "represent a progressive movement toward autonomy, which should be understood as the foundation for the capability for the reflexive monitoring of conduct" (p. 57). In each stage, the child learns to supplant motives that lead to distractions or blockages of activity, so that relevant anxieties are relocated into the unconscious, and simultaneously develops a new locus of bodily sensitivity, concern, and mastery (the oral-anal-genital progression of Freud. However, Giddens' special concern is to broaden the range of relevance of the body in child development. He notes the importance of locomotor skill in language development and use and the growing sense of importance of the face as a focus of interpersonal encounter and of shame or embarrassment.) Giddens does note, as Erikson does not, that the stages coincide with the child's developing levels of awareness of the agentive characteristics of others and of general linguistic ability, but neither author explores, at a theoretical level, the relational network or interactive practices that might help constitute the child's growing autonomy. Instead, Giddens emphasizes individual-level control of anxieties and of the body.

Those two emphases are maintained in Giddens' analysis of "the fabric of social activity," which is characterized as routinized social practice(s). His foci are indicated in the following passage: "An examination of routinization, I shall claim, provides us with a master key to explicating the characteristic forms of relation between the basic security system . . . and the reflexively constituted processes inherent in the episodic character of encounters" (1984, p. 60). He develops his analysis by analyzing "critical situations" in which the basic routines of life have broken down — his main example is Bruno Bettelheim's discussion in *The Informed Heart* (1960) of concentration camp effects on personality. In the camps, personal respect, autonomy of action, and dependable routines involving bodily nourishment and cleanliness were eliminated or used by the guards as topoi for abuse; the usual results were personality regression, a sense of meaningless isolation, and, often, a personality reconstitution based on identification with authority and with the rituals of degradation. Giddens argues that the camp experience systematically created a radical ontological insecurity, making a stable personality and rational behavior (and, we might add, even minimal interpersonal relatedness) impossible.

In contrast to such critical situations, daily life involves routines that sustain the security assumptions vital to its continuation. At a most basic level, these routines involve bodily stance, coordination, and mastery of gesture, through which a basically self-confident subject can maintain a posture of facing another person and so facilitate monitoring and signaling capacities. Routinely evidenced awareness of the significance of "facing" others is itself evidence of a capacity for reflexive monitoring and rationalization and, consequently, for responsible communicative agency. This Giddens sees as the basis for the importance of "face" and "facework" as analyzed by E. Goffman (1967) and is the reason that Giddens places considerable emphasis on Goffman's work.

Through his analysis of Goffman, Giddens segues from discussing routines of bodily posturing in space to routines that constitute interpersonal encounters. Giddens elaborates several of Goffman's themes. First is Goffman's emphasis on what Giddens calls "mutual reflexive monitoring," used through practices of attention and tact to secure the other's trust in one's ability and commitment to maintain involving interaction. Conversation is portrayed as an "arrangement by which individuals come together and sustain matters having a ratified, joint, current, and running claim upon attention, a claim that lodges them together in some sort of intersubjective, mental world" (Goffman, 1981, quoted in Giddens, 1984, p. 83). In an analysis of talk, he points out how mental health is signaled and judged by the trustworthy accountability of an agent's conversation.

The second theme involves Goffman's insights into the spatiotemporal features of interaction processes. Within the development of this theme, Giddens builds a basic argument about the macro-micro link: the important macroinstitutional forms and their fixity are "implicated in" the very structure and organization of encounters. He begins by reviewing Goffman's analysis of a range of types of social assemblage, especially the encounter or situation of focused face-to-face interactive engagement. He notes how encounters are bounded in space and serially ordered in time, how "front" and "back" regions are maintained and manipulated through often routine but always agentive work. From this analysis, he proceeds to discuss "positioning," his slant on the concept of a social position. The latter implies a social "'identity' [and linked role] within a network of social relations" (p. 83). In contrast, Giddens emphasizes a complex of "position-practice relations" and, specifically, positioning on three temporal scales: situations of copresence, the individual's life path, and "the broader regionalization of societal systems. . . . Individuals are positioned within a widening range of zones, in home, workplace, neighbourhood, city, nation-state, and a world-wide system, all displaying features of system integration which increasingly relates . . . daily life to social phenomena of massive time-space extension. . . . But it is the intersection between these forms of positioning and that within the *longue duree* of institutions which creates the overall framework of social positioning" (1984, p. 85).

After repeating the link of situatedness to routine and security and noting how the routine use of rules, even in ironic ways, contributes to social reproduction, Giddens (1984) does discuss social relations (which, he says, he will "not always be particularly careful to separate" from social interaction). Social relations are conceived as basic units for the analysis of system integration (the kind that integrates noncopresent collectives); "social relations concern the 'positioning' of individuals within a 'social space' of symbolic categories and ties," such as an array of kinship categories (p. 89). He ends the chapter by noting how social relational positioning shapes and depends on knowledgeability. In short, social relations conceptually lead to involvement with social structural rules and resources, not with other people.

Chapter 3 of *The Constitution of Society* is called "Time, Space, and Regionalization." It takes up the idea of positioning as an aspect of the process of social interaction and explores how the concept can be extended to cover expanses of time that go beyond single encounters. Giddens discusses the ideas of "time-geography" and how it treats individual life patterns in ways that have implications for macrosystem analysis. In short, the continuity in Giddens' discussion is based on positioning, moving from its empowering conditions to its importance within interaction to its implications as mobile action within a space of distanciated, institutionally embedded regions.

I think the theory of structuration achieves Giddens' goals very well. It sketches out a set of concepts that are coherent and quite wide-ranging but avoids the well-known problems of the standard assumptive bases of traditional and interpretive social science. The concepts lead our analysis in new and promising directions. Yet, as I have indicated, in formulating his metatheory, Giddens consistently has avoided moving toward personal relationships and the relational network as he develops his conceptual resources.

I would say that the structurational metatheory leaves open two questions that, affirmatively answered, would make fuller inclusion of a relational dimension in structurational studies valuable, if not mandatory. First, are relationally specific knowledge and interactive opportunity part of a society's produced and reproduced social structure? Giddens seems to be inconsistent in answering "no" to this question: if social groups have varying power because of differential access to certain rules and resources, why are pet names and personal familiarity not just as much power resources as aristocratic manners or technical knowledge? Second, how shall we treat the contribution of personal and group support to the development and stability of the agent? They are certainly included in self-identity, but are they not also involved in the deeper processes of stratification of the agent?

OVERVIEW OF GIDDENS' THEORY OF MODERNITY

Giddens' approach to theorizing about the modern era is to trace its underlying features and their consequences, rather than to determine its historical causes. One of his concerns is to argue against postmodernism; where the latter sees a new type of social pattern after a quite recent breakpoint, Giddens sees the coming of age of high modernity, as trends that began several hundred years ago intensify their development. Such trends (analyzed as "institutional dimensions of modernity") include capitalism, industrialization, rationalization, globalization, nationalism, and growing military and surveillance powers, but Giddens argues that all these have their roots in more basic sources. One basic source is the separation-recombination of time and space, so that localized routines of "the same place at the same time" are replaced by use of schedules and surveillance to extend day-to-day relevancies over global distances with flexible timing. A second, derivative but more important, source is the "disembedding" of social systems from local contexts of interaction to operate more generally, especially by means of two mechanisms: symbolic tokens (for example, money) and expert systems (with authority based on credentials rather than local knowledge). Both these disembedding mechanisms depend on trust, transformed from faith in routine or personal integrity to a generalized acceptance of social institutions. A third source of modern trends is called institutional reflexivity — "the regularized use of knowledge about circumstances of social life as a constitutive element in its organization and transformation" (1991, p. 20). Such reflexivity ranges from organizational and governmental controls based on surveillance and social science through democracy as control over the political and social milieu to the use of generalized knowledge by individuals in making lifestyle choices.

Giddens does spend time on the institutional consequences of emergent modernity, especially on the relations among the institutional dimensions mentioned above, growing globalization, and shifting patterns of risk that mark modernity. However, a lot of attention is paid to the way modernity organizes day-to-day life experience. In particular, he develops four relevant themes. First is a generalized view of trust. Modernity, Giddens argues, has brought a transformation of trust, now tied not to loyal personal bonds but to negotiated acceptance. Childhood development is now presented as developing trust by creating a "potential space" of routine practices manifesting independence from the caregiver, which has at its borders a "cocoon" of risks and threats treated as unreal. In adulthood, a similar structure supporting a sense of ontological security is achievable in nonroutine situations, over extended distances, and even for abstract systems, based partly on face-to-face performance by experts at what Giddens calls system "access points." In short, a new ontological character for trust may allow for typical trust-bearing relationships to be narrower and shallower.

A second theme about modern experience is the new form taken by personal or "self-identity." Identity is no longer a result of "place" in a physical locale or a kinship or communal structure. Instead, the self is a "reflexive project" of conscious and skilled concern to us (and others) as we build "a coherent and rewarding sense of identity" (Giddens, 1991, p. 75). Self-identity rests in part on a developmental narrative, an autobiography with plans into the future, fairly often revised and an important medium of reflexive self-control. The main trajectory of this narrative is self-actualization, as we go through "passages" in various "lifestyle sectors" of experience and surmount obstacles and inner conflicts to become who we are. The chief value guiding it is authenticity, not any more general moral vision, and although relational intimacy is a means to self-actualization and an important part of our narrative, personal integrity is oriented primarily toward each person's self. Giddens sees this version of self-identity as directly continuous with the reflexivity and disembedding that are characteristic of modernity.

Two other themes, although important, allow for briefer attention. First, Giddens argues that, as abstract systems gain control of more of life, the episodes or "fateful moments" when control seems inadequate — death, birth, irrational deviance, moral crisis — are separated out and hidden from view, in what he calls the "sequestration of experience," and are dealt with by experts rather than as a part of everyday life. This process disembeds us from the routine relationships that might be given significance by such moments; however, sequestration is inevitably incomplete, and issues raised by such episodes are increasingly focal in what Giddens calls "the return of the repressed." Those issues, and others important to the project of the self, are more and more public, political issues in a final theme of "lifestyle politics." This range of issues differs from the "emancipatory politics" of the past in being focused not on freedom from domination but on moral choice among the social parameters of lifestyle choices about sexuality, death, work, and the environment.

I have actually presented only a fragment of Giddens' theory of modernity, and in a number of works, he elaborates on the nature and development of today's institutions — economic, technological, social, and military. His analysis focuses on abstract process characteristics of modernity that work at numerous levels of analysis, thereby overcoming the macro-micro problem and promising relevance for analysis at the relational level. On the other hand, the features of modernity on which he focuses — disembedding, reflexivity, a self-narrative of personal integrity — seem to highlight the autonomy and isolation of modern life, not whatever we experience of interdependence and community. However, one especially relevant theme about day-to-day experience that he develops is the relation of modernity to personal relationships; for those ideas, we turn directly to his theory of contemporary personal relations.

MODERN INTERPERSONAL RELATIONS
AND DIALOGIC DEMOCRACY

In his most recent work, Giddens has aimed to build a theory of personal life and personal relationships compatible with his metatheory and his theory of modernity. His central work on these lines is *The*

Transformation of Intimacy (1992), developing themes begun in *Modernity and Self-Identity* (1991), but those works involve a concept of democracy in personal life that is elaborated in *Beyond Left and Right* (1994).

Giddens' central concept in the personal sphere is that of the "pure relationship." A pure relationship is "a social relation . . . entered into for its own sake, for what can be derived by each person from a sustained association with another; and which is continued only in so far as it is thought by both parties to deliver enough satisfactions for each individual to stay within it. Marriage — for many, but by no means all groups in the population — has veered increasingly toward the form of a pure relationship, with many ensuing consequences" (1992, p. 58). The "relationship" involved here is "a close and continuing emotional tie" (p. 58) and involves active participation in intimacy. For Giddens, intimacy is, well, intimately tied to his notion of modern reflexivity and implies egalitarian coparticipation in another's exploratory self-development, in construction of a narrative that sustains each sense of self. This enterprise, mentioned above as the "reflexive project of the self" (p. 62), Giddens sees epitomized in self-help manuals, 12-step groups, and talk shows. In intimacy, "each partner is prepared to reveal concerns and needs to the other and to be vulnerable to that other" (p. 61) but is "contingent" and holds "until further notice," only as long as each party benefits sufficiently from the relation (p. 63).

Giddens introduces the term "confluent love" for sexual love in the pure relationship, to replace the concept of romantic love. One difference of confluent love is its emphasis on sexual interaction: rather than taking sexual fulfillment to be the natural consequence of romantic pairing, it presents (mutual) sexual fulfillment as a key benefit sought through the instrumental development of sexual skills. However, in numerous other respects, the pure confluent relationship is a more modern, rationalized (in the Weberian sense) version of the romantic ideal. Giddens does note the modern cast and revolutionary impact of the concept of romantic love. He argues that it displaced the traditional sense of marriage as placement in a system of economic and reproductive roles and brought with it many elements that carry on today in the pure relationship concept. For instance, a romantic relationship implies intimacy and interpersonal communion, a relationship set off from social constraints, and a high level of reflexive self-interrogation and choice. The romantic ideal was used especially by women in their constructions of projected narratives of selfhood, and, in many cases, romantic involvement was taken to promise escape from the paternal household and life fulfillment — a promise that rarely worked out as the woman would have wished. This lack of realism is connected to one of the main problems that Giddens sees with the concept. The romantic ideal was tainted by the gender inequality of the times in which it was imagined and led women to ignore constraints that made its long-term realization through the institution of marriage nearly impossible. Moreover, in the idealized romantic relationship, the lovers often are represented as "uncompleted" without the other or "fated" for each other. Giddens sees this image as leading to what he calls "projective identification" and pathological dependence. He argues that the romantic ideal led to changes in marital and social institutions that made possible a more egalitarian sense of relatedness as "opening oneself out to the other" by self-secure, autonomous individuals.

In his other works on modernity, Giddens argues that pure and confluent patterns have become important as traditional relational bases have declined. The separation of time and space and the disembedding of social systems have helped fragment and undermine the sense of community as a site of unique local familiarity, and with mobility and interpenetration of networks, kinship relations have become fragmented and less relied on. Moreover, with the prominence of abstract systems and a new prototype for trust, what we seek and hope for in a personal relation has itself changed from honor to affectionate loyalty and from sincerity to authenticity (? — "A friend is not someone who always speaks the truth, but someone who protects the emotional well-being of the other" [1990, p. 119]). Instead of being parts of a stable relational support structure, friendships must be as autonomous as the individuals in them.

The idea of autonomy is central to Giddens' concept of democracy. He sees democracy as "free and equal relations" that foster development of individual potentials, protection from arbitrary or coercive power, authentic involvement in basic decisions, and access to needed resources. A more elaborate later version, the concept of dialogic democracy, includes an emphasis on public discussion and mutual tolerance and respect as carried by the growth of social reflexivity. All these ideas, Giddens argues, are consonant with that of the pure relationship. Free mutual choice of intimate relations by autonomous individuals is characteristic of modernity in the interpersonal realm.

Giddens notes that the genders are not equal in their acclimation to pure relationships. He sees women as the most important sources of change toward the more egalitarian form and heterosexual men as the main resistors. Women's growing political and economic equality has led them to protest domestic inequality, but the persistence of traditional roles and the romantic ideal, along with the psychodynamics of child experience, have led women to remain trapped in patterns of dependence on men. The absent, autonomous father represents the outer world and is identified with, in the search for autonomy, by both boys and girls. However, in this identification, the girls' experience is split: she retains a tie to the mother, which results in communication skills that she can use to try to win over the male "other," idealized yet dangerous and unreliable. The boy is treated more distantly by the mother and must split from her to enter the male adult world, but the pain and crippling effect of this loss is never overcome. As a result, men typically rely on women to do the emotional labor involved in relating and, faced with greater uncertainty and a demand for egalitarian participation in intimacy, are prone to destructive or violent responses. The extent to which these patterns apply to nontraditional childhoods or gender identifications is not discussed by Giddens; however, he does see homosexuals' relations, for both sexes, as exemplary in many cases of pure relationships.

Giddens (1992) identifies a number of problems or dilemmas faced by people involved in pure relationships, which he characterizes as "structural contradictions" of such relationships. Clearest is the opposition between the conditional and temporary limits of such relationships and the need for trust and commitment in order to support full disclosure, relational growth, and security. "It is a feature of the pure relationship that it can be terminated, more or less at will, by either party at any particular point. For a relationship to stand a chance of lasting, commitment is necessary; yet anyone who commits herself without reservations risks great hurt in the future, should the relationship become dissolved" (p. 137). Another contradiction involves the opposition of autonomy and dependence: as an intimate relationship develops, there is a tendency for a partner to develop emotional dependence or relational self-identification with the other and to use the relationship as a crutch or refuge from general social involvement. Yet, such patterns mean that at least one partner is failing to develop an autonomous and responsible self-narrative, with various destabilizings or pathological consequences, discussed below as codependence. A third contradiction involves sexual exclusiveness, often a support for growing trust and intimacy but threatened by the growing availability and appeal of transient or "episodic" sexuality. This appeal may be linked to a fourth condition, not exactly a contradiction: because both men and women today have psyches shaped by traditional relational and child-rearing patterns, sexual attraction itself is marked by characteristics (dominance, mystery) that are incompatible with or undermine pure relationships.

Giddens also explicates the pure relationship by contrasting it with two others: sexual addiction and codependence. Increased sexual liberality has transformed Don Juan–like seducers into sex addicts, highly skilled in initiating relationships but compulsively inclined to avoid intimacy. This addictive pattern is like the pure relationship in its instrumental version of relatedness, does achieve enough autonomous control to practice its pursuits, and does cope with the threat of insecurity through avoidance, but such addiction entails a deeper loss of rationalized, reflexive control over self and blocks construction of a coherent self-narrative. Giddens (1992) gives great emphasis to a second contrasting notion of relationship, that of codependency, which he generalizes to apply to any person who, "in order to sustain a sense of ontological security, requires another individual, or set of individuals, to define her (or his) wants; she or he cannot feel self-confident without being devoted to the needs of others" (p. 89). Such persons can be in relationships that are either codependent (with a compulsive other person) or fixated; in the latter case, "the relationship itself is the object of addiction" (p. 89). Fixated relationships are more common and differ from pure relationships precisely in stemming from inadequate maintenance of autonomy: at least one partner's self comes to depend on the other person or the relationship through projective identification. Dissolution of such relationships is merely personally devastating to women; in men, it leads to such pathologies as stalking and physical abuse.

Giddens' concept of intimate or pure relationships illustrates some of the promise implicit in his theory of modernity. Its main foundation and strength is its thorough development of the concept of reflexivity and reflexive control, as carried out by an agent more complex and realistic than that of the classically rational actor or the pure subject of phenomenological or hermeneutic theories. Giddens' stratified model of agency allows the use of developmental, psychodynamic analysis without commitment to determinism or mechanistic theory. Giddens' theory also has some deeper explanatory power because of the centrality of reflexivity and trust in his theory of modernity. He can take the themes of growing self-consciousness and equality and show their interdependence within broader currents of institutional reflexivity, trust in abstract systems, and democratization in his macroanalysis of modern societal development. These are desirable properties that any theory of relationships should seek to include, and Giddens shows fairly well how they should be integrated with more specific relational claims. Some specific themes in Giddens' analysis are also innovative and worthy of attention — for instance, his distinction between "opening outward" in a pure relationship versus "projective identification" as interactive processes and his (limited) attention to development of a self-narrative — these are concepts that deserve elaboration and test in communication research. Finally, I would explicitly acknowledge the concept of "pure relationship" enacting "dialogic democracy" as a theoretically grounded ideal that, elaborated as discussed below, could be highly useful to both couples and relational theorists.

Some of the utility of Giddens' theory can be illustrated by counterposing it to recent dialectical-dialogic theorizing; I will focus here on the work of L. A. Baxter and B. M. Montgomery (1996). These authors retain the senses of difference, process, and situated praxis that they find characteristic of dialectical theories but supplement it with concepts of multiple voices and centrifugal-centripetal tension that they find in M. M. Bakhtin's dialogic position. Rather than positing a determinate logic of development, they argue that "individuals are socially constructed in the ongoing interplay of unity and difference. Communication events, relationships, and life itself are ongoing and unfinalizable, always 'becoming,' never 'being.' . . . There is only an indeterminate flow, full of unforeseen potential that is realized in interaction" (Baxter & Montgomery, 1996, p. 47). I believe that Giddens would applaud this theory of interactive praxis with constitutive implications for identity and relationships; his metatheory seems fully consistent with it, and insofar as his pure relationship concept is like an ideal type, it is meant to variably resemble any real relationship — to be one (growingly but variably insistent) voice. However, Giddens' theories go beyond and supplement the dialogic view in several ways. First, like much postmodernist work, dialectic-dialogic decenters the agent and, therefore, cannot explain how people are able to engage in dialogue and have their selves constituted by it. We must not mistake an account of how a sense of self emerges in symbolic interchange for an explanation of agentive powers. Second, Giddens' concept of structural contradictions that can arise in relationship is on a different and important level than the dialogic contradictions described by Baxter and Montgomery. In recognizing multivocality, it is vital to recognize that some dialogues insistently drive themselves to monologue, silence, or conflict (Pearce, 1989); Giddens' notion of contradiction is flexible and open-ended enough to describe this possibility without denying conversational agency. Third, Baxter and Montgomery's conception of process seems so flexible that it renders all dialogues and relational processes equally probable. It does not offer an analysis or image of any type of relationship that is characteristic or symptomatic of life today (or anytime), relative to dominant patterns and forces in material reality. Giddens offers his concepts as touchstones with broad and systematically explained relevance.

However, Giddens' theory also involves a series of weaknesses or lacunae that I see as united under the theme undersociality. First, in emphasizing reflexivity, Giddens neglects other themes in his metatheory and analysis of modernity. The duality of structuration is never mentioned, nor is the general triad of power, meaning, and normativity — Giddens' metatheoretic emphasis on the omnipresence of power in interaction is not brought into play. More significantly, perhaps, the "separation of time and space" characteristic of modernity is noted only as fragmenting traditional relational nets. Increased mobility and more powerful technology have been suggested as sources of major changes in relational dynamics similar to those addressed by Giddens (cf. Bennis & Slater, 1968; Berger & Kellner, 1964), and Kenneth Gergen (1991) has constructed an elaborate theory of how changes in our spatiotemporal powers have led to changes in self-concepts and relationships. His basic theme is that the self today is "saturated" — overrun with relational implications and possibilities.

This neglect of the mediation of space and time is paralleled by the individualistic orientation Giddens takes toward relationships. For Giddens, agents may engage in relationships but are not (or should not be) engaged by them. His description of individuals involved in pure relationships is reminiscent of early social exchange analyses; his agents are socially constituted, but in relational interaction, they are no more essentially involved than are the atomized individuals of capitalist theories in market transactions. In a chapter on "Love, Commitment, and the Pure Relationship" (Giddens, 1992), commitment is discussed only in examples of the crippling effect on women of abandonment or widowhood. A lifelong bond is not discussed distinct from an open relationship of a few weeks' duration. Now, there is another option: individuals can make deep, self-defining commitments to relationships, but in doing so, they seem liable to fall within Giddens' category of codependence, fated to a stunted and pathological self-narrative.

In *Modernity and Self-Identity* (1991), Giddens does emphasize commitment more as necessary in a pure relationship. "Commitment is recognized by participants to buy time: to provide emotional support which is guaranteed to persist through at least some of the perturbations which the relationship might undergo (although returns will almost certainly be demanded for this). . . . The committed person is prepared to accept the risks which the sacrificing of other potential options entails" (1991, p. 93). Two problems are apparent: first, commitment is treated as merely one more service for which "returns" will be expected — not exactly the usual meaning or expected dynamic. Second, the theory does not account for the necessity or importance of commitment — it is certainly not necessary for openness, provision of good advice, sexual favors, or self-narrative help. In the end, Giddens does not integrate commitment as a basic or ontological potential of relationship.

Caught in this atomized treatment, it is perhaps predictable that Giddens neglects the larger social context, treating the isolated dyadic bond as the norm. There is no discussion of the fact that dyads are often and even constitutively embedded in groups of relatives, friends, or community members. No doubt this results from his stance that kinship and communal relations of the traditional sort have fragmented, but overwhelming evidence suggests that the fragmented ties that remain are prized, depended on, and, in many cases, reembedded. The valuable discussion of childhood experience within the traditional family is not paralleled by a discussion of the experience of parenting and coparenting, neither for traditional nor for "purely related" couples. The main discussion of parent-child relations occurs within the chapter on codependence, in which Giddens' first argument is that modern parental relations are more varied (in blended families and so on) and that, as a result, they are more likely to be negotiated and to approach the pure ideal. He argues that agentive negotiation is common at much younger ages than typically recognized and that, for very young children, the parent ought ethically to assume a "counterfactual" negotiating stance, recognizing how the child would reply if he or she were competent. However, Giddens' main argument has to do with parenting as the source of addictive and codependent behavior; one section is called "Toxic Parents?," and other sections quote at length from self-help descriptions of processes of overcoming parental abuse. The substantive nature of the child's role in the family and its negotiation (on multiple dimensions rather than simply the one of benefit versus abuse) in a context of multiple parents and children is not really addressed, and no argument for its irrelevance is given. Although Giddens' topic is not family relations, I think the pattern of foci is symptomatic: Giddens' perspective is constrained by the individual-society problematic of standard sociological theory and by his nonrelationally oriented metatheory.

CONCLUDING RECOMMENDATIONS

I believe that the theory of structuration has great potential as a foundation and a starting point for the investigation of relational communication, but I think that, in developing both metatheory and substantive theories,

Giddens has chosen roads of elaboration that limit the value of his contributions to the foundation of relational theory. I suggest several changes in the conceptual substructure of the theory of structuration to enhance its adequacy in the treatment of relationships.

First, I think Giddens' stratified model of agency needs to be supplemented in a way that explains the openness of individuals to committed relational involvement. Here, it is appropriate for me to formally avoid giving a clear and full definition of what I mean (or want structuration theory to mean) by "personal (or even social) relationship." However, I can suggest several broad defining clauses. I do not think it is sufficient to define a personal relationship, or commitment, by qualities like interdependence, exchange of benefits, level of objective investments, or mutuality of self-disclosure. One is interdependent with the owner of one's favorite grocery store and frequently exchanges important benefits with that owner as well; one can exchange the deepest self-disclosure with another guest on a talk show. These relations differ from commitment, I would claim, in being merely external, not involving the self of the person with the self of the other. R. Bhaskar (1979) distinguishes external from internal relations and argues that realism and similar positions (including structuration) can recognize internal relations as those involving the essential natures of the related entities. I am inclined to think that empirical investigation, plus theoretical work, would be required to determine what sort of personal relation a personal relation of commitment would involve. The most obvious and shallowest possibility, given Giddens' theory so far, would be that, in a committed personal relationship, a person begins to judge benefits from the point of view of both relational members, not just himself or herself — from the point of view of "we." This idea is even consistent with relatively recent versions of exchange theory (Kelley & Thibaut, 1978; Rusbult & Buunk, 1993). I do not think it is sufficient because it retains the rational, externally related, nonprocessual image of the individual agent and ignores the more fundamental things that relations can do to people.

A possibility more consonant with Giddens' central theoretical concepts is that such processes as self-narrative, reflexive monitoring, and even rationalization might themselves be dialogic in the sense developed by Baxter and Montgomery (1996) and might give a special place or voice to another person to whom we are committed. My sense of where I am would become a sense of where I am on a project about which we differ, or agree, and to which I feel responsible.

An emendation that is better known is that social relationships are essential to the development of agency. Giddens does give an important role to caregivers, but the main contribution of experience with them is to create enough of a sense of security to make the agent's conscious activity autonomous. After existential insecurities can be coped with, the agent is monological and seems like the rational economic (hu)man. An alternative is to accept a version of the position that agency is social — that the constitution of agentive powers and their structure depends on processes that are essentially nonmonological. Prototypes of this sort of position are legion — G. H. Mead, M. Buber, M. M. Bakhtin, C. Taylor. In Giddens' model of agency, we might argue that a sense of familiarity and membership with other agents is as important as and partly substitutable for a sense of routineness involving time-space settings and paths.

Second, I believe that Giddens' conceptual system also must recognize the full constitutive nature of interaction — an odd claim considering that Giddens' key book is *The Constitution of Society* (1984). His early openness toward poststructuralist writers (for example, 1979) has become increasingly negative (1987b) as he has defended the real and explanatory powers of agency against reductionistic attacks; however, in defending agency, I think he has overlooked the ways and extent to which agency, in its processes and consequences, is dependent on and shaped by social constitution. My own suggestion for a change in his conceptual substructure would be to add to the three dimensions of structuration (communication, norms, power) a fourth — call it constitution. By addressing another person, we are not just recognizing but also constituting them as an agent and a participating speaker (Althusser, 1971); just so, by saying "We're best friends," we are not just labeling but also bringing into fuller existence a relationship. Interaction has this power, which is not legitimately reducible to communication, power, or normative action. By separating this dimension from the others, we would be led to pay attention to interactional dynamics that transform the internal relation of personal relationship.

My third suggestion concerns Giddens' approach or avoidance of the macro-micro problem. By stressing the continuity of basic processes across system levels and the centrality of time-space, Giddens has reconceptualized and, if anything, focused social theorizing on the problem. After all, his theory of personal relationships uses characteristic processes of "modernity" as the ultimate level of explanation. However, in this reconceptualization, he has diverted attention from the relational context in which those processes proceed. "Family" or "friendship group" become, in the first instance, regions of time-space routine. I would suggest that structuration theory places renewed emphasis on reticular context as a dimension of equal importance with time-space. Routine in the space of social relationships is as much a ground of ontological security and a dimension along which integration works as is spatiotemporal routine. The final dimension noted above, systemic-functional complexity, is harder to think of as fundamental to interpersonal relationship, but aspects of J. Habermas' (1987) analysis of the life world and the relations of the institutionalized system to it might be useful elaborations of a theory that seeks to characterize modern relationships.

These changes would empower Giddens to deal with the central problem in his theory of personal relationships: that it is undersocialized and, so, leaves no room for a committed relationship between the instrumentally pure relationship and the unhealthy codependent one. Analyses of modernity or other social problems inevitably would implicate the agent's capacity, not just to act but also to relate. Additionally, the changes would enable him to discuss personal relationships within a more usual range of relational contexts: the family, the circle of friends, and so on, and they would lead to a focus of attention on the problem of commitment without codependence or domination — a plaguingly important one in our times.

NOTES

1.   Banks and Riley (1992) and L. Putnam (1992) have criticized use of the term "metatheory" by McPhee and Poole (1980) on grounds that I think involve a misunderstanding. They seem to think that, by metatheory, we mean a substantive theory that synthetically arrays a variety of other theories. On the contrary, we consistently use metatheory to refer to a level of theorizing that is more abstract than substantive theory and that covers broad conceptual, ontological, normative, and methodological issues that ground and constrain substantive theory. Aristotle's *Metaphysics* initiated this usage, and, in my experience, it is standard. I find it more accurate than "ontology of potentials," because ontology ignores Giddens' very important contributions to theory building and methodology (including his methodological postulate that ontological concerns should and do have priority over epistemological ones) and potentials misdescribes such inescapable conditions of social life as the duality of structuration and stratified agency.

2.   The distinction among "elements" is actually one dimension of a two-dimensional grid of distinctions; I have drawn from two different rows in composing my list of dimensions. The two rows involve Giddens' distinction between interaction and "modalities." To be brief, I consider the modalities to be incoherent with Giddens' theoretic emphasis on duality and definition of structure, trying to capture irremediably dual notions of process and structure in single, rulelike terms.

6

"But I Thought that We Were More than Error Variance": Application of the Social Relations Model to Personal Relationships

Sandra Metts

Anyone who has been interested in the phenomenon known loosely as close or personal relationships, whether as participant or scientist, has been struck by the complexity of relational life. The conversations of ordinary people are peppered not only with references to members of their relational network, such as friend, lover, dating partner, husband or wife, parents, and other category designations, but also with more discerning expressions, such as "just a sexual relationship," "only a study partner," "a good friend but not best friend," a "fishing buddy," and so forth. Moreover, traditional role and kin relationships are sometimes defined as personally selected, for example, "my mother (brother, sister, father) is my best friend," and carefully distinguished, for example, "He's my biological father but not my real dad."

Clearly, something in the nature of these interactions and their interpretations are identifiable and consequential to people as they go about their daily affairs. Similarly, people observe the interactions of those around them and reveal their insights by reference to relationship properties. For example, coworkers or academic colleagues who spend considerable time working together may be observed to deviate from the norms of polite discourse, to use shorthand expressions and personal idioms, to complete each other's sentences, to co-construct stories or edit each other's stories, and to have similar attitudes about social objects, events, and other people. Observations of these interactions by outsiders may evoke the spontaneous comment, "You two act like a married couple," or even more descriptive, "like an *old* married couple." In all these cases, relationship participants and observers are acting like "naive scientists." They are making connections among particular types of interactions, particular people in those interactions, and evidence of consistency in patterns and content of interactions that lead them to conclude that a relationship is present.

The purpose of this chapter is to provide a more formal analysis of the connections that laypersons make in their daily observations. The social relations model (SRM) (Kenny, 1994a, 1994b, 1996; Kenny & Kashy, 1991) will be presented as a statistical representation of the general concept of relationship. Certainly, not all questions about personal relationships invite statistical analysis nor require use of the SRM. As with any method, the choice should be based on the types of questions that motivate the research. However, when the researcher is interested in isolating "purely relational phenomena," the SRM provides a useful means toward that end (Kenny, 1994a, 1994b).

With that caveat in mind, the remaining pages of this chapter will be used to introduce D. A. Kenny's SRM and illustrate its utility to researchers who are interested in how to study the unique qualities of a relationship. Because the SRM emerges from several traditions in the social sciences that have struggled with how a relationship should be conceptualized and how it should be measured, background on these traditions is useful for understanding the contributions and limitations of the SRM. Therefore, the chapter will proceed in four sections. First, it will orient the reader to the general scope of the chapter by suggesting the types of methodological issues in studying personal relationships to which the SRM responds. It then will summarize three research traditions in personal relationships that are most relevant to the conceptual underpinnings of the SRM; each of these traditions offers an insight into the type of research problem or concern that the SRM addresses. Third, the fundamental assumptions that underlie the SRM, particularly those that help us understand relationship interdependence, will be elaborated. Finally, the chapter will close with comments on the utility of the model for scholars interested in quantitative analyses of personal relationships.

METHODOLOGICAL ISSUES IN STUDYING PERSONAL RELATIONSHIPS

The conceptual and methodological challenges of studying personal relationships have drawn the attention of scholars from a number of disciplines. As a psychological phenomenon, for example, a relationship can be studied as partners' mental representations and subjective states. As a communication phenomenon, a relationship can be studied as the manifest structure of partners' interactions. The SRM does not advocate any particular disciplinary orientation to relationships, but it does advocate statistical practices that separate the qualities and behaviors unique to a relationship from the qualities and behaviors characteristic of the persons involved in the relationship.

Although this distinction is intuitively reasonable, it is not necessarily evident in research practices. For example, scholars routinely make theoretical claims about relationships based on data collected from individuals. According to S. Duck (1990), "Most 'theories of relationships' — and there are not many — are focussed at an individual level of analysis and deal with individual attributions about relational events, individual processing of information about others, individual characteristics and their effect on relational partners, or individual strategies and plans for or about relationships" (p. 6).

Building theories of relationships from individual-level data has been criticized on the grounds that it fails to recognize the emergent and interdependent nature of relationships (Baxter & Montgomery, 1996; Duck & Sants, 1983; Robins, 1990). The practice continues, however, because traditional research methods are not typically adapted to relationship-level questions motivating the research. In some circumstances, a researcher might well want to know what individuals think, feel, or believe about their relationships. However, when a researcher is interested in the unique properties of a relationship, attempts to generalize individual level perceptions to relationship properties require attention to methodological issues.

Several such issues can be illustrated with an example. When responding to a questionnaire, an individual might report a high rate of negative partner behavior, such as complaining, and also might report a low level of relationship satisfaction. If this pattern holds generally true for a large sample of respondents, a likely conclusion is that complaints lead to relational dissatisfaction. Although this conclusion might, indeed, be true, it is not necessarily substantiated from the self-reports of individuals.

First, persons in close relationships tend to respond to their relationships emotionally. These generalized positive or negative affects can influence how a person perceives and subsequently reports his or her partner's communicative behavior. The correlation between partner's complaints and respondent's dissatisfaction may be, in part, because of the consistency between two self-report measures, both completed by the same person (that is, common method variance) (see Weiss & Heyman,

1990, for more detailed treatment of this point). This "halo effect" may inflate measures of association between relational satisfaction and partner's complaints. Analyzing the interactions between the partners and coding the occurrence of complaints is one way to determine how much of a respondent's satisfaction or dissatisfaction is attributable to partner's complaints (although causality still is debatable). Additionally, coding both members' messages may reveal that the respondent's partner only complains when the respondent does a certain type of action. This level of analysis then would reveal interactional or dyadic-level linkages.

A second issue concerns the treatment of variation within the sample. When respondents' scores deviate from the average of the group, that is, a person reports relatively high satisfaction but also reports relatively high rates of partner complaints, this variation is typically assigned to the error term, as either random error or measurement error. If, however, a researcher assessed a respondent's general tendency to see all comments, regardless of who is talking, as complaints, this traitlike predisposition could be controlled for in the analysis. In the absence of such a distinction, the unique effect of perceived level of partner's complaints on a particular respondent's level of relational satisfaction is not verified.

Issues of variability can arise in an analogous fashion even in research that purports to study relationships rather than individuals. In experimental and survey research, for example, respondents often are placed in groups for the purpose of analysis. Ordinary language labels, such as married, dating, friends, and coworkers, are used to reflect presumably common (and stable) features within groups and provide meaningful distinctions between the groups when compared with each other. This practice ignores the fact that relationships within any category might, themselves, differ on very important dimensions. Some marriages have little sexual or emotional interdependence, whereas others have a great deal; some friendships are primarily communal and some primarily exchange oriented; some coworkers are very close friends, and some roommates are hardly more than acquaintances (Fitzpatrick, 1991; Fitzpatrick & Badzinski, 1994). In much the same way that variations in individual scores are assigned to error variance, variation on scores within relationship types often is considered error variance. The possibility that it represents the unique consistency of a particular dyad is seldom explored.

The SRM offers one response to the methodological issues that concern relationship scholars. In several articles and book chapters (for example, Kenny, 1988, 1994b, 1996; Kenny & Kashy, 1991) and in a recent book (Kenny, 1994a), Kenny has presented techniques for isolating properties that are uniquely relational. Although primarily formulated in response to limitations in the research on interpersonal perception, the implications of Kenny's SRM are germane to relationship processes more broadly construed. In order to set the stage for a discussion of the SRM, the next section reviews the prominent research traditions that are most amenable to this type of analysis. Each of these traditions provides a piece of the relationship puzzle that Kenny distills.

THREE RESEARCH TRADITIONS

Reflections on the development of the close relationships field since the 1970s indicates three broad traditions guiding research: the behavioral perspective, the cognitive perspective, and the system perspective. Although there is variability among scholars who work within these broad categories, each tradition has a core set of assumptions about what a relationship is and how it should be analyzed. In addition, although there is overlap among these perspectives in concepts and methods, they can be distinguished, at least for the purposes here, by the point of entry to the relationship. This review is not intended to be exhaustive but to be illustrative of the types of research that represent each tradition.

Behavioral Perspective

Few researchers in the behavioral tradition would argue that subjective states and cognitions of relationship partners are unimportant (Gottman, 1979). Indeed, several studies have systematically linked the content and structure of relational talk with the affective responses of participants (for example, Weiss & Summers, 1983) and compared observer judgments with participant judgments to determine consistency (Birchler, Clopton, & Adams, 1984). However, analyses are decidedly "bottom-up" (behavior to affect or cognition) rather than "top-down" (affect or cognition to behavior). In general, the assumption is that the behavioral manifestations of how couples use their time, coordinate their activities, and talk to each other provide both couples and researchers with a meaningful map of a relationship territory and, when appropriate, serve as evidence for inferring subjective states.

Research Practices

The behavioral perspective assumes that relationships exist in patterns of behavior that distinguish personal relationships as a group from nonpersonal (or social) relationships and distinguish certain types of personal relationships from other types (for example, distressed from nondistressed marriages, close friends from best friends, communal relationships from exchange relationships). The types of behaviors examined range from microlevel behaviors (for example, eye gaze, speech dysfluency) and episode types (self-disclosure, conflict, sexual intercourse) to larger spans of time and activity (for example, leisure time activities, household tasks). Although, in theory, all behavior is observable, the units of behavior that are analyzed are not necessarily obtained from direct observation. Depending upon the nature of the research question guiding the study, a researcher might use self-report data provided by respondents, observational data, or a combination of both types of data.

Self-report data can be collected with a variety of measurement instruments. Common among these are questionnaires that ask respondents to describe behaviors occurring in recollected events, highly structured or open-ended diaries that ask respondents to record patterns of behavior over time, or records of daily events. H. T. Reis (1994) further specifies three procedures for collecting data for daily events: at predetermined intervals established by the researcher, in response to signals (for example, telephone calls, pagers) from the researcher, or participant recording each time a targeted event occurs.

In many cases, participant self-reports are the appropriate, and often the only, way to access a behavior or event (Metts, Sprecher, Cupach, 1991; Robins, 1990). Sexual episodes, for example, are difficult to study in ways other than through self-report methods. However, as the time between an event's occurrence and its reporting increases, the likelihood of recall bias and post hoc interpretation based on current affective states also increases (Miell, 1987).

Even self-reports of current behavior can be confounded with subjective states, particularly when the targeted behavior or event implicates affective states (for example, conflict or argument). For example, E. A. Robinson and M. G. Price (1980) placed observers in the homes of married couples to record the frequency of "pleasurable behaviors" spouses displayed and received. Spouses also recorded the frequency of pleasurable behaviors they expressed and received during the time observers were present. Results indicated a moderate correlation between spouses' recordings of pleasurable behaviors and those of observers. However, dissatisfied spouses underestimated rates of pleasurable events by about 50 percent compared with satisfied spouses. In addition, spouses were more accurate in recording the pleasurable behaviors they sent than in recording the pleasurable behaviors displayed toward them by their partner. These findings are consistent with several behavioral studies suggesting that, in general, people are able to report their own behavior more accurately than a partner's or family member's behavior, perhaps because generalized affect influences attention and recall (see also Noller & Ruzzene, 1991; Sullaway & Christensen, 1983).

In addition to self-report measures, research in the behavioral tradition draws heavily on analysis of behaviors that are directly observed by relational partners or by the researcher, usually preserved as audio- or video-taped interactions. These patterns typically are identified in conversational interaction with four types of measurement procedures (alone or in combination) (Cappella, 1991). These procedures include coding, where trained coders or mechanical recording devices register the presence or absence or quantity of a type of behavior in a segment of interaction; rating, where trained coders assign values, often on Likert-type scales, for amount or degree of behavior exhibited; participant judgment, where untrained but involved persons assign values according to the meaning inferred from a segment or episode (for example, hostile-affiliative); and observer judgment, where trained or untrained persons who are not involved assign values according to the meaning inferred from a segment or episode based on generally shared cultural knowledge.

Examples of each of these types of measurement are available in the literature. The long tradition of research on the conversational control patterns of married couples, for example, makes use of trained coders who code each turn in the conversation for the presence or absence of control moves. Based on the relational communication coding scheme developed by L. E. Rogers and her colleagues (for example, Millar & Rogers, 1987; Chapter 4 of this book), each conversational turn is coded for the direction of relational control that it manifests; a one-up move, a one-down move, or a one-across move. Pairs of turns, or interacts (A-B–B-A–A-B), are then categorized according to the symmetry or complementarity in the sequence of control moves manifested in the interact. A one-up move, for example, might be followed by a one-up move (symmetrical pattern), by a one-down move (complementary pattern), or by a one-across move (neutral pattern). In general, patterns of control are systematically associated with relationship satisfaction, communication satisfaction, and perceived understanding.

The work by J. M. Gottman and colleagues over the past two decades exemplifies the use of both coding (mechanical measures of affect) and rating (trained coders' assessment of affect) in marital couples' and families' conversations during problem-solving and conflict episodes (see Gottman, 1979, 1982a, 1982b, 1994; Markman & Notarius, 1987 for reviews; also, Gottman & Levenson, 1986; Levenson & Gottman, 1983; Notarius & Johnson, 1982). In these studies, both physiological behavior (that is, heart rate, skin conductance, sweating, and somatic activity) and observer-coded emotional states using the specific affect coding system (Gottman & Levenson, 1986) are measured. In general, results indicate that husbands are less likely to discharge negative affect through verbal and nonverbal expression and that negative affect reciprocity (both physiological measures and observer-coded affect) is predictive of marital satisfaction over time.

The work of S. Planalp and A. Benson (1992) employs noninvolved observer judgments to identify behavioral indicators of cultural level relationship schemata. College students were asked to distinguish audiotaped conversations between friends from audiotaped conversations between acquaintances and to specify the basis of their decision. Students were able to distinguish the conversation with some degree of accuracy (79 percent) and could specify the behaviors that led them to their decision. In general, friends were identified as "more relaxed, more intimate, more informal, to share floortime more equally, to interrupt each other more often and to talk about a single topic more often than acquaintances" (p. 493).

Implications

For scholars interested in understanding properties that characterize relationships rather than individuals, the assessment of behaviors that occur (or occurred) when relationship partners are in each other's presence offers an important advantage. It allows researchers to identify sequences of contingent behavior between relational partners that presumably represent relationship interdependence. To the degree that a relationship exists as patterns of mutual influence, the ability to identify these patterns is important. According to J. N. Cappella, "If x's behaviors do not affect y's uniquely and mutually, then contingent responsiveness is not present and y cannot be said to be observably sensitive to alterations in x's actions" (1987, p. 188). This definition captures the essence of a relationship as behaviorally manifested. Cappella's own work with nonverbal and vocalic synchrony in mother-child dyads and adult dyads (for example, Cappella, 1981, 1988; Cappella & Palmer, 1990) illustrates this perspective, as does Rogers' work with relational control moves in married couples' conversations and Gottman's work with conflict episodes described previously.

In addition, once contingent sequences have been identified, behavioral analyses can provide ways to categorize relationships based on interaction patterns, rather than common relationship labels (for example, married, close friends) or evaluative designations (for example, distressed couples). For example two mothers might pick up their babies about the same number of times, but a ratio of the proportion of times a mother picks up her baby only when it cries might reveal that one mother tends to initiate contact spontaneously whereas the other mother provides contact only in response to the infant's distress. A classic study of interaction patterns between rhesus monkey mothers and their infants by R. A. Hinde and M. J. Simpson (Hinde, 1979) serves as an excellent illustration of how ratio data might be used. Ratio measures of the number of times the mother spontaneously initiated contact with her infant and the number of times that the mother rejected the infant's spontaneous attempts at contact with her yielded four types of mother-infant relationships: rejecting (low mother initiation, high rejection of infant's attempts), possessive (high mother initiation, low rejection of infant's attempts), controlling (high mother initiation, high rejection of infant's attempts), and permissive (low mother initiation, low rejection of infant's attempts) (pp. 74–75).

Similar patterns have been observed in the interactions of human mothers and their infants. The origin of attachment theory (see Ainsworth, 1972, 1982; Bowlby, 1979, 1982), for example, was in the observations of mothers and their infants in both clinical and nonclinical settings. In the "secure" attachment pattern, babies explored the environment freely and consistently received comforting from their mothers when distressed. In the "avoidant" attachment pattern, babies explored the environment freely but either avoided mother or received little comforting when distressed. In the "anxious-ambivalent" attachment pattern, babies were hesitant about exploring the environment and, when distressed, received inconsistent comforting (that is, were as likely to be rejected as to receive comforting). Although these behavioral patterns were presented by J. Bowlby and others as the foundation of an infant's mental "working model" of attachment and eventually presented as the basis of adult relationship predispositions known as attachment styles (for example, Collins & Read, 1990; Hazan & Shaver, 1987; Shaver, Collins, & Clark, 1996), their initial formulation was derived from the behavioral patterning of mother-child interactions.

In sum, the study of behavioral patterns in various types of relationships provides an important piece of the relationship puzzle. It reveals linkages among behaviors that characterize relationships but that might not be recognized by participants in those relationships. However, what the study of behavior alone does not reveal is the meaning of those linkages for participants. Much of behavioral minutia of a close relationship succumbs to an efficiency model of processing. It is collected and stored as a gestalt, a mental image of "the relationship." To better understand this level of relationship, scholars often study relationship cognitions.

Cognitive Perspective

Researchers aligned with the cognitive perspective are interested less in the frequency or sequencing of observable behaviors than in the "sense" that relational partners make of those behaviors. Because social events in general, and relationship events in particular, are not "brute facts" nor "undigested interactions" (Duck & Sants, 1983), any particular relationship is presumed to be the enactment of partners' abstract mental representations. Consequently, the direction of analysis tends to be top-down, from cognition to behavior. From this perspective, communication is not merely the manifestation of relationship regularities but a more active arena that partners use "to develop accurate relational knowledge . . . , to ensure that they share the same relational knowledge, and to discover the limits of their common knowledge and each one's specialized knowledge" (Surra & Bohman, 1991, p. 302).

Research Practices

The most common research practices in this tradition are the use of interviews and participants' written descriptions as a means to characterize cognitive structures, followed by experimental or quasi-experimental designs to study how the structures operate in processing and recalling relationship relevant information. The operations of a cognitive structure typically are inferred by the researcher from systematic variation in processing and recalling details of a relational stimulus (for example, a media portrayal of a relationship or a researcher-generated vignette or scenario) (for example, Fehr, 1993; Fitzpatrick, 1991).

Although a number of concepts are employed to describe cognitive properties, two concepts imported from the social cognition literature have been particularly useful to relationship researchers: prototypes and schemata. These mental structures are presumed to function both as generative mechanisms, guiding the types of behaviors that a person might enact in a relationship (Baxter, 1987; Surra & Bohman, 1991), and as interpretive mechanisms, guiding the patterns of inference and attribution that a person might associate with the behaviors of a partner (Surra, Batchelder, & Hughes, 1995).

B. Fehr's systematic investigation of love and commitment illustrates both the nature of prototypes and how they function in relationships. Fehr (1988) isolated a cluster of core and peripheral features associated with the concepts of love and commitment in the descriptions of respondents. For example, core attributes of love are those associated with companionate love (caring and affection); peripheral attributes are those associated with passionate love (sexual attraction and lust). Core attributes of commitment are loyalty, responsibility, and faithfulness; peripheral attributes are security and feeling trapped.

Recall data from researcher-generated descriptions of relationships indicated that prototype attributes are associated in both vertical and horizontal clusters. Thus, when a prototype was activated by the presence of relevant attributes (particularly core attributes) in a relationship description, respondents "remembered" that other attributes were present as well, even when they are not present in the descriptions (vertical association). Likewise, when attributes for one prototype were present (or absent) in a relationship description, subjects inferred the presence (or absence) of attributes for the other (horizontal association). Fehr (1988) concludes that, in ongoing relationships, prototypes function not only to sort and organize observed stimuli but also to construct mental representations of the relationship that depend heavily on inference to achieve internal coherence.

Several theoretical and empirical investigations of relationship schemata are available in the literature as well. Schemata are usually distinguished from prototypes on the basis of their broader, more complex, and causally integrated representation of relationships. Schemata have been used to characterize both general relationship knowledge and relationship-specific knowledge. C. A. Surra and T. Bohman (1991) define "general schemata" as those cognitive structures that contain "beliefs about what a relationship is typically like, normative beliefs about what makes a relationship good or bad, and rules for appropriate behavior" (p. 288). General schemata are heavily influenced by social conventions, the media, observations of one's parents, other network members, and one's unique history in various types of relationships.

One example of a general relationship schemata is that proposed by W. W. Wilmot and L. A. Baxter (described in Wilmot & Shellen, 1991). Based on ethnographic interviews, Wilmot and Baxter formulated the relationship schemata model, which consists of three elements: "a natural language label, a set of criterial attributes which typify the prototype, and communicative indicators of criterial attributes" (p. 423). When describing friendship, for example, respondents not only supplied various types of labels (casual, good, and best friend) but also specified the criteria by which these categories of friendship were differentiated. Moreover, some of the criterial attributes for friendship were identical to those used for characterizing romantic relationships (for example, trust, respect, ease in communicating, and openness), whereas others were unique to romantic relationships (for example, mysticism or inexplicableness, sexual intimacy, more direct talk about the relationship, greater effort, and more exclusivity). The communicative indicators of criterial attributes were difficult for respondents to specify, but among those generated were willing to be open, willing to keep a secret, and listen to other's problems.

Relationship-specific schemata are adaptations of the general schemata to the specifics of a particular relationship. According to Surra and Bohman (1991), they are "an organized representation of traits, beliefs, behaviors, and action sequences that are relevant to a particular other person and to one's relationship with that person" (p. 288). M. W. Baldwin (1992, 1995) further specifies that the representation of "self-with-other or self as experienced in that relationship" is processed as an "if-then formulation, 'If I get angry my spouse will withdraw from me'" (1995, p. 548).

M. A. Fitzpatrick's typology of marital couples illustrates a particularly systematic examination of relationship-specific schemata (see Burrell & Fitzpatrick, 1990; Fitzpatrick, 1988; Fitzpatrick & Badzinski, 1994; Noller & Fitzpatrick, 1993). The relational dimensions inventory taps three dimensions of married life: ideology (for example, traditionalism, uncertainty), interdependence and autonomy (for example, sharing time and space), and communication (for example, conflict avoidance and assertiveness). Couples' scores on the relational dimensions inventory indicate the extent to which they are one of three marital types (traditionals, separates, or independents) or a combination of marital types (for example, husband is traditional and wife is separate). According to Fitzpatrick (1990), "marital schemata operate to specify the nature and organization of information relevant to the partner and the marriage, and to plan and direct activity relevant to the schemata" (p. 443). Messages that do not "prime" the schemata or messages that are considered irrelevant to the schemata are not processed through the schemata. However, once the schemata is primed, "relevant messages are processed for consistency and inconsistency. . . . Consistent marital messages are processed in a mindless or scripted manner and probably trigger similar scripted responses from the spouse" (p. 444). Inconsistent messages stimulate attributional processes and other types of sense-making analyses.

Two processes associated with schemata are of special interest to relationship scholars: the process by which an individual's general relationship schemata is particularized to a specific relationship and the process by which two partners achieve some degree of overlap or agreement in their relationship-specific schemata. Although neither process is fully understood, several explanations have been offered.

One description of the process by which an individual's general relationship schemata is adapted to a specific relationship is offered by Planalp (1987; Planalp & Rivers, 1996). She depicts the general schemata in much the same way that Fehr presents the love and commitment prototypes, as a structure of "interconnected slots" that sort and systematize abstract relationship information. As information about a particular relationship is acquired, it fills relevant slots and instantiates the schemata. If a particular type of relational information is not available (or observed), default values are filled in. For instance, a woman might assume that her partner would continue to work after marriage (care for the children, avoid infidelity, and so on), even if these issues were not explicitly stated, if these assumptions were fundamental premises of her relationship schemata. Planalp refers to this process as "assimilation," whereby schemata shape the interpretation and recall of ambiguous information. On the other hand, schemata also are themselves subject to adaptation when new information overrides the default option or proves to be inconsistent with the existing relationship-specific schemata. Planalp refers to this process as "accommodation" and notes that it may occur gradually or abruptly.

Both assimilation and accommodation are probably activated by the more general human motivation to seek coherence. As L. C. Miller and S. J. Read (1991) contend, seeking coherence "provides the underlying dynamic in the development of individuals' mental models of interactions, other persons, self, and relationships in the world" (p. 71). To the extent that people perceive their relationship-specific model to be internally coherent and consistent with other outside information, they should be more likely to feel that they understand relationship events.

The second process that concerns cognitive theorists is how the two relational partners achieve some level of overlap or agreement in their relationship-specific schemata (Surra & Ridley, 1991). In some cases, agreement need not be "achieved" at all because it arises naturally from the overlap in preexisting relationship general schemata (Montgomery, 1988). In these cases, knowledge and expectations are synchronous, and the need for adaptation in the relationship-specific schemata is relatively small. However, to the extent that preexisting schemata are different and perhaps incompatible, partners will need to negotiate agreement through more or less overt means.

Research on the process by which relational cognitions are revealed and negotiated is entailed in much of the conflict literature, although not necessarily cast in those terms (see Canary, Cupach, & Messman, 1995, for a review). In addition, the fact that couples create their own rules to set parameters on when and how they will engage in conflict (Honeycutt, Woods, & Fontenot, 1993; Jones & Gallois, 1989) suggests that they are attempting to create a "joint script"or behavioral and interpretive framework. This script functions as a domain-specific instantiation of a mutually generated relationship-specific schemata.

Finally, the research suggests that the process of achieving agreement and overlap in relationship schemata is both the cause and the effect of relationship satisfaction: agreement in relationship schemata contributes to relationship satisfaction, and relationship satisfaction facilitates the communicative processes that lead to greater agreement (for example, Sillars & Scott, 1983). Conversely, when couples have little agreement in their schemata, they may attend to different stimuli and process relational information in different ways. To the extent that this results in poor communication, the inability to reach consensus about the nature of the relationship may contribute to lower satisfaction, and lower satisfaction may diminish both ability and willingness to engage in further communication about relationship differences (Sillars, Folwell, Hill, Maki, Hurst, & Casano, 1994).

Implications

Understanding the relatively stable cognitive structures that guide the "sense-making" process of relationship partners provides a second piece of the relationship puzzle. It reminds researchers that relationship partners store, organize, and retrieve relationship events in characteristic ways. When partners share the same mental representation of the expectations, rights, obligations, roles, and symbols for their relationship, it might be said that their relationship *is* that common mental structure. Cognitive theorists also remind researchers that "contingency" in the manifest behaviors of interaction may be only one level of linkage between partners. Linkages also may be represented as contingency between behavior and cognition, both within and between partners. Exploring the nature of these second-order linkages is central to the research agenda of scholars in the system perspective.

System Perspective

As implied previously, the distinction between the behavioral and cognitive approaches to relationships is a fuzzy one. Both approaches recognize that behavior and cognition are not easily separated. However, neither approach locates the relationship uniquely in the vortex of these two forces. Scholars who explicitly focus on the systemic quality of relationships do exactly that. Indeed, this tradition is often referred to by its proponents as the interdependence perspective. However, in order to avoid confusion with Kenny's specific and methodological use of the term "interdependence," the label system has been selected to designate the perspective described below.

One of the earliest renderings of personal relationships as a system emerged in the 1970s with the seminal work of G. Levinger and his colleagues (for a review, see Levinger, 1994). Incorporating both behavior and cognition, Levinger and J. D. Snoek (1972) argued that close relationships exist in the interdependence or mutuality of the partners: "partners have shared knowledge of one another, assume some responsibility for each other's outcomes, and at least begin to regulate their association upon a mutually agreed basis," creating unique overlap in actions, views, and experiences (p. 5).

This representation of relationships was echoed in the description of relational phenomena detailed in Hinde's (1979) landmark text. He describes relationships as "intermittent interaction between two people, involving interchanges over an extended period of time. The interchanges have some degree of mutuality, in the sense that the behavior of each takes some account of the behavior of the other." He adds, "To understand relationships fully, . . . it is necessary to come to terms not only with their behavioral but also with their affective/cognitive aspects and to do so whilst recognizing that they are inextricably interwoven" (pp. 14–15).

In the early 1980s, H. Kelley and colleagues (1983) began to formalize the notion of mutuality by restricting it specifically to contingent sequences or "causal interconnection" between events (that is, acting, thinking, feeling). The premise of the model is that "events are causally connected within each person's chain, and events are causally connected between the two persons' chains, this last being the basic feature of interpersonal relationships" (p. 31).

More recently, the chain metaphor has been abandoned, but scholars continue to view relationships as interdependent systems. E. Robins (1990), for example, argues that interdependence exists at two levels: the interactional level and the psychological level. "At the interactional level, each partner's actions (interpersonal events) affect the subsequent actions and covert responses (subjective events) of the other. At the psychological level, mutual influence is apparent in each partner's having developed somewhat stable attitudes and beliefs about the relationship and the partner (subjective conditions). . . . The two levels of interdependence are causally interrelated in an ongoing, cyclical manner" (pp. 60–61). Clearly, Robins' description of interactional interdependence is consistent with much of the research in the behavioral tradition, and his description of psychological interdependence is consistent with much of the research in the cognitive tradition (for example, relationship-specific schemata).

A similar perspective is evident in the contextual model of marital interaction developed by T. N. Bradbury and F. D. Fincham (1989, 1991). This model, like others described in this section, attempts to represent the complex interplay among the several types of influences on partners who are interacting. One set of influences are those elements of the immediate environment, or "proximal context," to which each person responds. For example, the behaviors of each partner are processed in light of moment-to-moment, transient thoughts and feelings. This leads to a behavioral response that, in turn, stimulates the partner's processing and behavioral response. In addition, another set of factors that influence the processing stage are part of the "distal context." These are relatively stable individual predispositions to process relationship information in certain ways. These factors might include personality, chronic mood states, beliefs about relationships generally, beliefs about this particular relationship, beliefs about self, beliefs about the partner, and so forth. Importantly, the connection between the distal and the proximal contexts is bidirectional: relatively stable dispositions can influence how an interaction is processed, and processing during interaction can modify relatively stable dispositions. Finally, attributions that arise in any particular interaction may continue to influence how partners think or feel over time, often becoming a salient feature of the preinteraction environment in which a subsequent interaction occurs.

Research Practices

Given the complexity of the models in the system perspective, research that attempts to tap all dimensions simultaneously is rare. However, a common research practice is to conduct a series of studies that test aspects of the cognitive, affective, and behavioral associations in the relationship system and, thereby, move systematically toward confirmation of a theoretical model. For example, Bradbury and Fincham have confirmed their expectation that attributions made by partners about particular relationship problems are related to sequences of behaviors displayed during the discussion of that problem (for example, Bradbury & Fincham, 1989), to emotional responses experienced during those discussions, and to long-term relational satisfaction (Bradbury & Fincham, 1991; Fincham & Bradbury, 1987).

Likewise, the systematic series of studies conducted by C. E. Rusbult and her colleagues on responses to dissatisfaction in relationships has contributed substantially to understanding interdependence in relationships (see Rusbult, Yovetich, & Verette, 1996, for a review). This program of research initially was stimulated by the recognition that some responses to relational problems are not manifested as overt or discrete behavior. For example, a spouse may choose to simply ignore a partner's behavior, may remain silent rather than make a comment, or may perform actions other than spoken messages that are hurtful to the partner. This led to the formulation of four broad strategies of response mode distinguished along the two dimensions of active-passive and constructive-destructive. These response modes were termed "exit," "voice," "loyalty," and "neglect" (Rusbult, Johnson, & Morrow, 1986).

Subsequent research indicated that individual-level factors (for example, psychological gender) and relationship-level factors (for example, investment) influenced the use of these strategies. Additional research also indicated that the use of these strategies was associated with relationship quality. Importantly, however, the accumulated research revealed that, although destructive response strategies (exit and neglect) consistently contributed to poor couple functioning, positive strategies (voice and loyalty) did not consistently contribute to healthy couple functioning. In an effort to understand why this might be the case, Rusbult and colleagues recently proposed an accommodation model to explain why some partners accommodate to the negative actions of their partner whereas others retaliate (Rusbult, Yovetich, & Verette, 1996). Essentially, the accommodation model proposes that partners sometimes "transform" an automatic self-interested response into a partner-interested or relationship-interested response. Various features of the interaction, the individual, and the relationship then are incorporated into the model to predict the likelihood of accommodation.

Perhaps the best example of research that consistently employs the methods suggested by a system position is the research conducted by W. Ickes and his colleagues (Ickes & Tooke, 1988; Ickes, Robertson, Tooke, & Teng, 1986). Using a method that allows researchers to obtain both behavioral and subjective-cognitive data, Ickes and colleagues typically employ a three-step procedure. First, couples are videotaped while they interact. Second, participants view their tape (usually separately) to mark segments of the conversation where they experienced an affective or cognitive response. Third, participants view the tape a second time and are directed to respond to the segments marked by their partner (for example, by noting their own affect or cognitions or by inferring those of their partner). In addition, noninvolved observers can be used to code interaction sequences for comparison purposes.

In one study, Ickes and colleagues (1986) found that behavioral measures of dyadic involvement coded by outsiders, such as directed gazes, were positively correlated with the amount of partner's self-reported thoughts and feelings and the amount of positive thoughts and feelings. The results suggest that one partner's behavioral responses may stimulate increased subjective activity on the part of the other and that increased subjective activity may generate involving behavioral responses. In another study, Ickes, Tooke, Stinson, Baker, & Bissonnette (1988) found evidence of intersubjectivity or similarity in the content of partners' thoughts and feelings that develops from interaction.

Implications

The models articulated by scholars in the system perspective are theoretically coherent representations of the complexity of personal relationships. They remind researchers that relationships are not only behavioral structures and not only cognitive structures but also an arena in which these two forces are equally important.

Unfortunately, the multiple influences operating in relationships require careful attention to multiple sources of variation in statistical analyses. If the unique qualities of a couple are to be identified, a researcher must identify not only what occurs between the couple but also what occurs when the individuals are in other situations. A recent study by Hancock and Ickes (1996) illustrates the importance of this concern. In a test of the taken-for-granted assumption that the personalized knowledge of friends contributes to accurate inferences of thoughts and feelings, Hancock and Ickes compared ratings of three perceivers who viewed a videotaped interaction between strangers: an uninvolved observer, one of the interactants, and a friend of the other interactant who was brought to the lab for this purpose. Hancock and Ickes found that friends were no more accurate than observers or stranger-interactants in inferring thoughts and feelings of the "friend" interactant. In fact, the single most important variable was the "readability" of the target; some targets were easy to read for all observers, whereas others were difficult for any observer to read.

This finding is at the heart of Kenny's concern with much existing research that purports to study dyadic or relational effects. He argues that the characteristics of individuals, both behavioral and cognitive, that are relatively stable across situations must be accounted for if truly dyadic effects are to be isolated. Certainly, this argument is not new to Kenny. In each of the three research traditions reviewed above, scholars have struggled with how to find, identify, measure, and represent the elusive phenomenon called relationships. What is significant about the arguments advanced by Kenny is that they have been systematized into a method of analyzing relationships that helps researchers detect patterns of affect, attitudes, and behaviors that can be attributed with some confidence to the relationship, rather than to the amalgam of the individuals. The SRM provides an explanation of Kenny's approach to the issue of distilling the relationship.

THE SOCIAL RELATIONS MODEL

The SRM is a statistical model designed to isolate the "residual unique qualities of relationships" (Kenny & Kashy, 1991). As Kenny admits, the statistics are complicated and closely tied to assumptions about how the data in each case are related (Kenny, 1994a). However, the conceptual premises of the model are intuitive and provide an analytic framework that can be used to examine relationships. Therefore, the following discussion summarizes the conceptual, rather than the statistical, implications of the model.

The Nature of Interdependence

The fundamental assumption of the SRM is that relationships are characterized by interdependence (for example, attitude similarity, affect reciprocity and compensation, conversational synchrony and enmeshment). This assumption certainly is not unique to this model. As evident in laypersons' naive assessments and in the several research traditions reviewed previously, the relational partners are believed to exhibit behavioral and cognitive familiarity that can be observed and measured. However, the SRM is uniquely responsive to the conceptual and methodological implications of assuming an interdependence model. As Reis notes in the forward to Kenny's (1994a) book,

Researchers who study the diverse phenomena of attraction, communication, interaction, and relationships have lacked paradigms for identifying and isolating the various components that contribute to a given observation. Consider a single data point: Jack loves Jill. Is this because Jack generally loves others? Is it because people generally love Jill? Or is it because there is something about Jack's feeling for Jill that transcends his usual lovingness and her typical lovability? A moment's reflection reveals that the conceptual implications of this distinction are more significant than mere methodological refinements would be.

That is, substantive conclusions about this data point will vary markedly, depending on which interpretation is the right one. (pp. x–xi)

Reis' point is well taken. The love between Jack and Jill is not conceptually meaningful unless it is differentiated from Jack's generalized predisposition to love (actor effects), from Jill's generalized predisposition to be loved (partner effects), and from the random effects that might occur in the measuring of their love (random error). The same consideration holds for communicative behavior as well.

In order to determine whether the SRM is relevant to a set of couples' scores, Kenny begins with three questions. First, is there evidence of interdependence? Statistically, this would be indicated if couple scores on some measure of perception, affect, cognition, or behavior are correlated. The existence of even moderate overlap between partners warrants the use of the dyad as the unit of analysis. Using the individual as the unit of analysis would violate the assumption of independence inherent in most inferential statistics (see Kenny & Judd, 1986).

The second question is, what type of interdependence is theoretically appropriate to examine? Kenny distinguishes two types of interdependence (Kenny, 1996; Kenny & Kashy, 1991). "Within-dyad interdependence" is sequential interdependence in that a behavior or cognition from one partner elicits a behavior or cognition from the other partner. For example, a complaint by one partner might elicit a countercomplaint from the other. Within-dyad interdependence is measured for the same dyad over time. "Between-dyad interdependence" refers to comparisons of one partner's scores on a variable to the other partner's scores on a variable across pairs, for example, the degree to which marital satisfaction scores for wives are related to marital satisfaction scores for husbands. For this purpose, data can be collected at one point in time and the same measure used across couples. The importance of distinguishing between these types of interdependence is that they answer very different types of questions. For example, conversational constraints on interactants' ability to match turn length, self-disclosure, emotional support, and similar interactional phenomena might actually yield a negative correlation within a dyad but yield a positive correlation across relationships because the general tendency to equalize turn length, self-disclosure, and emotional support occurs, on balance, over time. Likewise, a comparison of scores for husbands and wives or other relational partners across groups may miss important interactional information. For example, the fact that overall levels of some variable are correlated more highly for certain relationships (for example, husbands and wives are more similar in their level of social support than men and women in dating couples) may be less informative than the fact that husbands' social support follows only a solicitation cue from wives, whereas in dating couples, solicitation cues are not related to the occurrence of social support.

A third question to be addressed is whether statistical evidence of interdependence can be attributed legitimately to emergent qualities of the relationship. Because of assortive mating practices and educational tracking, for example, married couples and close friends often share similar educational, social, and economic backgrounds. Consequently, similarity in values, attitudes, and predispositions are individual factors that exist prior to and independently of their relationship ("compositional effects"). Likewise, because partners often share a common environment, they may be exposed simultaneously to some independent causal factor ("common fate" effect) that creates or intensifies similarity. By contrast, interdependence that is interaction based reveals the mutuality of influence that characterizes relationships. Interdependence may be conceptualized unilaterally or reciprocally. Unilateral interdependence is evidenced when one partner's behavior or attitude affects the other (for example, husband complaints affecting wife's satisfaction). Reciprocal interdependence is evidenced when each partner's satisfaction affects the satisfaction of the other. Each of these types of interdependence necessitates an appropriate analysis technique, detailed in Kenny (1996). These procedures are designed to help researchers clarify the nature of the interdependence they believe they have uncovered.

Components of the Social Relations Model

The SRM argues that the unique effects of the relationship can be confirmed only by removing other sources of variance that might account for these regularities at a particular point in time (moment of study). The first source of variance that must be eliminated is variance attributable to generic predispositions or patterns of behavior (or attitudes, perceptions, attributions) characteristic of a person across situations. Because these consistencies in behavior and cognitions are not unique to the interaction with partner, they are known as "actor effects" or, in the case of perception studies, "perceiver effects." For example, some people disclose more readily than others, some people interrupt more often than others, and some people are generically untrusting, unhappy, or withdrawn.

The second source of variance that must be eliminated is that attributable to the relatively consistent responses that people receive from others. Because these consistencies also are not unique to the interaction with actor, they are designated as "partner effects" or, in the case of perception studies, "target effects." For example, attractive people tend to receive positive responses from others, affiliative people tend to receive self-disclosure from others, and people high in argumentativeness tend to elicit counterarguments from other people. Both actor and partner effects are individual level effects in that both refer to qualities, habits, or dispositions of individuals.

Two sources of variance remain after the individual effects are removed. One source of variance is attributable to the unique pattern of affect or behavior found in a particular dyad. This is known as "relationship effects" and reflects the extent of actual interdependence between partners. The second source of variance is error variance because of measurement error or randomness in the behavior of an interactant on some variable of interest. Relationship effects can be distinguished from measurement and random error if couples are observed interacting at two or more times, are observed interacting with other people (in a round robin or block design), or are measured with two or more measures.

Kenny (1994) and Kenny and D. A. Kashy (1991) provide several examples of how the partitioning of variance in the SRM can be interpreted. One example taken from Kenny and Kashy is used here to illustrate. J. Levine and H. Snyder (1980) asked two classes of children (five to six years old) to rate their classmates on how much they wanted to "sit with, work with, and share with him or her." These items were considered multiple measures of liking and, therefore, allowed error variance to be distinguished from relationship variance. Partitioning the variance indicated that 24 percent of the variance in liking was simply error; however, 50 percent of the variance in liking was because of relationship effects, with about 20 percent because of actor effects (some children generally liked others and some children generally disliked others). Popularity of the target (partner effects), or how much other children generally liked the target, accounted for a relatively small amount of variance, only 7 percent.

Partitioning of the variance in this way indicates the unique contribution of the relationship to the overall variance estimate. However, it does not specify whether a particular attitude, affect, or behavior is reciprocal within a dyad. Reciprocity would be indicated if a person who especially likes his or her partner is especially liked by his or her partner (Kenny, 1994a; Kenny & Kashy, 1991). This is represented by correlating the two partners' relationship effects, that is, the relationship effect for Partner A is how he or she feels about (or acts toward) Partner B after removing his or her own actor effects and his or her partner's partner effects. The relationship effects for Partner B are the corresponding residual effects for that person. These two relationship effects then are correlated to assess reciprocity (a positive association should emerge if both partners are similar toward each other, but a negative association should emerge if partner evaluations or behaviors are discrepant). In essence, then, the SRM not only identifies interactional properties unique to couples but also permits analysis of the nature of reciprocal influences.

Limitations and Implications

Personal relationships are complicated and dynamic constructions. They originate in the goals, needs, and experiences of their members but exhibit qualities that transcend individual influences. Although each of the research traditions reviewed in this chapter contributes substantially to our knowledge of relational processes and properties, a fully articulated statistical model is necessary to isolate patterns of interdependence and reciprocity that are unique to a given relationship. If behavior exhibited by a couple is no different from their behavior individually, then unique dyadic effects have not been identified. If the shared relationship schemata of a couple could be predicted from similarity in their individual schemata before they even met, then a uniquely relational schemata has not been identified. If a friend's ability to infer emotion or intentions is no greater than an observer's ability, then a unique relational effect has not been identified. The SRM provides researchers with a systematic and statistical confirmation for the existence of dyadic and relational effects.

The SRM, however, is not without its limitations. One particularly perplexing limitation is how the statistical evidence of dyadic effects is to be interpreted conceptually, that is, if a relationship is found to have properties above and beyond those attributable to the individuals, their common backgrounds, or the random patterns that emerge during a particular interaction, what does this mean? Do higher levels of unique variance mean that a couple has more of a relationship, a more personal relationship, a more intimate relationship, or a more enmeshed or interdependent relationship? Perhaps more problematic, does the absence of unique variance suggest that a couple has no relationship?

A second limitation of the model, or more accurately, a limitation of its use to date, is its restricted range of application. Kenny (1994) notes that the most extensive application of the SRM has been to person perception research. He admits that only 5 of the 50 studies reviewed as the basis of his book were focused on people in long-term relationships. He acknowledges that extending the model to couples' behavior will be difficult, especially in cases in which multiple relationship partners (for example, spouse, friend, and coworker) are needed to control for effects because of the composition of the dyad.

Finally, the ability of researchers to use the SRM is somewhat limited by the need for special computer programs that are not yet widely available. Unlike traditional designs that rely on a comparison of means that are calculated directly from the scores of members in a group, the SRM uses special variances and correlations that are not computed by conventional means. As a result, "variances can be negative and the correlations can be larger than 1" (Kenny, 1994a, p. 213). Understanding the implications of derived measures and uncommon statistical values presents important conceptual, as well as analytic, challenges to a researcher. For example, correlation values typically cannot exceed one, a value that represents perfectly parallel distributions of scores (that is, each time a value increases for one variable, the value for a second variable increases to a comparable degree). A correlation greater than one is difficult to conceptualize for researchers familiar with the traditional notion of correlation.

These concerns aside, however, the SRM is a promising approach to several relational phenomena that have eluded communication scholars for some time. For example, one common indicator of relationship familiarity to casual observers is the tendency for relational partners to violate social rules of formality, particularly norms of politeness (Brown & Levinson, 1987) and other forms of facework (Goffman, 1967). However, the nature and extent of these violations are not consistently demonstrated in the literature (Baxter, 1984; Cupach & Metts, 1994; Metts, 1997). The SRM offers an alternative to the common practice of using researcher-generated scenarios that manipulate the type of relationship (for example, close friend, casual acquaintance) that a respondent is supposed to envision. Relational partners could be paired with each other and also with same-sex and other-sex interactional partners performing similar tasks or discussing similar topics. If modification of politeness norms manifests itself as a relational effect, it should emerge from the analysis.

A similar approach could be taken with other supposed indicators of relationship familiarity, such as person-centered emotional support, accounts used to justify untoward behavior, teasing and play, self-disclosure, and even sentence completion. Likewise, the taken-for-granted assumption that communication changes in developing and dissolving relationships along such dimensions as personalness and flexibility can be assessed by systematically comparing elements of talk both within and between dyad interactions, thereby isolating relationship effects from individual effects.

Although the SRM is not suitable for all investigations, its conceptual and statistical coherence recommends it as a viable option for these and related questions about the form and function of communication in personal relationships. Its implementation requires considerable effort and statistical expertise, but the information it yields is not likely to be available otherwise.

7

Narrative, Dialectic, and Relationships
Richard L. Conville

In 1971, Paul Ricoeur published an essay entitled "The Model of the Text: Meaningful Action Considered as a Text." He argued that human action, because of its textlike qualities, may be interpreted by the human sciences using the same hermeneutical tools as those employed to interpret literature. A straightforward application of this program would be to investigate interpersonal communication (and its primary by-product, relationships) by employing those same interpretive tools. However, it is not that simple.

Because Ricoeur's notion of discourse is central to his essay, I believe that the essay's subtitle is more accurately rendered as "Meaningful Action Considered as Discourse." The purpose of this chapter is not to turn Ricoeur's subtitle exactly on its head but to tilt it rather obliquely so that it reads something like "Discourse Considered as Meaningful Action." My hypothesis is that discourse of a particular kind, the sort that depicts human relationships, provides a window onto interpersonal communication and insight into the meaning of "relationship." I am proposing that discourse itself be a site both for the observation of interpersonal communication and for the application of those interpretive methods Ricoeur had in mind. Thus, rather than treating the human action of interpersonal communication as if it had certain attributes of discourse (Ricoeur's position), investigators would take a rather more direct approach and examine discourses themselves for their portrayals of interpersonal communication.

However, Ricoeur's position should not be lightly dismissed. It furnishes a platform for the alternative perspective I am outlining here. The question Ricoeur posed was, "What is it to understand a discourse?" (1971, p. 531). Ricoeur reasoned that if human action is enough like discourse then interpretive procedures used to understand that "language-event or linguistic usage" called discourse (p. 530) can be used to understand human action.

Understanding discourse, Ricoeur further reasoned in answer to his own question, consists of understanding how basic traits of discourse manifest themselves in actual narratives. By analogy, so his argument went, understanding human action would consist of investigating those four traits of discourse as they manifest themselves in human action. However, in my oblique version of the subtitle, if discourse depicts interpersonal communication in a meaningful way, then understanding discourses would be one means of understanding interpersonal communication and its natural progeny, relationships.

First, I will elaborate on Ricoeur's analogy between discourse and human action. This will lay the groundwork for constructing my rendering of it, the focus of this chapter. Next, I will raise two questions about the study of relationships, "Where shall we look for relationships to study?" and "How shall we examine relationships, once located?" In the process of answering these questions, I then will demonstrate a hermeneutical method consistent with Ricoeur's analogy between discourse and human action. It is a dialectical-narrative-structural method for deducing constitutive elements of relationships from discourse. Finally, I will make some observations on the findings as they regard dialectical thinking and as they shed light on relationships and the interpersonal communication that constitutes them.

RICOEUR'S LINGUISTICS OF ACTION

Ricoeur begins his argument that human action shares with discourse certain constitutive similarities by asserting that discourses are marked by four basic traits. First, both discourses and human actions occur in time and, therefore, uniquely reflect "the times" in which they occur. Second, they both have a speaker-writer-doer and, in various ways, refer back to him or her. Third, both discourses and human actions are always about something. Fourth, they are addressed to some kind of audience.

Ricoeur proceeds. Discourses may be spoken or written, and the four traits of discourse manifest themselves quite differently in the two modalities. Specifically, spoken discourse is more closely tied to this indigenous social occasion than is written discourse. Relative to spoken discourse, written discourse is freed from the ostensive reference of the moment; the author's intended meanings are much less important in written discourse than in spoken; in written discourse, the "something" that the text is about is potentially much larger than the shared situation of communicants in spoken discourse; and in written discourse, the addressees are all who can read, not just those within earshot. Written discourse, therefore, is relatively more free from those four aspects of the social occasion that evoke spoken discourse: the times, the speaker-writer, the topic, and the audience.

Spoken discourse occurs in the immediacy of those four aspects of the social occasion. Although written discourse is freed from that immediacy, human action itself is even more autonomous. Ricoeur continues and elaborates the distinctions between written discourse and action. First, written discourse captures the otherwise transient in human action. It stops time. However, normally transient human action also may be "captured." Traces of its occurrence may remain, held in others' memory and detached from the event of the action. The marriage of Michael Jackson and Lisa Marie Presley and their subsequent divorce were no doubt their own actions, but they also are actions that have become the property of the popular culture.

Second, written discourse refers back to a writer, even though it may be a "distended and complicated" connection. However, human action may take on a life of its own apart from the actors' intentions. Indeed, we often cannot forsee or control the effects of our actions, and those effects may become the property of society if they are institutionalized as reputation or as policy. For example, former President Carter's widely publicized work with Habitat for Humanity is perceived as making a statement about his values, and congressional efforts to balance the federal budget often are seen as "sending a message" to citizens at large, to the financial markets, and to other nations' leaders.

Third, written discourse is always about something, but that something is the "world" the discourse calls forth from readers, not the idiosyncratic topic of a conversation. So, too, "the meaning of an important event exceeds, overcomes, transcends, the social conditions of its production" (Ricoeur, 1971, p. 543). The broader social meaning of Martin Luther King's assassination continues to be a subject of reflection and debate in this country.

Fourth, written discourse is addressed, potentially, to all who can read, not simply to a single listener or a small group, as with speech. In like manner, human actions may be "read" or interpreted by observers to whom they were not directed: "like a text, human action is an open work, the meaning of which is 'in suspense'" (Ricoeur, 1971, p. 544). In the wake of fiftieth anniversary celebrations of the end of World War II, contemporary audiences have renewed discussions of the wisdom of using the atomic bomb on Hiroshima and Nagasaki.

Thus, freed from the constraints of occasion even more so than written discourse is, human action must, nevertheless, be tamed, or at least captured, in order to be investigated. "The four traits," Ricoeur concludes, "taken together constitute the 'objectivity' of the text" (1971, p. 546). This taming seems to be what Ricoeur means, in part, by his claim for "objectification:" "action . . . may become an object of science, without losing its character of meaningfulness, through a kind of objectification similar to the fixation which occurs in writing" (p. 538).

Because human action and discourse share the four basic traits of discourse, it follows that discourse, as it depicts relationships, also shares with human action a common communicative structure, the four traits.

Ricoeur continued, "By this objectification, action is no longer a trans-action to which the discourse of action would still belong. It constitutes a delineated pattern which has to be interpreted according to its inner connections" (1971, p. 538). Human action may be, thus, "objectified" or held in place for further examination by depicting it in discourse and abstracting the four traits delineated above. Hence, we return to that reformulation of Ricoeur's subtitle, "Discourse Considered as Meaningful Action." I am arguing that scholars may elucidate relationships by analyzing discourses that have captured depictions of interpersonal communication. What is more, "a relationship to another person is itself not an element of nature but something that is given meaning and existence by relaters, perceivers and modes of action, including discourse" (Duck, 1995, p. 539). In short, one modality of relationships' existence is by virtue of discourses about them.

LOOKING FOR RELATIONSHIPS

Investigators often find that their access to human action is through accounts of it, or discourse (that is, that their access to interpersonal communication and the relationships constituted by it is through participants' narratives about those relationships). Thus, we come full circle to my proposal in this chapter, based on the oblique reading of Ricoeur's subtitle, "Discourse Considered as Meaningful Action," that discourse itself be considered a site both for the observation of interpersonal communication and the application of appropriate interpretive methods.

Relationships can hardly be pointed to, although evidence of their existence abounds, ubiquitous, as the waving of tree branches is evidence of the wind. Consider an example. If we wish to ascertain the dean's relationship with his or her colleagues, we may observe him or her interact with them or we may administer an instrument to measure their relationship. However, that observed interaction is not their relationship any more than the results of a paper and pencil test are their relationship. Those observations and measurements point to a relationship (as waving branches indicate wind), but they are hardly the relationship itself.

Likewise, accounts, but more. Like the moving branches that indicate the movement of wind, stories proclaim the presence of relationships. The dean and his or her colleagues' stories that they tell about each other not only point to their relationships but also portray their relationships in all their rich variety. Their accounts preserve their relationships in oral or written discourse so others may have access to them, and their relationship narratives provide a path forward into which their relationships may grow. "Stories and relationships are thus inextricably intertwined . . . in the sense that people come to define themselves and others through the stories they tell" (LaRossa, 1995, p. 555). So, in answer to the first question above, Where shall we look for relationships to study, I would look for relationships in the stories that relational partners tell as opposed to looking for them in either the minds or the actions of relational partners (Spitzberg, 1993; Conville, 1997, in press).

There are several advantages to this approach. Left to their own devices, relationships are transient and evanescent, but once captured as discourse in stories, they are stored away in memory or in text and can be brought out again and again for worry or analysis or interpretation. What we lose in up-to-date accuracy when we capture a relationship thusly, we gain in ability to examine it closely and repeatedly.

However, if our object is to understand a specific, ongoing relationship, perhaps to make recommendations for its management, such loss may be unacceptable. The relationship may have changed before we can analyze the narrative, and our results may be useless. However, if our object is to understand relationship as a theoretical concept or as a universal human accomplishment, then the relationship preserved in a story can be made a case study and used for theorizing and its inner workings applied to many relationships.

Looking for relationships in stories is also advantageous in dealing with the problem of change. Relationships change, and stories about relationships change with them. The rhetorical dimension of our stories allows them to reflect our present conditions and social roles as well as project our futures (LaRossa, 1995). Thus, relationship stories change over time with the same person, and at a given time, relationship stories change depending on the person telling them. The flexibility of stories gives them the potential for being dependable indicators of relationships.

If stories point to relationships, portray relationships, preserve relationships, and direct the course of relationships, as I am suggesting, then a reasonable question is, What, exactly, is it in stories that is relationship-like. I will outline a dialectical-narrative-structural method of discourse analysis that gets at that very question. The upshot of the procedure is what R. Barthes (1972) has called a "simulacrum," or likeness, of the story that highlights the interaction of the relational partners and that otherwise would have "remained invisible, or . . . unintelligible in the natural [unanalyzed] object [story]" (p. 149): Ricoeur's "delineated pattern that has to be interpreted" (1971, p. 538). Further, the investigator produces an "interested *simulacrum*" (Barthes, 1972, p. 149), one that is constructed with a view toward a certain end, in this case, the revelation of dialectical dimensions along which partners move in the story, thus, constituting their relationship.

One kind of storytelling that has been employed somewhat as I am suggesting is the novel (Alberts, 1986; Kougl, 1983; Ragan & Hopper, 1984). A certain degree of verisimilitude is necessary for fictional writing to be taken seriously by readers, and many authors are quite skilled in bringing it off. However, there remain questions, if not problems, regarding the representativeness of the interactions depicted in fiction as well as the observational skills of the writers (Ulrich, 1986).

However, there is one kind of discourse that has as its avowed purpose the accurate depiction of human affairs — documentary writing. "Documentary is the presentation or representation of actual fact in a way that makes it credible and vivid to people at the time" (Stott, 1986, p. 14). It "gives information to the intellect" and "informs the emotions" (p. 12).

Relationship stories are latent in much documentary writing. Even a cursory reading of such works as Robert Coles' *Children of Crisis* (1967), William Carlos Williams' *Doctor Stories* (1984), Melissa Greene's *Praying for Sheetrock* (1991), or Alex Kotlowitz's *There Are No Children Here* (1991) will confirm this assertion. Moreover, documentary writing seems to be an appropriate genre of discourse on which to focus in this chapter, given the perspective I am developing. The object of the documentary writer is to accurately present the experience of others; thus, as data, documentary narrative is relatively "clean" compared with other narrative forms, such as fiction or polemical essays. Because the focus of the documentary writer is preservation of human experience, his or her products constitute naive data in that the relationship stories found there are there because they are merely a part of the discursive picture being drawn, not because they have been singled out for attention as relationships for scholarly examination.

The undisputed classic in U.S. documentary writing is James Agee and Walker Evans' (1988) *Let Us Now Praise Famous Men*. The curious title comes from a passage in the forty-fourth chapter of Sirach (one of the Apocryphal books in the English Bible, King James Version), which is a tribute to the virtues of ordinary persons. In the summer of 1936, *Fortune* magazine's managing editor Eric Hodgins sent Agee south, Harvard-educated Tennessean that he was, to do an article on cotton tenant farmers — another Depression piece. He wanted "a verbal and photographic record of the daily living of an 'average' or 'representative,' family of white tenant farmers" (Stott, 1986, p. 261). Agee requested Walker Evans to join him as photographer, and Evans was granted a two-month leave from the Farm Services Administration. What Hodgins and the world got was anything but a set of sentimental pictures and tepid narrative about the Depression for casual upper-class readers. Rather, they were delivered starkly honest pictures of the "Poor naked wretches, . . . / That bide the pelting of this pitiless storm" and embarassingly introspective and egocentric narrative that pressed the question, "How shall your houseless heads and unfed sides, / Your loop'd and window'd raggedness, defend you / From seasons such as these?" (from Shakespeare's *King Lear*, quoted by Agee [1988] on the page behind the Contents).

Fortune did not publish the article or Evans' photographs. For five years, the manuscript and pictures languished because of Agee's vacillation and various publishers' lack of enthusiasm. Finally, Houghton Mifflin agreed to publish the work, by now book length, but by September 1941, the reading public had had its fill of Depression documentaries, and besides, the Battle of Britain was raging. The book languished again, without critical acclaim and unsold (Stott, 1986). However, resurrected by the social strife of the times, Houghton Mifflin reissued the book in 1960, "hailed by critics as a great 'lost' work" and, in retrospect, a precursor of the New Journalism and "harbinger of the decade's social upheavals and reforms" (Bergreen, 1984, p. 261). Indeed, the newest (1988) edition is testimony to the book's enduring popularity among scholars and students in fields as diverse as literature, sociology, anthropology, and history.

The section of *Let Us Now Praise Famous Men* that I have chosen for analysis records the first encounters of Agee and Evans with the alien world of cotton tenantry, populated by white landowners, overseers, and tenants plus black laborers. It is entitled "July 1936," starts on page 25 of the 1988 edition and runs through page 43, and is divided into three parts, "Late Sunday Morning," "At the Forks," and "Near a Church." The three scenes provide a geographic and demographic context for Agee and Evans' study of the three sharecropper families encountered later in the book and called Gudger, Ricketts, and Woods. Moreover, the three scenes recount the experience of Agee and Evans in their initial contacts with persons across the deep cultural divides of race, class, and region. Sixty years later, the problems of negotiating those chasms dominate the news and commentary of the nation's media outlets as well as occupy extensive scholarly attention.

EXAMINING RELATIONSHIPS

The second question guiding this inquiry is, How shall we examine relationships, once found. If we believe that relationships are depicted in discourse in meaningful ways, then an approach that is particularly fitting is the dialectics of relational transition (Conville, 1991, 1997). The dialectics of relational transition is a narrative-structural-dialectical approach to knowledge about relationships: Narrative — relationships endure as narratives. Discourse captures the transience of relationships and makes them accessible to others; moreover, relationship stories depict the interaction of partners and record their subjectivity. Structural — the analytical procedures are based on C. Levi-Strauss's (1963) "The Structural Study of Myth" (without the philosophical baggage of structuralism). Dialectical — the structural analysis of relationship stories exposes dialectical oppositions that constitute the relationships.

A dialectical approach searches out "oppositional patterning," that is, occasions where the constituents of human action are deployed in such a configuration "that the two opposed items (people, social classes, etc.) would take meaningful definition, *one from the other*" (Rychlak, 1984, p. 370). Such dialectical relationships, thus, are marked by process and contradiction (Baxter, 1988). W. W. Wilmot speaks of the "dynamic *interplay*" between dialectical opposites (1987, p. 167): a process brought about by the opposed items' standing in contradiction to one another. The upshot of such dynamic interplay is change "caused by the struggle and tension of contradiction" (Baxter, 1988, p. 258). As B. M. Montgomery has summarized, "Relationships take shape in *the interplay of conflicting and interconnected forces* evident in the partners' behavioral patterns, motivational dynamics and contextual environments" (1993, p. 206).

Structural analysis of relationship narratives amounts to a discovery procedure for ferreting out dialectical oppositions that may be operating there. Details of the procedure are given in my *Relational Transitions* (Conville, 1991; see also Conville, 1997). Step one is to produce a chronological list of the most significant episodes in the story, those episodes on which the narrative depends and whose presence shapes the story. A focus on episodes amounts also to a focus on the four basic traits of discourse delineated above. Each episode, or coherent action sequence, exhibits "(1) the fixation of the meaning, (2) its dissociation from the mental intentions of the author, (3) the display of non-ostensive references, and (4) the universal range of its addressees" (Ricoeur, 1971, p. 546).

Figure 7.1 is the list I propose, based on my reading of the three scenes from Agee and Evans' study. Episodes 1–4 are from "Late Sunday Morning," 5–12 from "At the Forks," and 13–21 from "Near a Church."

FIGURE 7.1
Chronological List of Significant Episodes in Agee's
"July 1936" from *Let Us Now Praise Famous Men*

---

1. Landlord met Agee and Evans and drove with them out to his tenants' "settlement." As they approached the tenant houses, it was clear that they had interrupted a visit by relatives.

2. A male trio out of the group was on their way to church but was summoned by the landlord to sing for Agee and Evans.

3. The trio sang. [Agee said "that was fine. Have you got time to sing us another?" (p. 29).]

    [A request to sing and the trio's compliance occurred three times.]

4. Agee gave the leader 50 cents and said he was sorry they had been delayed and hoped they weren't late for church.

    [See Note below for an elaboration of Agee's uncertainty here.]

5. Agee and Evans stopped at a fork in the road to ask directions. Agee walked up to the front porch where three people were sitting.

6. Agee was momentarily paralyzed by the penetrating stares from the young white couple sitting on the porch.

7. Agee was surprised when he was confronted by the animal noises of the somewhat older white man who, despite being disabled in mind, body, and speech, tried to speak to him.

8. The young woman told their story of Depression hardships, her husband's asthma (and inability to work), and the help they had received from the settlement of equally destitute African-Americans down the road.

9. The older white man offered Agee a rolled-up farm magazine, which Agee took willingly when the young woman explained that is what he wanted.

10. The couple warmed to Agee and they continued to talk; "happiness burst open inside [Agee] like a flooding of sweet water" (p. 37).

11. Agee took his leave with a "Better luck to you, . . . unable to communicate to them at all what my feelings were" (p. 37).

12. As they drove away and Agee looked back, "The young man lowered his head slowly and seriously, and raised it. The young woman smiled, sternly beneath her virulent eyes, for the first time" (p. 37).

13. Agee and Evans came upon an astonishing photographic subject beside the road, a white frame church.

14. A young African-American couple walked by on the road as they were setting up the photographic equipment and figuring out how to get into the church building.

15. Agee, uncomfortable over the prospect of breaking into the church, walked after the couple to ask about getting permission to enter the church, then broke into a trot, anxious to overtake them before they disappeared down the road.

16. Agee's foot slipped on the gravel as he neared them, and the sound startled and terrified the couple.

17. Agee stopped abruptly and slowly approached them, abjectly apologetic: "I'm *very sorry*! I'm *very* sorry if I scared you! . . . I wouldn't have done any such thing for anything" (p. 42).

18. Agee asked about getting into the church.

19. They did not know.

20. Agee thanked them once more, "and was seized once more and beyond resistance with the wish to clarify and set right, . . . with my eyes and smile wretched and out of key with all I was able to say" (p. 43).

21. Agee walked back to the church.

Note: "Meanwhile, and during this singing, I had been sick in the knowledge that they felt they were here at our demand, mine and Walker's, and I could communicate nothing otherwise; and now, in a perversion of self-torture, I played my part through. I gave their leader fifty cents, trying at the same time, through my eyes, to communicate much more, and said I was sorry we had held them up and that I hoped they would not be late" (p. 31).

Step two of the analytical procedure is to arrange the episodes into a rows-and-columns grid in which similar episodes comprise the columns and rows present different types of episodes. The basic operation of the procedure is to consider each succeeding pair of episodes and ask the question Are they the same (or nearly so), or are they different? Therefore, with regard to episodes 1 and 2 in Figure 7.2, in my judgment, the answer is "different." Different people were involved in the episodes, their activities differed, and different privileges and prerogatives obtained among them. Thus, the two episodes were placed in two different columns. The same question is asked about each succeeding episode paired with each previously considered episode. Thus, for example, I judged episode 5 to be different from episode 4 and also different from episodes 3 and 2 but not different from episode 1. So, episode 5 was placed in the same column as episode 1 to signify their similarity. Both episodes (along with

FIGURE 7.2
Dialectical Structure of Agee's "July 1936" in
Let Us Now Praise Famous Men

I	II	III	IV	V	VI	VII
1	2	3	4			
5			6	7		
				8		
				9	10	
			11		12	
13				14		
	15	16	17			
	18	19	20			21

```
          Dominant-----Submissive
               Compelled--------------------Volunteered
                    Closed-------------------------------------Open
```

Indigenous Dialectics
   Dominant-Submissive   Columns II and III
   Compelled-Volunteered   Columns III and V
Conventional Dialectics
   Closed-Open   Columns III and VI
Dialectical Stasis   Column IV

episode 13) recount Agee and Evans' initiatives in contacting local subjects, which meeting presaged relationship stories.

The columns in the grid, thus, represent types or classes of episodes from the narrative. For example, the episodes in column IV (4, 6, 11, 17, and 20) have in common their depiction of Agee in stunned uncertainty, not knowing how to act in the face of an unexpected interaction. For example, in episode 11, Agee bade farewell to the young white couple on the porch, and the best he could come up with was the trite, "Better luck to you," when there was so much more that he felt but could not enunciate under the circumstances.

Figure 7.2 is the grid that reflects my reading of the set of three episodes. Numbers on the grid refer to the episodes in the chronological list of Figure 7.1. The grid classifies the episodes while preserving their chronological order.

Step three of the analytical procedure is to interpret the grid. Inspection of the grid ideally leads the analyst to detect one or more dialectical propositions that are at work in the story and, by extension, in the relationship depicted in it. The dialectical oppositions, taken together, comprise Barthes' simulacrum of the narrative, its latent structure, now revealed. In the lower part of Figure 7.2, I have enumerated three dialectical oppositions I believe to be operating in Agee's narrative — dominant-submissive, compelled-volunteered, and closed-open. The dominant pole of the first dialectic is composed of episodes of summoning, asking, and an attempt to ask (episodes 2, 15, and 18) and comprises Column II of the grid. Its dialectical opposite (submissive) is found in Column III of the grid and is composed of episodes depicting forms of response to those requests, episodes 3, 16, and 19. Exemplary are the landlord's and then Agee's requests for the trio to sing (episode 2) and their compliance (episode 3), a pattern repeated two more times early in the narrative. So, one kind of relationship Agee depicted in his narrative was characterized by the dialectical opposition of dominance and submissiveness, with Agee, uncomfortably, in the dominant role.

From another perspective, however, episodes in Column III (3, 16, and 19) depict those occupying subservient roles as compelled to act in a certain way. The social position of those African-American farm workers (near-serfs) in Alabama's sharecropper system in the 1930s made a request by a foreman or an upper-class white (Agee) tantamount to a command. Hence, singing, when requested, was hardly a matter of choice. So, in this second dialectical relationship, their being compelled to act upon request is contrasted with those episodes that comprise Column V (7, 8, 9, 14), in which actors volunteered information. Examples include the young African-American couple (episode 14) who simply and openly walked by, not hiding themselves from Agee and Evans, and the disabled, older white man who tried to speak with Agee (episode 7). Thus, Agee also reported being involved in relationships that were characterized by the dialectical opposition, compelled-volunteered, himself occupying, at various times, either pole of the dimension. He was both the one who compelled and the one to whom information was volunteered.

From yet another perspective, the episodes in Column III depict relational partners as being closed in contrast to other episodes in the discourse that depict them as being open (Column VI, episodes 10, 12). The smile from the young woman and nod from her husband (episode 12) stand in stark contrast to the stiff obedience of the singing trio (episode 3) and the terror of the young African-American couple (episode 16). By their gestures, the former subtly disclosed something of their private selves to Agee and Evans, but the latter acted strictly within the roles dictated to them by prevailing social practices. The dialectical opposition, closed-open, marked yet another kind of relationship in which Agee participated and that he reported. He was the target of his relational partners' closedness as well as their openness.

OBSERVATIONS

First, in Figure 7.2, I have labeled one of the dialectical dimensions, closed-open, as conventional, that is, the open-closed dialectic has been reported by a number of investigators to obtain across a wide variety of relationships and is considered standard in the literature (Baxter, 1988; Rawlins, 1992; Masheter, 1994). The present study supports these findings.

Second, as I have argued elsewhere (Conville, 1997), orthodoxy must not be allowed to govern our observations as investigators. In order to remain true to the uniqueness of human interaction, we must allow for the appearance of dialectical dimensions that are indigenous to particular episodes and discourses. Hence, two of the dimensions are classified as indigenous in Figure 7.2, dominant-submissive and compelled-volunteered. Thus, we may say that Agee's recounted interpersonal communication shared with other persons' interpersonal communication a fundamental similarity: it constituted relationships that varied along a dimension whose poles were anchored by closed and open. However, the analysis also showed that Agee's relationships were unique to their particular circumstances. Those circumstances produced other relational dimensions peculiar to this discourse, dominant-submissive and compelled-volunteered.

Third, the episodes in Column IV of Figure 7.2 present themselves as an anomaly to dialectical thinking. Normally, tension is created by the opposing forces represented by the poles of the dialectic, and a relationship is pulled between these two extremes, but Column IV appears to be a dimension that has collapsed into its center. Lacking poles to move between, Agee was frozen in place at that center. For example, in episode 4 (plus the gloss at the foot of Figure 7.2) Agee loathed the role of "white master" bestowed upon him by the situation, but lacking viable alternatives, he played out the role while swallowing his true feelings and uttering platitudes. Again, in episode 17, Agee has approached the African-American couple to ask a question and inadvertently frightened them. He can merely stammer and grovel an apology, unable to retreat or advance.

Here, we have a case of dialectical stasis, an instance in which the dynamic of dialectical opposition comes to an abrupt halt. In the narrative, Column IV serves as an antidialectic, forming an oppositional pole for the three dialectical dimensions. In its placement at the center of Agee's narrative (IV of VII), it creates a kind of armature or nearly still pivot around which the rest of the discourse frantically circulates.

Fourth, the multiple roles occupied by the episodes in Column III also present an anomaly to dialectical theory. Typically, dialectical dimensions are independent in the sense that they occupy different semantic spaces. Yet, here, one dialectical pole seems to occupy three spaces at once: submissive, compelled, and closed. The singing trio and the young African-American couple were depicted at various times as having a part in relationships in which they were submissive, were compelled, and were closed. If Column IV is like an armature in Agee's discourse, Column III is like a false echo. When submissive was called out across the great cultural divide that separated his tenant subjects from Agee, he heard back compelled and closed. When compelled was called out, he heard submissive and closed. When closed was called out, he heard submissive and compelled. This tightly packed semantic space seems to define the plight of those with whom Agee was trying to converse: submissive, compelled, closed.

Finally, Column III (episodes 3, 16, 19) serves as a kind of hinge for the discourse under consideration. As noted above, the episodes comprising Column III partake of three dialectical oppositions — dominant-submissive (Columns II and III), compelled-volunteered (Columns III and V), and closed-open (Columns III and VI), that is, all three dialectical dimensions are anchored by Column III. Thus, one could say, quite literally, that Agee's narrative turns on Column III. From one point of view, the singing trio (episode 3) and the young black couple (episode 16) were submissive in the face of requests from those who were more powerful. However, in contrast to the voluntary actions depicted by the young white couple (episodes 7, 8, 9) talking to Agee on their porch and the young black couple (episode 14) when they passed by Agee and Evans at the church, the trio (episode 3) and the couple startled by Agee (episode 16) seemed not only submissive but also compelled to act as they did — as if they had no choice. Finally, the singing trio (episode 3) and young African-American couple (episode 16) were also closed when seen in contrast to the relatively open responses of the young white couple (episodes 7, 8, 9).

SUMMARY

My objective has been to demonstrate a unique approach to the study of relationships, a qualitative approach that is at once dialectical, structural, and narrative. To summarize, the approach began with Ricoeur's (1971) essay subtitled "Meaningful Action Considered as a Text," in which he differentiated action from discourse and, within discourse, oral from written. Given this basis, I argued that a simpler and more direct way to bring the resources of discourse studies to relationship studies required reversing Ricoeur's subtitle to read, "Discourse Considered as Meaningful Action." Then, I claimed that documentary narrative depicts relationships and, thus, provides a unique means of observing the interpersonal communication that constitutes them. Finally, I conducted a dialectical, structural, narrative study to illustrate some of the kinds of insights into relationships afforded by the approach.

Specifically, the analysis revealed three dialectical dimensions at work in the relationships under consideration: Agee's conversations across daunting differences in race, class, and region. Agee's discourse depicted his relationships as oscillating between the polar oppositions of dominant-submissive, compelled-volunteered (indigenous ones), and closed-open (conventional). These intercultural relationships swept back and forth across the dialectical dimensions, creating the social domain or field of play on which the relationships were contested.

By contrast, the analysis also revealed an instance of dialectical stasis where, momentarily, normal dialectical movement halted in the face of a relational impasse. Also, contrary to dialectical thinking, the analysis revealed a multiple layering of dialectical dimensions in which all three polar oppositions were anchored by the same set of narrative episodes.

These findings suggest several observations on the meaning of relationship:

that some dialectical dimensions are quite portable, appearing across a wide variety of relationships (that is, they are conventional);

that some dialectical dimensions may be unique to particular relationships (that is, they are indigenous);

that the dialectical movement of relationships may be less predictable than typically thought (that is, dialectical stasis may occur);

that a relationship's dialectical dimensions may not be independent but, rather, may share semantic space with other dimensions; and, finally,

that relationships conducted across racial, class, and regional divides may be constituted by their members' participation in movement along dialectical dimensions anchored by dominance and submissiveness, compelled and volunteered, closed and open.

Documentary narrative, the kind of discourse that has been the focus of this study, is written to be read as an authentic picture of the world. Reading such texts is a way of reading the world. However, the world — of human action, of relationships, for example — does not yield to our gaze so easily.

One "reads" the world. What provides that "reading" are the clues that one is capable of "seeing" and of interpreting. The suggestive virtuosity of a Sherlock Holmes came not only from "seeing" the inobvious clues that others did not "see," but also from piecing together a story out of what would otherwise be merely the "asides" — the titillating, but irrelevant, stuff the rest of us "see." (Thayer, 1994, p. 5)

When we think we "see," the wisdom of U. Eco's (1980) William of Baskerville constrains our hubris: "All the world's creatures are like a book and a picture to us in a mirror" (p. 18).

8

Making Meanings with Friends
William K. Rawlins

In 1994, Cindy Marshall, a scholar with whom I work, returned home to Maine for the summer. We had talked several times about my interest in studying recordings of friends actually talking together, an approach to understanding friendships that, ironically, as a communication scholar I had only minimally attempted for professional research purposes. She was kind enough to speak with several people in Maine who might be interested in tape recording some of their time spent talking with a close friend. She informed these persons that their words would be closely scrutinized and written about by me, a professor with whom Cindy worked and an authority on friendship. Many of them were surprised to learn that scholars actually were studying how friends communicate with each other but were eager to participate in the project. The discourse of one pair of these amenable participants, Karen and Christine, provides the primary basis for my discussion. There was no interview protocol or schedule of questions guiding their interaction other than the fact that they knew I was interested in their friendship; their talk went where they took it during their shared vivid present. Everything I say about these friends I have gleaned from listening to them talk with each other and studying their transcribed words.

By their own reckoning early in the conversation, Karen and Christine have been friends for some "thirty years and counting." One late summer day, it rained in Maine, and Karen took the afternoon off from her job at a local swimming pool. She and Christine convened at her home; Karen put a microphone in a coffee cup on the table between them and turned on and tested the cassette tape recorder, and they began to talk about their lives and their friendship. The tape machine clicked off after the first 45 minutes, whereupon they cooked a meal together, sat down to eat, flipped the cassette over, turned the recorder back on again, and talked for another 45 minutes.

Amid the sounds of utensils scraping dishes, talking with mouths full, a cat meowing, and trips back and forth into Karen's kitchen, I have selected a 12-minute segment from the second side with which to interact for the purposes of this chapter. There are numerous vibrant, touching, funny, mundane, and panoramic moments throughout the recorded talk of these two women. In many respects, while listening attentively to, transcribing, and contemplating their interaction, I have been reminded of the film *My Dinner with Andre* and was similarly carried off into their respective life adventures and predicaments. I am fascinated by the depth and variety of meanings that their interaction creates and exhibits. I have studied relational communication for 20 years yet am struck once again by just how nested each woman's life is with the other's — their families, memories, trips, jobs, judgments, disappointments, and possibilities. At several points, I have taken out maps of Maine and the United States, even a globe, trying to visualize their mentioned locations and travels. Among other topics, I have reflected on sailing, parenting, and breaking and mending bones, hearts, and homes. I have heard laughter and strained and absent voices, personal and shared worlds being constructed, rebuilt, presupposed.

I am convinced that it is impossible to say anything that remotely approaches the richness and vitality of their interaction as it occurred, much less objectively describes and predicts it or accounts for its "variance." Moreover, I am not interested in analyzing the routine methods these women ostensibly utilize to accomplish the sequence of talk I present here. Instead, I want to re-present a portion of their discourse and develop an interpretation of some of the communicative practices and features these women seem to draw upon and accomplish in their talk with each other as friends. Thus, I seek to hear through their voices and see through their words how one extended segment of their conversation expresses aspects of their friendship. In doing so, I, in turn, will be saying some things about the character of communication and meaning making in this relationship. Clearly, I also am performing specific relationships with the discourse provided by these women, as well as with you, the reader. After enacting those relationships through the words I write, I will reflect on and thematize my perceptions of their characteristics.

At this point in the tape, Karen and Christine have been talking about their relationships with their adult children, their children's relationships with each other, and the difficulties of coordinating family get-togethers. To get an uninterrupted feel for their conversation, you may first want to read all of the excerpts from their discourse in sequence, skipping over my commentary. In this way, you have a chance to derive some of your own meanings in relation to their discourse before my voice becomes too intrusive.

A VISIT WITH A VISIT

K: (to her cat) Are you a nice kitty? Are you a nice kitty?

C: (almost to herself) Anyway, I decided not, decided not to think about it, 'cause whatever will happen, will happen.

K: (to her cat) Okay, check it all out. Put your nose right on it. See, there's nothing there that you want. Nothing.

C: Tell you what I'm getting into more lately is, (pause) not doing anything . . .

K: (chuckles in a low-pitched, almost encouraging way)

C: (laughs briefly)

K: (chuckles in the same cadence as before, yet higher pitched)

C: about, not feeling that I have to make things, I have to somehow help things along.

K: Um hm.

C: I've just; I've gotten to the point where I'll, you know?, I sort of whipped myself into a frenzy when I was there, that bad week that last week that I was there, and I was so depressed, getting the house ready, that somebody might come, that some friend might come, or Loretta might come, or some unknown person might come, and, and I went around sweeping and . . .

K: My God, Chris.

C: dusting . . .

K: That *is* depressing.

C: And, I wanted to have the house look nice and then I, I kinda got a hold of myself and I thought . . .

K: Hahahaha (rapid high-pitched laugh)

C: You know!?

K: Yeah.

C: Really here! Um. You know, I don't even *know* if anybody's coming, and, and, and it's beautiful weather, and you know I don't want to be doing this. And I got sort of mad at myself and mad at the house, and, and so since then I've sort of got this idea like, whatever happens, you know, then Julie started in about maybe cousin Alice coming from Georgia, and when could I get her out there, and I said, "Julie, I can't do anything about, given the information that I have, I can't do anything about it, I, uh, I'm glad for you to stay there. For Alice to stay there, whoever comes, that's good. But I can't make any more efforts over it; I've just had a summer of planning for things that didn't happen and getting ready for things that didn't happen, and I can't do, and I don't want to do that anymore."

K: Mmm.

C: I mean I didn't say it in that way to her; but that's the way I feel, basically. I'm just gonna look after what I have to do for myself and for my cat.

K: Yeah.

C: And keep myself there. And if they fall into place, good; if they don't, too bad, you know?

K: Yeah.

It may seem odd to start an examination of this conversation with Karen speaking to her cat, but talking about pets and talking to Karen's cat were integral moments of this visit. At various points in the conversation, talking to the cat seemed to provide a "breather" in their conversation, which often allowed a new topic to emerge. For example, immediately prior to this passage, the women had been discussing how their families would converge on their homes during Labor Day weekend and some of the problems involved. Karen's talk to the cat attends a transition into a more general discussion of doing less for company.

Listening to this passage, I notice the significance of laughter in the friends' dialogue and the challenges it poses to me in re-presenting this discourse to readers. Laughter is a vital part of their interaction — there are low, almost mocking chortles; metered laughs, like Karen's in the previous excerpt, that increase in pitch and seemingly urge the other woman to continue and to feel good about what she is saying; wheezy, surprised laughs that turn into coughs and then more laughter; wary, questioning laughs that sound unsure about where the talk is turning and at whose expense. Laughter adds gusto and a risky, joyful timbre to their talk. In its ambiguity and teetering emotions, it sounds from the depths of a robust and longstanding connection. M. M. Bakhtin usefully worried how we render in words the singularity of such intonation at the heart of communicating in relationships (Todorov, 1984).

Of course, multiple voices intersect as these friends speak. Note, for example, how Christine quotes her own utterances to her daughter Julie in her talk with Karen. I find intriguing her admission that the version spoken here is an altered one. In this reenactment, Christine seems to dramatize for her friend what she really felt (or is now feeling if she were) addressing Julie. Thus, this quotation of herself embedded in her talk with Karen allows Christine to speak more candidly in relation to her daughter than she may have in the actual circumstances. Further, Christine appears to be rehearsing a more decisive and assertive identity and position on family visitors through this rendering of herself to Karen. On her part, Karen responds throughout in actively confirming ways. Their dialogue continues.

C: I mean it was, I just got burned out when I tried to get Mary out, that was one thing with Mary, you know I felt like I was under the gun the whole time!

K: Well . . .

C: I had to try to get out and, you know, worked up a gigantic phone bill. Both of us tryin' to make connections and tryin' to go. Finally, I just said, "Well, you know, somebody up there is telling us the word is no" — HmHmHmHm (chuckles quietly, rising slightly in pitch)

K: Hm (laughs briefly)

C: — "and I'm willing to listen to that." HmHa, and Mary really wasn't, 'cause of course she wanted to go so bad. And I didn't blame her, I understood exactly how she felt and said, "There's gotta be a way." Um. I threw in the towel first because over the years I've learned that when it comes up no, seven or eight times, that you better listen. Is that what it is, what the answer is is NO? (laughs)

K: Yeah.

C: No way.

K: Yeah.

C: And it just kinda, and I just like blew a gasket I guess, and just thought, "I can't go through this anymore; (quietly) I don't do this anymore. I don't."

K: (big sigh) I don't know, I can't get ready for things; I, I don't, it's been a long time since I've been willing to get ready for things.

C: Really?

K: No.

C: I've started, this has been quite sudden with me, 'cause usually that's what I spend half my life, getting ready for things, and see . . .

K: I mean for people . . .

C: No, I do too, yeah!

K: visitors, you know, coming to this house. (Walks into the kitchen) Hey, they take it as they find it.

C: Oh, I, well . . .

K: And if they don't like it, I can show them where the door is. (She's running water, doing something in the sink.)

C: Right. Well, I guess it wasn't so much the house, it was, uh, I was upset about everything on the island anyway, and then . . .

K: Yeah, well, you deserved to be.

C: And that was another feature of it that (long pause) I just . . .

K: Here, look out the door (talking to the cat).

C: (laughs) (to the cat) Look at the rain.

K: (to the cat) Yeah, right, it's like getting your playpen.

C: Hahahahun.

K: (to the cat) Do something besides whine at me; what's the matter with you? Ho God!

C: Ha ha ha, I think he probably resents this other person here.

K: No, she doesn't, it's just, it's a, it's a need for attention, I don't know, I don't . . .

C: Yeah, but if she maybe doesn't have your full attention or something. Are we still on this thing here? (referring to the tape recorder)

K: Yeah.

C: Oh jeez me, why don't we, we've got to talk about, I've got . . .

K: We're supposed to be talking about friendship, but . . .

C: We got Harlingen right.

K: Harlingen, but . . .

I hear a variety of things transpiring during this excerpt. For me, some of the understated drama of their conversation is nicely displayed. Christine is still talking about the effort involved in receiving visitors at her island summer home. With vigorous phrases, she recounts how she got "burned out," feeling "under the gun" and working up a "gigantic phone bill" in trying to arrange Mary's visit. Finally, she quotes herself as citing "somebody up there" as intervening in this mythic quest and the other woman's reluctance to accept the answer "no." She characterizes the episode as blowing a gasket for her and meditatively quotes what her immediate thoughts were to Karen, "I can't go through this anymore." At first, it sounds like a conclusion she reached in her mind at that time.

However, when she repeats it quietly, "I don't do this anymore. I don't," it sounds like she once again is contemplating a new personal policy out loud to Karen, rather than reporting on her reactions in the past. Her present expression of these thoughts is quite pensive and conclusive in tone.

Beginning with a large sigh, Karen echoes her frustration about the time involved with "getting ready for things," that is, visitors to her home, and observes spunkily that "Hey, they take it as they find it" or are shown the door. She also emphatically endorses Christine's distress about recent events at the island, stating explicitly, "Yeah, well, you deserved to be." In short, it appears they have had a fairly thoughtful discussion about their attitudes toward preparing for company. However, when Christine seems to continue this topic ("And that was another feature . . ."), Karen responds to her cat's meowing to go outside. Then both friends laughingly tease the cat about the rainy conditions, subtly establish its gender, and critique its apparent need for Karen's "full attention." The cat has occasioned comic relief and perhaps a new topic of conversation.

Interestingly, at this point, Christine asks whether they are still being taped. Her surprised and somewhat flustered reaction to Karen's affirmative answer is intriguing to me as the would-be eavesdropper embodied by the machine. It appears that she had forgotten that their conversation was being recorded, which supports my perceptions of the uninhibited and authentic qualities of their interaction. Karen reminds her they are "supposed to be talking about friendship." Christine observes, "We got Harlingen right," which I surmise refers to the scene of a serious quarrel during a vacation together to which they alluded toward the end of the first side of the tape. At that point, they also admitted that, during this taping session, they were addressing this memorable event for the first time since it occurred. Their exchanges opening the tape's second side lead me to believe that they actually discussed this incident further while they were preparing their dinner and the tape was not running. They also promise themselves to return to it during this second side of the cassette but never do. I am left wondering, What happened at Harlingen, Texas, between these two friends? Did they resolve it the afternoon of this taping? How did they decide to limit their recorded talk about it? What would their discussion reveal about their friendship's communicative practices if I could have heard it? I comfort myself with the thought that I am fortunate to be able to listen to the dialogue they have shared with me.

Christine then initiates a poignant dialogue about Karen's unavailability and minimal communication the previous winter. They address a predicament in their friendship that calls to mind what I have written about elsewhere as one of the central dialectical tensions facing close friends (Rawlins, 1983). I have identified the dialectic of the freedom to be independent and the freedom to be dependent as a pivotal tension in numerous interviewees' descriptions of their friendships, as well as in fictional depictions (Rawlins, 1992). I have stated, "Time apart can be interpreted either as an assertion of friends faith in their bond or the possible beginning of a new period of separateness that may jeopardize the friendship. During the period of separation, there is really no way of telling exactly which is the case, except by renewing contact" (p. 261). Imagine how intrigued I was to stumble on these two friends explicitly considering the lived dynamics of this dialectical principle because of Christine so pointedly raising them as a concern.

C: Well, the other thing, I've got to say this before we get back into that (laughs) Harlingen (laughingly said) who-knows-what,

K: (laughs with Christine)

C: but I have to tell you now. Last winter, after, after last fall (long pause) you were going to Portland for the, for the first time . . . (serious tone)

K: Yeah.

C: and . . . getting an apartment, all that stuff. And we, I went down to see you once. (slow, measured pace and tone)

K: Right. (quickly inserted)

C: And then, um, we had a few, I don't know how you pronounce it, desultory?

K: Desultory.

C: Letters. (brief laugh)

K: Um hm.

C: (laughs) missives floating back and forth.

K: I get the feeling here that there's something between us? (said with a quizzical expectant laugh)

C: Then . . . a little longer silences and longer silences.

K: Yeah.

C: And I got quite upset.

K: I know; it was my fault. (quickly interjected)

C: Well, I'm not saying fault, but the thing is, Karen, that I decided that the crux of it was that (puts food in her mouth) we're friends of this long and good standing, (pause) and I didn't know what the *hell* was going on. I didn't know if you were dead or alive.

K: I was pretty near dead.

C: Or in the hospital, or what. But I had no way of, I mean except to call your son and say, you know, "Is your mother okay?"

K: Did you?

C: No. I didn't.

K: Oh. Yeah, well; I don't know whether he could've answered you or not.

The above excerpt opens with a distinctive mix of laughter and deliberately paced interaction, momentarily achieving a questioning, ambivalent atmosphere. After laughing about Harlingen, Christine clearly wants to talk with Karen about their (but mainly Karen's) actions the previous winter. She initiates the topic of their gradually losing contact in a markedly measured sequence of turns, even dwelling on the correct pronunciation of "desultory" in recalling their letters. Karen responds to each of these speaking turns promptly and tersely, which functions to magnify their segmented quality. After Christine seems to laugh a little nervously, Karen senses "that there's something between us?" registering this questioning observation with a watchful laugh. Christine then asserts that the "little longer and longer silences" made her "quite upset," and Karen instantly replies, "I know; it was my fault."

In my opinion, less than ideal contact is a condition many adult friends face (Rawlins, 1994), but it is primarily a relationally negotiated pattern and responsibility that may be handled by friends in multiple ways ranging from ignoring to explicitly addressing the issue. Evidently, Christine cares enough about the matter to raise it with Karen but is not interested in assigning blame or "fault." It is a reasonably sophisticated communicative challenge for her to bring up this concern without hurting or angering Karen, which may be why she began the discussion in the way she did. Once the issue is on the table, however, she immediately clarifies that "the crux of it was we're friends of this long and good standing," that she was uninformed, and that her worries centered on her friend's well-being. In my judgment, a vexing past situation in this friendship has been opened sensitively for their present discussion as friends.

Yet, as someone who has listened to this conversation many times, I read these and the next few lines as initial expressions of some rather deep-seated themes in their ensuing dialogue. Specifically, Christine states, "I didn't know if you were dead or alive," to which Karen replies, "I was pretty near dead." Then Christine observes that the only way she felt she could learn if Karen was okay would be to call her son. Karen immediately asks if she did; Christine says no; and Karen states, "Yeah well; I don't know whether he could've answered you or not." Here is my interpretation of these lines: Christine was worried about Karen because she cares for her and can be anxious about her health. Even so, she respects her privacy and freedom within their friendship and recognizes that an unobtrusive way to inquire about Karen would be through her son, although she chose not to do so. Karen, in fact, acknowledges the legitimacy of Christine's concerns when she says she was "pretty near dead," however literally the expression is meant. Then, Karen momentarily puts Christine on the spot and seemingly tests her sincerity by verifying whether she did contact her son, then immediately excuses Christine by doubting whether he could have answered Christine. Her wry expression of this last statement could imply a variety of meanings: he might not know because he was not in touch with his mother either; he was in touch with his mother, but neither he nor she knew for sure whether she was "okay;" he knew his mother was not okay but would be hesitant to convey that to Christine. Regardless, it seems that Karen is confirming the validity of Christine's worries last winter as well as Christine's reluctance to contact Karen directly or indirectly.

C: Well the thing was, I thought (long pause) and then finally, I guess it was Julie, my daughter, said, something about that you were hav-, were in one of your stages where you didn't wanta communicate, you were withdrawing and whatever, whatever.

K: Yeah, I was.

C: And I thought, "Well that's okay; everybody has these times when they feel this way." But I feel like you should *alert* people that *care* about you (laughs) to the fact that this is what is going on . . .

K: (laughs) Yeah . . .

C: "I'm going into my cave. See ya in the spring," or whatever. Or "I don't wish to have anything, writing or any communications for a while. Not to worry. Adios. Bye to everybody, Hasta la vista or whatever."

K: Yeah.

C: Or something, because I (pause), I (pause), I . . .

K: You were worried.

C: It was very hard on me to not know and then to hear third hand, I mean maybe I, I didn't take the responsibility of following it up or making any, after a couple, writing a couple of times; but I felt like it would be a help to me to know that, not to know that you were having a depressed, hard time, but to know that you, you didn't want to be bothered with having to write or correspond, or to talk on the phone or see anyone, or whatever it was. But even a, a postcard to say this, or to say, you know, "Leave me alone" (laughs) or whatever.

K: (laughs in a quiet, understanding way)

C: And, or whatever you were thinking, (pause) would have been a help to me, because I find, I felt like you know maybe we're never gonna talk again, maybe we'll never see each other. I didn't know what exactly was going on. And I . . .

K: Well, I didn't know what was going on either.

C: No, I know you didn't.

At this point, Christine recalls thinking and her daughter observing that maybe Karen merely wanted to withdraw from social contact for awhile. After Karen agrees, Christine quotes her thoughts to herself at the time that such feelings are commonplace and "okay." Even so, she believes that Karen "should *alert* people that *care* about you to the fact that this is going on." They both laugh at this rather paradoxical recommendation to communicate to significant others that she does not intend to communicate with them. Christine rehearses two voices for Karen here: a humorous one that trades on a hibernation metaphor, and then a more serious and explicit statement with Spanish flourishes at the end that seem to add color and a comical, mock cosmopolitan flavor. As Karen affirms this idea, however, Christine surrenders her comic tone and makes the frank request, "Or something," haltingly trying to offer her reasons, "I (pause), I (pause), I . . . ," which Karen completes for her, "You were worried." In short, she once again recognizes the emotional basis of Christine's concerns and, by implication, legitimates Christine's suggested policy for communicating social withdrawal.

Christine then further elaborates her anxieties about not knowing about Karen or learning of her through others and acknowledges that she was partly responsible for losing contact by not following up on her early letters. Even so, she repeats her desire to be informed when Karen "didn't want to be bothered with having to write or correspond, or to talk on the phone or see anyone, or whatever it was." The friends laugh together at the suggestion that Christine would prefer "even a, a postcard" or a brusque, "Leave me alone" to ambiguous silence. She remarks that, last winter, she was not sure if they would ever talk or visit again, that she "didn't know exactly what was going on." Once again, Karen responds, "Well I didn't know what was going on either," implying that her being on the "sending" side of her own silence was possibly as frustrating and confusing as being on the "receiving" side. Christine immediately confirms Karen's reflection, saying, "No, I know you didn't."

C: But the thing is. (pause) However much you want to struggle through things on your own, and I know that every now and then we have to do this on a lot of things, (pause) but I, I would just hope that you could say, "I need to be by myself, I need to be incommunicado;" or whatever. However you phrased it. And then I'd say, "Oh yeah. Well that's good. I know that. That's what's happening to Karen now; and that whatever it entails I don't know, but I know that that's the way, that's her pleasure right now to do this time, to frame it out this way." Now I can accept that, I have always accepted everything else that . . .

K: (laughing sardonically) Ha heh. "She's thrown my way."

C: No, I mean between us, both of us, back and forth have accepted pretty much, may have been some bumpy spots and all, but we could live with it, and we could go on. And then, and so I felt that, well, one of the worst things anybody can do to *me* is from, prior history, is to not let me know what the hell is going on.

K: Yeah, I can understand why you would feel that way.

C: That is the worst thing that could, if, I don't care, I can cope, if I (heh heh) . . .

K: I'll just get this.

C: (chuckles) I'm spitting rice on the floor.

K: Hahahaha. (laughs quietly in a little bit of a high-pitched titter)

C: Um, and then you know since my father's illness and death and all when I wasn't told, and I've always had that feeling that (long pause) if you lay it on me I can somehow get a handle on it, I can work at least on doing that. If I don't know, and if it's secret and I'm not supposed to be told anything, that is devastating . . . to me. So there. (The passage beginning with, "if you lay it on me" is quite emotional in tone and then gradually tapers back into a more ordinary conversational one.)

Once more, Christine acknowledges Karen's and most persons' need to "struggle through things" independently while also repeating her hope that Karen will inform others when she feels that way. Then, Christine rehearses what she would say to herself upon learning "That's what's happening to Karen now." These statements clearly endorse Karen's actions. Christine then comments on her ability to accept Karen's needs to be alone, as well as "everything else that . . ." As Christine searches for words, Karen supplies a fairly cynical conclusion to the sentence in a sarcastically laughing manner, "Ha heh. 'She's thrown my way.'"

In my opinion, this can be heard as a rather complex occurrence in their conversation. Basically, Karen is ventriloquizing Christine's voice here in nuanced yet telling ways. First, by using the third person ("She's" instead of "You've thrown my way."), Karen grammatically converts the implied trajectory of the sentence to resemble Christine's previous statements *about* Karen in the past or a hypothetical situation, rather than something she is now saying *to* Karen. Through this formulation, Karen seems to subtly suggest that Christine is reluctant to address Karen directly. Second, using the word "thrown," rather than the cautious, diplomatic wording Christine has used up to this point, colors Christine's statement as possibly one that recalls unpleasant surprises. Thus, Karen's version changes Christine's statement from one about acceptance into one of judgment. Having Christine say, "I have always accepted everything else she's thrown my way," in a sardonic tone significantly shapes the spirit and implied meaning of her unfinished sentence, in my opinion. In this version, Christine is not accepting Karen; she is judging her, and in the third person no less.

Christine seems to pick up on this characterization, protesting, "No," and proceeds to describe "bumpy spots" occurring in their relationship, "between us," that "both of us, back and forth have accepted pretty much." Even so, her initiation of this overall segment of the conversation does constitute a judgment of Karen's actions last winter, and despite Christine's desire to grant Karen the freedom to be independent, Karen's unannounced and extended silences did trouble her. Accordingly, Christine restates what, early in the conversation, she, without assigning blame ("saying fault"), deemed "the crux" of the issue. Using almost identical words as before, she states, "One of the worst things anybody can do to *me* is from, prior history, is to not let me know what the hell is going on." Interestingly, however, she does not emphasize the word "hell" this time, and the entire statement is said in a way that seems to announce that her point is a repeat of an important one she has already made. Karen realizes its significance and says empathetically, "Yeah, I can understand why you would feel this way."

As Christine begins to discuss this "worst thing" she has mentioned, a brief humorous interlude occurs because of her "spitting rice on the floor." Then we learn that, because of the secrecy surrounding her father's death, Christine feels quite strongly about not being told things. One of the most emotional passages in this talk is her statement, "If you lay it on me I can somehow get a handle on it, I can work at least on doing that. If I don't know, and if it's secret and I'm not supposed to be told anything, that is devastating . . . to me." With Christine's personal and historical associations registered, the significance of her feelings about not hearing from Karen is thrust into a new light. The immediate result in the dialogue is that Karen now begins to explain her actions.

K: Well, see I wasn't consciously trying to keep secret; I, I, I certainly was not thinking about anything but myself.

C: No,

K: Right, you know . . .

C: No.

K: I wasn't thinking about, you know, my effect on you . . .

C: No, of course not.

K: and I wasn't thinking about my effect on Cindy either . . .

C: No.

K: and I didn't communicate with her any more than I communicated with you . . .

C: No, it was everybody, and I understand that.

K: No, and now that it's later, I am ashamed of that, but, at the time I just didn't want to do anything except, you know, sit in my chair and take my daily Prozac.

C: Yeah.

K: Which was a disaster. (said with a brief scornful laugh)

C: Was it?

K: Oh yeah, Christ.

C: How long did you take it?

K: I took it for about four or five months.

C: Really, Kar? (asked in a quiet, deeply concerned voice)

K: Yeah. And at the end of it, I was beginning to think, you know, "Hey, why bother?"

C: Yeah.

K: "Why bother at all?"

C: Yeah.

K: And at that point I thought, "Why don't you just stop this?"

C: Yeah.

K: You know so, I just call, I just stopped taking it . . .

C: Yeah.

K: and uh, I did call the doctor, and say, "You know, it uh," and left a message on her, I don't know, with her nurse or some damn thing, but I was . . . you know, not getting the benefit . . .

C: Was this a medical doctor that had given you this?

K: Yeah,   Yeah,   Yeah. Yeah.

C: Oh.   Hmm. (harmony occurs on "Oh" and "Hmm" with each "Yeah" of Karen's appearing directly above)

K: (brief mocking laugh) Jean thought I was, what a heart attack waiting to happen, you know and all those lovely things.

C: Right.

K: I don't know; it was just a bad . . .

C: a bad time.

K: a bad time.

C: Oh yeah. Must have been awful for you.

At the beginning of this excerpt, Karen immediately addresses Christine's use of the word "secret," asserting that "trying to keep secret" was never her conscious goal. Secrecy suggests deliberately concealing information or selectively excluding others. In contrast, during this period, Karen recalls being focused only on herself without considering the "effect" of her seclusion on Christine or Cindy, another close friend of hers; further, she describes being equally uncommunicative with both women. After responding supportively to virtually every point Karen makes here, Christine acknowledges the blanket nature of Karen's retreat, saying, "No, it was everybody, I understand that." Removed in time, Karen admits being "ashamed" of seemingly abandoning her friends but now adds that her self-absorption included daily use of Prozac, "which was a disaster."

As she listens to her friend here, Christine proceeds to ask brief, interested questions and to give positive minimal responses (Maltz & Borker, 1982) that may facilitate Karen recounting this lamentable period lasting "four or five months." Karen reenacts her thoughts "at the end of it" to Christine when she concluded to herself, "Why don't you just stop this?" She reports, "I just stopped taking it," and narrates leaving a message for her doctor to that effect. Sounding critically concerned, Christine asks, "Was this a medical doctor that had given you this?"

At this point, a brief exchange occurs that I want to describe in detail because it illustrates the rhythm and musicality of these friends' conversation and my extreme limitations in trying to render it for readers. As my transcription above tries to depict, here is what happens: After Christine asks this question, Karen says, "Yeah," then in a gentle manner repeats, "Yeah," this time accompanied by Christine saying "Oh" in soft, higher-pitched harmony, followed immediately in the same cadence with Karen saying "Yeah" again, this time with Christine simultaneously voicing "Hmm" in the same dulcet harmony, and then Karen utters one last solo

"Yeah." It is a musical coda of sorts for the story just told, followed by Karen's piqued observation that "Jean thought I was a heart attack waiting to happen; you know, and all those lovely things." Then ensues an interaction confirming the negative nature of this period, which both friends concur was "a bad time" for Karen. Christine observes compassionately, "Must have been awful for you."

K: And I didn't, you know, the only people that I knew were like Michael and Tina and the kids.

C: Right.

K: And that was all I wanted to know.

C: That was all you could do . . .

K: If they had anybody over for dinner, you could be damn sure I wasn't there.

C: Right. (walks into kitchen) No, I know how you can't deal with anybody, and don't want to. (from another part of the room) I'm gonna have some more rice, now.

K: So . . .

C: I don't know how I could still be hungry, but I am . . . Well . . .

K: Chris, I apologize. I apologize, and I . . .

C: No, I, it's not a thing for an apology, I'm just saying, in the *future* when the storms come, don't . . .

K: I'll do it, ha ha.

C: Try to raise the pennant and say "Storm signals are flying here."

K: "Storm signals are flying," okay. (said mostly to herself seemingly in rehearsal)

C: Or some such ilk, and um, and just so I can say, "Okay." And I, I would do the same, I mean . . .

K: Ah, but you, dear heart, are going to be at sea.

C: (talking with food in her mouth) Only 19 days, I mean not for the rest of the winter, (laughing a little) ha ha, ha ha ha I hope, unless we're blown way off course!

K: Noo, I, I, I hope I sincerely hope for my sake that this winter will be purposeful.

C: Yeah.

K: And maybe even interesting? Nah.

C: Well, why not?

K: (whispers) That's too much.

C: You've got all of Portland at your feet! (laughs)

During the above segment, Karen indicates that her only contacts during this time were her son and his family, who live in the immediate vicinity, and only if they did not have guests for dinner. Christine validates Karen's need for limited social contact on both accounts and, walking into the kitchen, voices her understanding that "I know how you can't deal with anybody, and don't want to." While Christine is in the kitchen announcing she will "have some more rice," Karen tries to begin a statement, "So . . ."

Wondering aloud how she "could still be hungry," Christine returns to the table. At this point, Karen, calling her friend by name, says quite sincerely, "Chris, I apologize. I apologize, and I . . ." Karen seems to be registering her realization that, even though her retreat was painful and understandable and accepted by her friend, she hurt Christine when she provided no indication of what she was going through. The friends have returned to "the crux" of their discussion after considering in depth each woman's experiences of "last winter."

This being so, Christine cuts short Karen's statement, once again insisting, "It's not a thing for apology." Instead, Christine apparently wants to establish a forward-looking practice in their friendship and, dwelling on the coast of Maine as they do, uses nautical terms, "I'm just saying, in the future when the storms come, don't . . ." Before hearing the rest, Karen laughingly interjects, "I'll do it." Christine continues, "Try to raise the pennant and say, 'Storm signals are flying here,'" which Karen immediately appears to rehearse aloud to herself. Christine states that such a signal will allow her to respond, "Okay," and that she will indicate likewise, should she require solitude.

Having agreed on this procedure, Karen promptly steers their conversation to the fact that soon Christine literally will be "at sea." Chuckling and with her mouth full, Christine replies that she will sail for "Only 19 days" and not the entire winter "unless we're blown way off course!" Karen, in turn, wistfully hopes for a purposeful and interesting winter, to which Christine encouragingly replies. Just beyond this transcript, the women begin to analyze Karen's constraints and opportunities in Portland during the approaching season.

REFLECTIONS ON MEANINGS MADE

I think it is worthwhile to be reminded about what it can mean to converse in a close, longstanding friendship. As enacted by Karen and Christine, the meanings of this kind of relationship are active, collaborative, ongoing, and cumulative accomplishments. They frequently are created by one or both parties from highly nuanced behaviors, prosodic cues, or word choices. Meanwhile, these meanings presuppose and symbolically reproduce mutually experienced or recognized events that have occurred or are unfolding in real time, concrete settings, and with genuine consequences for the friends or persons about whom they care.

In my research, I have investigated the dialectics of communicating in friendships primarily by listening to and looking at the discourse of persons talking *about* their friends and then trying to situate their descriptions in moments of the life course (Rawlins, 1992). In writing this chapter, I have been listening to two longtime friends, each talking *with* her friend. Thus, when I entitle this chapter "Making Meanings with Friends," I intend at least two meanings based on two sorts of relationships: first, the activities re-presented here of these two friends making meaning with each other on a summer afternoon and, second, my own written attempt at making meanings with these friends' recorded discourse.

This chapter addresses only a brief excerpt from these two women's afternoon conversation, which in turn is but a fleeting episode in their friendship of some 30 years. However, like gazing into a tide pool, perusing this slice of life reveals much about the ebbs and flows of communicating with friends. This discourse illustrates the enjoyment of conversing with a friend and, for these women in particular, a shared appreciation of the drama of everyday life, its continuous production of comic and tragic events, and the desire and need to make sense of them. It should not be surprising, then, to witness a range of emotions in their dialogue from worried self-reflection to exuberant laughter. In fact, the terrain of their talk is sprinkled with many species of laughter. For these two friends, to speak with one other is to speak with feeling.

An atmosphere of encouragement shapes and reflects much of their dialogue as well. This ambiance is probably because of several communicative practices richly evident in their talk. Many risky or disclosive comments are met with confirming responses. Each woman explicitly recognizes the legitimacy of the other's experience at various points. They actively listen to each other, providing frequent verbal and nonverbal responses and asking relevant questions. Concerns are expressed where concern seems warranted by the other's narrative. Seemingly unselfconsciously, they appear to exhibit effort and empathy in trying to recognize, if not understand, what someone else is feeling or saying at that moment. Although I acknowledge the ways in which these practices resemble canonical emphases of humanistic communication, they all seem to be meaningful features of how these friends communicate in this discourse.

Other aspects of their interaction appear to draw on these supportive tendencies. For one, these friends seem to feel free to experiment stylistically and with multiple voices in their talk. Throughout this discourse, they quote their own thoughts and statements and those of others in stylized, colorful, and sometimes admittedly fictional ways. It is as if each feels encouraged to "narrativize" and dramatize events in ways that allow her to role play, rehearse new identities, explore different characters. Meanwhile, the moral or practical consequences of these choices are open to scrutiny and reaction by her friend.

Here enters my interpretation of how they enact the dialectic of judgment and acceptance that I have discussed in depth elsewhere (Rawlins, 1989, 1992). At different points in their talk, an identifiable tension emerges between each woman's confidence that the other will accept her and give her the benefit of the doubt in most instances and her expectation that deserved judgments and critiques will be conveyed when deemed necessary. This dialectical tension is enacted notably in their discourse as they deal with the issue of Karen cutting off contact with Christine the previous winter. As I mentioned above, this matter itself turns on the dialectical tension between granting and experiencing the freedom to be independent and the freedom to be dependent in close friendship (Rawlins, 1983).

Weaving in and out of critical and accepting discourse, the two women express and examine in detail Christine's legitimate concerns about Karen's seclusion and Karen's understandable needs for privacy. Judging and thinking together in this way, they seem to establish successfully and sensitively a new policy for dealing with such circumstances in the future. Interestingly, it is a paradoxical policy asking each friend to communicate to the other when she is feeling the need not to communicate. The other, in turn, is expected to hear and respect this desire for what it is.

Much of the contemporary study of communication in relationships owes its impetus to the thinking of Gregory Bateson, and if Bateson, (1972) insisted on anything, it was that nothing ("no-thing") possesses or expresses meaning in and of itself. All meanings are processes and products of relationships. Even the meanings of the relationships themselves emerge in relation to other relationships, constructed and noticed by observers who assume particular relationships within and with them (Bateson, 1979).

A diverse array of embodied as well as textual relationships configure themselves in the meaning making of this chapter. Thus far, I have considered Karen and Christine's communicative relationship with each other, which is mediated by numerous other relationships — with children, in-laws, prior spouses, friends, coworkers, employers, and so on — a fraction of which are alluded to in this discourse.

My relationship with their discourse also is mediated by numerous other embodied and textual relationships. Only a few of these are mentioned here, including our mutual relationship with Cindy Marshall, who arranged the taping, the various texts I have cited, and, of course, the editors of this book. I want to emphasize that my understandings and interpretations of their communicative activities, self-identities, and relationship with each other say as much or more about my relationships with them and with other persons and discursive formations as their relationship with each other. For example, based on my own scholarly work, I was delighted to encounter, scrutinize, and thematize their grappling with and discussion of the dialectic of conjunctive freedoms and their enactments of the dialectic of judgment and acceptance. So, these exchanges became facets of their interaction that I keyed on in depth in this chapter.

As I have been studying Karen and Christine's interaction, I have wanted to write about and dialogue with the entire 90 minutes they recorded, not just the 12 minutes I chose to present here. I am fascinated by how their conversation builds on itself, with events, people, and places cross-referenced and indexed multiple times as they co-tell the stories of each other's lives and relationships. So, I have entered arbitrarily into a conversation that has been happening for some 30 years. Moreover, separating out a segment of its sounds and voices for transcription and analysis feels like cutting into a musical piece. In many respects, I have found it helpful to think of this afternoon conversation in musical terms, remaining attuned to its various moods, rhythms, harmonic textures, and melodies. I have experienced the extended portion examined above as composing a significant movement in the overall conversation, taken as a musical piece. Indeed, much of my understanding of Karen and Christine's relationship as expressed on the tape derives from the qualities I have described as musical.

I do not want simply to lament the absence of sounds in this chapter because of the silent limitations of writing. I have tried to listen carefully to them and talk about them. Even so, it truly is difficult to reproduce in written form the intonation of their utterances. Adverbs describing laughter, complex emotions, and vocal tones evocatively and precisely are hard to come by; yet, such features contribute considerably to the friends' communicative relationship as well as my relationship with their discourse.

I, therefore, want to emphasize that any assertion made in this chapter like, "Laughter is a vital part of their interaction" merely registers my opinions and observations about this discourse. I am judging them and positioning their interaction with each other through virtually every statement I make. Such sentences create an illusion of factuality in (especially written) discussions of others' activities and experiences. Accordingly, I want to remind you, the reader, to test the utility of any of the interpretations I offer here in relation to your own experiences. You also should test the appropriateness and validity of my comments in relation to the representations I have provided of these women's discourse. There is, of course, some circularity in this latter process, because I selected the passages and have written all the textual descriptions regarding their nonverbal behaviors, which are themselves interpretations. Even so, their spoken words are transcribed verbatim here and are open to agreement or alternative interpretations by readers, based on their specific relationships with them.

Finally, I am proposing different relationships and am seeking to make different meanings with you, the reader, than I might in a standard chapter. I am asking you to "listen" to two women talk together and to read my commentary to gain some insights about what it means to communicate in their friendship. I realize that this discourse could remind you of some things that you already know, moments you have experienced and shared with others, and your experiences cannot help but influence your relationships with this chapter, with these friends. Authors define multiple relationships with their readers, consciously and unconsciously. Compare the meanings we make here with the meanings you make in relationships with other authors. If you know me personally, and perhaps are even an actual friend of mine, how does that affect your reading and meaning making with this chapter? What if you are a "perfect stranger?" What if you are critical of me? *Our* relationship will contribute substantially to the meanings you make with this chapter.

ACKNOWLEDGMENTS

I thank Karen and Christine for taping and sharing their conversation with me and Cindy Marshall for arranging their participation. I also thank Annette Markham, Cindy Marshall, and Sandy Rawlins for carefully reading and commenting on this chapter.

References

Agee, J., & Evans, W. (1988). *Let us now praise famous men*. New York: Houghton Mifflin.

Ainsworth, M.D.S. (1972). Attachment and dependency: A comparison. In J. L. Gewirtz (Ed.), *Attachment and dependency* (pp. 97–137). Washington, DC: Winston.

Ainsworth, M.D.S. (1982). Attachment: Retrospect and prospect. In C. M. Parkes & J. Stevenson-Hinde (Eds.), *The place of attachment in human behavior* (pp. 3–30). New York: Basic Books.

Alberts, J. K. (1986). The role of couples' conversation in relational development: A content analysis of courtship talk in Harlequin romance novels. *Communication Quarterly, 34*, 127–142.

Althusser, L. (1971). *Lenin and philosophy and other essays*. New York: Monthly Review Press.

Ames, S. A. (1993). *Multiple spoken and written channels of communication: An ethnography of a medical unit in a general hospital*. Unpublished doctoral dissertation, State University of New York at Buffalo.

Aristotle (1941). *The basic works* (Richard McKeon, Ed.). New York: Random House.

Bakhtin, M. M. (1986). *Speech genres and other late essays* (V. W. McGee, Trans.). Austin: University of Texas Press.

Baldwin, M. W. (1992). Relational schemas and the processing of social information. *Psychological Bulletin, 112*, 461–484.

Baldwin, M. W. (1995). Relational schemas and cognition in close relationships. *Journal of Social and Personal Relationships, 12*, 547–552.

Banks, S., & Riley, P. (1992). Structuration theory as an ontology for communication research. In S. Deetz (Ed.), *Communication Yearbook 16* (pp. 167–196). Newbury Park, CA: Sage.

Barnhart, R. K. (1988). *The Barnhart dictionary of etymology*. New York: H. W. Wilson.

Barthes, R. (1972). The structuralist activity. In R. T. DeGeorge & F. M. DeGeorge (Eds.), *The structuralists from Marx to Levi-Strauss* (pp. 148–154). Garden City, NY: Doubleday.

Bateson, G. (1935). Culture, contact and schismogenesis. *Man, 35,* 178–183.

Bateson, G. (1951). Information and codification: A philosophical approach. In J. Ruesch & G. Bateson (Eds.), *Communication: The social matrix of psychiatry* (pp. 168–211). New York: Norton.

Bateson, G. (1972). *Steps to an ecology of mind*. New York: Ballantine Books.

Bateson, G. (1973). *Steps to an ecology of mind*. New York: Paladin.

Bateson, G. (1979). *Mind and nature: A necessary unity*. New York: E. P. Dutton.

Bavelas, J. B., & Segal, L. (1982). Family systems theory: Background and implications. *Journal of Communication, 32*(3), 99–107.

Baxter, L. A. (1984). An investigation of compliance-gaining as politeness. *Human Communication Research, 10,* 427–456.

Baxter, L. A. (1987). Cognition and communication in the relationship process. In R. Burnett, P. McGhee, & D. Clarke (Eds.), *Accounting for relationships: Explanation, representation and knowledge* (pp. 192–212). London: Methuen.

Baxter, L. A. (1988). A dialectical perspective on communication strategies in relationship development. In S. Duck (Ed.), *Handbook of personal relationships* (pp. 257–273). Chichester: John Wiley & Sons.

Baxter, L. A., & Montgomery, B. M. (1996). *Relating: Dialogues & dialectics*. New York: Guilford.

Bennis, W., & Slater, P. (1968). *The temporary society*. New York: Harper Colophon.

Berger, P. L., & Kellner, H. (1964). Marriage and the construction of reality: An exercize in the microsociology of knowledge. *Diogenes, 46,* 1–25.

Berger, P. L., & Luckmann, T. (1966). *The social construction of reality*. New York: Doubleday.

Bergreen, L. (1984). *James Agee, a life*. New York: E. P. Dutton.

Berlo, D. K. (1960). *The process of communication*. New York: Holt, Rinehart, and Winston.

Bernstein, R. J. (1985). *Beyond objectivism and relativism: Science, hermeneutics, and praxis*. Philadelphia: University of Pennsylvania Press.

Bettelheim, B. (1960). *The informed heart*. Glencoe, IL: Free Press.

Bhaskar, R. (1979). *The possibility of naturalism*. Atlantic Heights, NJ: Humanities Press.

Bickerton, D. (1990). *Language & species*. Chicago, IL: University of Chicago Press.

Birchler, G. R., Clopton, P. L., & Adams, N. L. (1984). Marital conflict resolution: Factors influencing concordance between partners and trained coders. *American Journal of Family Therapy, 12,* 15–28.

Birdwhistell, R. L. (1970). *Kinesics and context.* Philadelphia: University of Pennsylvania Press.

Birdwhistell, R. L. (1977). Some discussion of ethnography, theory, and method. In J. Brockman (Ed.), *About Bateson* (pp. 103–141). New York: E. P. Dutton.

Birtchnell, J. (1993). *How humans relate: A new interpersonal theory.* Westport, CT: Praeger Publishers.

Boesch, C., & Boesch, H. (1983). Optimization of nut-cracking with natural hammers by wild chimpanzees. *Behaviour, 83,* 265–286.

Boesch, C., & Boesch, H. (1984). Mental map in chimpanzee: An analysis of hammer transports for nut cracking. *Primates, 25,* 160–170.

Boesch, C., & Boesch, H. (1990). Tool use and tool making in wild chimpanzees. *Folia Primatologia, 54,* 86–99.

Bonner, J. T. (1980). *The evolution of culture in animals.* Princeton, NJ: Princeton University Press.

Bostrom, R., & Donohew, L. (1992). The case for empiricism: Clarifying fundamental issues in communication theory. *Communication Monographs, 59,* 109–129.

Bowlby, J. (1979). *The making and breaking of affectional bonds.* New York: Tavistock.

Bowlby, J. (1982). *Attachment and loss: Vol. 1. Attachment.* New York: Basic Books.

Bradbury, T. N., & Fincham, F. D. (1989). Behavior and satisfaction in marriage: Prospective mediating processes. In C. Hendrick (Ed.), *Close relationships* (pp. 119–143). Newbury Park, CA: Sage.

Bradbury, T. N., & Fincham, F. D. (1991). A contextual model for advancing the study of marital interaction. In G.J.O. Fletcher & F. D. Fincham (Eds.), *Cognition in close relationships* (pp. 127–150). Hillsdale, NJ: Lawrence Erlbaum.

Brown, P., & Levinson, S. (1987). *Politeness: Some universals in language usage.* Cambridge: Cambridge University Press.

Bruner, M. L. (1996). Beyond the modern imaginary: A rhetorical theoretical response to the crisis of representation. Unpublished manuscript, University of Washington Department of Speech Communication, Seattle.

Buber, M. (1958). *I and thou* (R. G. Smith, Trans.). New York: Charles Scribner's Sons.

Buber, M. (1965a). *Between man and man* (R. G. Smith, Trans.). New York: Macmillan.

Buber, M. (1965b). *The knowledge of man* (M. Friedman, Ed.; M. Friedman & R. G. Smith, Trans.). New York: Harper.

Buber, M. (1967). Replies to my critics. In P. A. Schilpp & M. Friedman (Eds.), *The philosophy of Martin Buber* (pp. 689–744). LaSalle, IL: Open Court.

Buber, M. (1970). *I and thou* (W. Kaufmann, Trans.). New York: Charles Scribner's Sons.

Buber, M. (1973). *Meetings* (M. Friedman, Ed.). LaSalle, IL: Open Court.

Burgess, E. W. (1926). The family as a unity of interacting personalities. *Family, 7,* 3–9.

Burghardt, G. M. (1991). Cognitive ethology and critical anthropomorphism: A snake with two heads and hog-nose snakes that play dead. In C. A. Ristau (Ed.), *Cognitive ethology: The minds of other animals* (pp. 53–90). Hillsdale, NJ: Lawrence Erlbaum.

Burrell, N. A., & Fitzpatrick, M. A. (1990). The psychological reality of marital conflict. In D. D. Cahn (Ed.), *Intimates in conflict: A communication perspective* (pp. 167–186). Hillsdale, NJ: Lawrence Erlbaum.

Byrne, R., & Whiten, A. (1988). Tactical deception of familiar individuals in baboons. In R. Byrne & A. Whiten (Eds.), *Machiavellian intelligence* (pp. 205–210). Oxford: Clarendon Press.

Canary, D. J., Cupach, W. R., & Messman, S. J. (1995). *Relationship conflict: Conflict in parent-child relationships, friendships, and romantic relationships.* Thousand Oaks, CA: Sage.

Capra, F. (1982). *The turning point: Science, society and the rising culture.* New York: Simon and Schuster.

Cappella, J. N. (1981). Mutual influences in expressive behavior: Adult-adult and infant-adult dyadic interaction. *Psychological Bulletin, 89,* 101–132.

Cappella, J. N. (1987). Interpersonal communication: Definitions and fundamental questions. In C. R. Berger & S. Chaffee (Eds.), *The handbook of communication science* (pp. 184–238). Beverly Hills, CA: Sage.

Cappella, J. N. (1988). Interaction patterns and social and personal relationships. In S. W. Duck, D. F. Hay, S. E. Hobfoll, W. Ickes, & B. M. Montgomery (Eds.), *Handbook of personal relationships: Theory, research and interventions* (pp. 325–342). Chichester: John Wiley & Sons.

Cappella, J. N. (1991). Mutual adaptation and relativity of measurement. In B. M. Montgomery & S. Duck (Eds.), *Studying interpersonal interaction* (pp. 103–117). New York: Guilford.

Cappella, J. N., & Palmer, M. L. (1990). Attitude similarity, relational history, and attraction: The mediating effects of kinesic and vocal behaviors. *Communication Monographs, 57,* 161–183.

Chadwick, D. H. (1992). *The fate of the elephant.* San Francisco, CA: Sierra Club Books.

Chapple, E. D. (1940). Measuring human relations. *Genetic Psychology Monographs, 22,* 3–147.

Cheney, D., Seyfarth, R., & Smuts, B. (1986). Social relationships and social cognition in non-human primates. *Science, 234,* 1361–1366.

Cheney, D. L., & Seyfarth, R. (1982a). How vervet monkeys perceive their grunts: Field play back experiments. *Animal Behaviour, 28,* 362–367.

Cheney, D. L., & Seyfarth, R. (1982b). Recognition of individuals within and between groups of free-ranging vervet monkeys. *American Zoologist, 22,* 519–529.

Cheney, D. L., & Seyfarth, R. (1990). *How monkeys see the world: Inside the mind of another species.* Chicago, IL: University of Chicago Press.

Cheney, D. L., & Seyfarth, R. M. (1991). Truth and deception in animal communication. In C. A. Ristau (Ed.), *Cognitive ethology: The minds of other animals* (pp. 127–151). Hillsdale, NJ: Lawrence Erlbaum.

Chevalier-Skolnikoff, S., & Liska, J. (1985). Personal observations of elephant behavior in Samburu, Kenya.

Chevalier-Skolnikoff, S., & Liska, J. (1993). Tool use by wild and captive elephants. *Animal Behaviour, 46,* 209–219.

Clark, A. L. (1976). Martin Buber, experience, and dialogue. Written in dialogue with H. M. Felton (J. Stewart, Ed.). Unpublished manuscript, University of Washington Department of Speech Communication, Seattle.

Clark, K., & Holquist, M. (1984). *Mikhail Bakhtin.* Cambridge, MA: Harvard University Press.

Cohen, I. (1989). *Structuration theory: Anthony Giddens and the constitution of social life.* New York: St. Martin's Press.

Coles, R. (1967). *Children of crisis.* Boston, MA: Little, Brown.

Collins, N. L., & Read, S. J. (1990). Adult attachment, working models, and relationship quality in dating couples. *Journal of Personality and Social Psychology, 58,* 644–663.

Conville, R. L. (1991). *Relational transitions: The evolution of personal relationships.* Westport, CT: Praeger.

Conville, R. L. (1997). Between spearheads: *Bricolage* and relationships. *Journal of Social and Personal Relationships, 14,* 373–386.

Conville, R. L. (in press). Telling stories: Dialectics of relational transition. In L. A. Baxter & B. Montgomery (Eds.), *Dialectical approaches to studying personal relationships.* Mahwah, NJ: Lawrence Erlbaum.

Cronen, V. E. (1995). Coordinated management of meaning: The consequentiality of communication and the recapturing of experience. In S. J. Sigman (Ed.), *The consequentiality of communication* (pp. 17–65). Hillsdale, NJ: Lawrence Erlbaum.

Cupach, W. R., & Metts, S. (1994). *Facework.* Thousand Oaks, CA: Sage.

Dance, F.E.X. (1977). The rhetorical primate. *Journal of Communication, 27,* 12–16.

Danziger, K. (1976). *Interpersonal communication.* New York: Pergamon.

Dasser, V. (1988). A social concept in Java monkeys. *Animal Behaviour, 36,* 225–230.

Davies, B., & Harré, R. (1991–92). Contradictions in lived and told narratives. *Research on Language and Social Interaction, 25,* 1–35.

Dawkins, R. (1986). *The blind watchmaker.* New York: W. W. Norton.

Dawkins, R. (1989). *The selfish gene.* Oxford: Oxford University Press.

Day, C. (1936). *This simian world.* New York: Alfred A. Knopf.

Dell, P. (1983). Researching the family theories of schizophrenia: An exercise in epistemological confusion. In D. Bagarozzi, A. Jurich, & R. Jackson (Eds.), *Marital and family therapy: New perspectives in theory, research and practice* (pp. 236–261). New York: Human Sciences Press.

Derrida, J. (1978). *Writing and différence* (A. Bass, Trans.). Chicago, IL: University of Chicago Press.

de Saussure, F. (1986). *Course in general linguistics* (C. Bally & A. Sechehaye, Eds.) (R. Harris, Trans.). LaSalle, IL: Open Court.

de Waal, F.B.M. (1982). *Chimpanzee politics.* New York: Harper & Row.

de Waal, F.B.M. (1988). The communicative repertoire of captive bonobos (*Pan paniscus*) compared to that of chimpanzees. *Behavior, 106*, 183–251.

de Waal, F.B.M. (1995). Bonobo sex and society. *Scientific American, 27*, 82–88.

Diamond, J. (1992). *The third chimpanzee.* New York: HarperCollins.

Douglas-Hamilton, I., & Douglas-Hamilton, O. (1975). *Among the elephants.* New York: Viking Press.

Duck, S. (1990). Relationships as unfinished business: Out of the frying pan and into the 1990s. *Journal of Social and Personal Relationships, 7*, 5–28.

Duck, S. (1995). Talking relationships into being. *Journal of Social and Personal Relationships, 12*, 535–540.

Duck, S., & Montgomery, B. M. (1991). The interdependence among interaction substance, theory, and methods. In B. M. Montgomery & S. Duck (Eds.), *Studying interpersonal interaction* (pp. 3–15). New York: Guilford Press.

Duck, S., & Sants, H.K.A. (1983). On the origin of the species: Are personal relationships really interpersonal states? *Journal of Social and Clinical Psychology, 1*, 27–41.

Dyson-Hudson, N. (1972). Structure and infra-structure in primitive society: Levi-Strauss and Radcliffe-Brown. In R. Macksey & E. Donato (Eds.), *The structuralist controversy* (pp. 218–241). Baltimore, MD: Johns Hopkins University Press.

Eco, U. (1980). *The name of the rose.* New York: Warner Books.

Elia, I. (1988). *The female animal.* New York: Henry Holt.

Ellis, D. (1982). The epistemology of form. In C. Wilder & J. Weakland (Eds.), *Rigor and imagination: Essays from the legacy of Gregory Bateson* (pp. 215–230). New York: Praeger.

Erber, R., & Gilmour, R. (Eds.). (1994). *Theoretical frameworks for personal relationships.* Hillsdale, NJ: Lawrence Erlbaum.

Ervin-Tripp, S. (1972). On sociolinguistic rules: Alternation and co-occurrence. In J. J. Gumperz & D. Hymes (Eds.), *Directions in sociolinguistics: The ethnography of communication* (pp. 213–250). New York: Holt, Rinehart and Winston.

Featherstone, M. (1991). Georg Simmel: An introduction. *Theory, Culture and Society, 8*, 1–16.

Fehr, B. (1988). Prototype analysis of the concepts of love and commitment. *Journal of Personality and Social Psychology, 55*, 557–579.

Fehr, B. (1993). How do I love thee? Let me consult my prototype. In S. Duck (Ed.), *Individuals in relationships* (pp. 87–120). Newbury Park, CA: Sage.

Fincham, F. D., & Bradbury, T. N. (1987). The impact of attribution in marriage: A longitudinal analysis. *Journal of Personality and Social Psychology, 53*, 510–517.

Fisher, B. A. (1978). *Perspectives on human communication.* New York: Macmillan.

Fitch, K. L., & Sanders, R. E. (1994). Culture, communication, and preferences for directness in expression of directives. *Communication Theory, 3*, 219–245.

Fitzpatrick, M. A. (1988). *Between husbands and wives.* Newbury Park, CA: Sage.

Fitzpatrick, M. A. (1990). Models of marital interaction. In H. Giles & W. P. Robinson (Eds.), *Handbook of language and social psychology* (pp. 433–450). New York: John Wiley & Sons.

Fitzpatrick, M. A. (1991). Understanding personal relationships through media portrayals. *Communication Education, 40*, 213–219.

Fitzpatrick, M. A., & Badzinski, D. M. (1994). All in the family: Interpersonal communication in kin relationships. In M. L. Knapp & G. R. Miller (Eds.), *Handbook of interpersonal communication* (2d ed.) (pp. 726–771). Thousand Oaks, CA: Sage.

Fogle, J.A.L. (1992). *Testing social communication theory through an analysis of participant-respondent data.* Unpublished doctoral dissertation, State University of New York at Buffalo.

Foucault, M. (1972). *The archaeology of knowledge and the discourse on language.* (A. M. Sheridan Smith, Trans.). New York: Pantheon Books.

Gadamer, H.-G. (1989). *Truth and method* (2d rev. ed.) (J. Weinsheimer & D. G. Marshall, Trans.). New York: Crossroad.

Gallup, G. G., & Suarez, S. D. (1983). Overcoming our resistance to animal research: Man in comparative perspective. In D. W. Rajecki (Ed.), *Comprising behavior: Studying man studying animals* (pp. 5–26). Hillsdale, NJ: Lawrence Erlbaum.

Galvin, K. M., & Cooper, P. (1996). *Making connections: Readings in relational communication.* Los Angeles, CA: Roxbury Publishing.

Garfinkel, H. (1984). *Studies in ethnomethodology.* Cambridge: Polity Press.

Garfinkel, H., & Wieder, D. L. (1992). Two incommensurable, asymmetrically alternate technologies of social analysis. In G. Watson & R. M. Seiler (Eds.), *Text in context: Contributions to ethnomethodology* (pp. 175–206). Newbury Park, CA: Sage.

Geertz, C. (1973). *The interpretation of cultures.* New York: Basic Books.

Gergen, K. (1991). *The saturated self: Dilemmas of identity in contemporary life.* New York: Basic Books.

Giddens, A. (1976). *New rules of sociological method.* New York: Basic Books.

Giddens, A. (1979). *Central problems in social theory.* Berkeley: University of California Press.

Giddens, A. (1981). *A contemporary critique of historical materialism, Vol. 1: Power, property and the state.* Berkeley: University of California Press.

Giddens, A. (1984). *The constitution of society: Outline of the theory of structuration.* Berkeley: University of California Press.

Giddens, A. (1985). *The nation-state and violence.* Berkeley: University of California Press.

Giddens, A. (1987a). What do sociologists do? In *Social theory and modern sociology* (pp. 1–21). Stanford, CA: Stanford University Press.

Giddens, A. (1987b). Structuralism, poststructuralism, and the production of culture. In A. Giddens & J. Turner (Eds.), *Social theory today* (pp. 195–223). Stanford, CA: Stanford University Press.

Giddens, A. (1990). *The consequences of modernity.* Cambridge: Polity Press.

Giddens, A. (1991). *Modernity and self-identity.* Stanford, CA: Stanford University Press.

Giddens, A. (1992). *The transformation of intimacy: Sexuality, love, and eroticism in modern societies.* Stanford, CA: Stanford University Press.

Giddens, A. (1994). *Beyond left and right: The future of radical politics.* Stanford, CA: Stanford University Press.

Godzich, W. (1994). *The culture of literacy.* Cambridge, MA: Harvard University Press.

Goffman, E. (1959). *The presentation of self in everyday life.* Garden City, NY: Doubleday.

Goffman, E. (1963). *Behavior in public places.* New York: Free Press.

Goffman, E. (1967). *Interaction ritual: Essays on face-to-face behavior.* New York: Pantheon.

Goffman, E. (1972). *Relations in public.* New York: Harper & Row.

Goffman, E. (1981). *Forms of talk.* Philadelphia: University of Pennsylvania Press.

Goffman, E. (1983). The interaction order. *American Sociological Review, 48,* 1–17.

Goodall, J. (1986). *The chimpanzees of Gombe: Patterns of behavior.* Cambridge, MA: Harvard University Press.

Goodwin, B. (1994). *How the leopard changed its spots: The evolution of complexity.* New York: Charles Scribner's Sons.

Gottman, J. M. (1979). *Marital interaction: Experimental investigations.* New York: Academic Press.

Gottman, J. M. (1982a). Temporal form: Toward a new language for describing relationships. *Journal of Marriage and the Family, 44,* 943–962.

Gottman, J. M. (1982b). Emotional responsiveness in marital conversations. *Journal of Communication, 32*, 108–120.

Gottman, J. M. (1994). *What predicts divorce? The relationship between marital processes and marital outcomes.* Hillsdale, NJ: Lawrence Erlbaum.

Gottman, J. M., & Levenson, R. W. (1986). Assessing the role of emotion in marriage. *Behavioral Assessment, 8*, 31–48.

Gould, S. J. (1991). Of mice and mosquitoes. *Natural History, 7*, 12–20.

Gould, S. J. (1995). Boyle's law and Darwin's details. *Natural History, 8*, 8–11, 68–71.

Greene, M. F. (1991). *Praying for sheetrock.* New York: Ballantine.

Guthrie, W.K.C. (1971). *The sophists.* Cambridge: Cambridge University Press.

Habermas, J. (1987). *The theory of communicative action, Vol. 2: Lifeworld and system: A critique of functionalist reason.* Boston, MA: Beacon Hill Press.

Hamilton, P. (1984). Editor's foreword. In D. Frisby, *Georg Simmel* (pp. 7–9). London: Tavistock Publications.

Hancock, M., & Ickes, W. (1996). Empathic accuracy: When does the perceiver-target relationship make a difference? *Journal of Social and Personal Relationships, 13*, 179–199.

Havelock, E. A. (1982). *Preface to Plato.* Cambridge, MA: Harvard University Press.

Hazan, C., & Shaver, P. (1987). Romantic love conceptualized as an attachment process. *Journal of Personality and Social Psychology, 52*, 511–524.

Heidegger, M. (1959). *An introduction to metaphysics* (Ralph Manheim, Trans.). New Haven, CT: Yale University Press.

Heidegger, M. (1971). *On the way to language* (P. D. Hertz, Trans.). San Francisco, CA: Harper & Row.

Heidegger, M. (1972). *On time and being* (Joan Stambaugh, Trans.). New York: Harper Torchbooks.

Hepper, P. G. (1991). *Kin recognition.* Cambridge: Cambridge University Press.

Heritage, J. (1984). *Garfinkel and ethnomethodology.* Cambridge: Polity Press.

Hess, R. D., & Handel, G. (1959). *Family worlds: A psychosocial approach to family life.* Chicago, IL: University of Chicago Press.

Hinde, R. A. (1979). *Towards understanding relationships.* London: Academic Press.

Hinde, R. A. (1987). *Individuals, relationships & culture: Links between ethnology and the social sciences.* Cambridge: Cambridge University Press.

Hinde, R. A. (1995). A suggested structure for a science of relationships. *Personal Relationships, 2*, 1–15.

Holldobler, B. (1977). Communication in social hymenoptera. In T. A. Sebeok (Ed.), *How animals communicate* (pp. 418–471). Bloomington: Indiana University Press.

Honeycutt, J. M., Woods, B. L., & Fontenot, K. (1993). The endorsement of communication conflict rules as a function of engagement, marriage and marital ideology. *Journal of Social and Personal Relationships*, *10*, 285–304.

Hopper, R., & Drummond, K. (1991). Accomplishing interpersonal relationship: A message-intrinsic perspective. Paper presented to the International Communication Association, Chicago.

Hrdy, S. B. (1981). *The woman that never evolved*. Cambridge, MA: Harvard University Press.

Hymes, D. (1974). *Foundations in sociolinguistics*. Philadelphia: University of Pennsylvania Press.

Ickes, W., Robertson, E., Tooke, W., & Teng, G. (1986). Naturalistic social cognition: Methodology, assessment, and validation. *Journal of Personality and Social Psychology*, *51*, 66–82.

Ickes, W., & Tooke, W. (1988). The observational method: Studying the interaction of minds and bodies. In S. W. Duck, D. F. Hay, S. E. Hobfoll, W. Ickes, & B. M. Montgomery (Eds.), *Handbook of personal relationships: Theory, research and interventions* (pp. 79–97). Chichester: John Wiley & Sons.

Ickes, W., Tooke, W., Stinson, L., Baker, V. L., & Bissonnette, V. (1988). Naturalistic social cognition: Intersubjectivity in same-sex dyads. *Journal of Nonverbal Behavior*, *12*, 58–84.

Insel, T. R., & Carter, C. S. (1995). The monogamous brain. *Natural History*, *8*, 12–14.

Jacoby, S., & Ochs, E. (1995). Co-construction: An introduction. *Research on Language and Social Interaction*, *28*, 171–183.

Jolly, A. (1985). *The evolution of primate behavior* (2d ed.). New York: Macmillan.

Jolly, A. (1991). Conscious chimpanzees: A review of recent literature. In C. A. Ristau (Ed.), *Cognitive ethology: The minds of other animals* (pp. 231–252). Hillsdale, NJ: Lawrence Erlbaum.

Jones, E., & Gallois, C. (1989). Spouses' impressions of rules for communication in public and private marital conflicts. *Journal of Marriage and the Family*, *51*, 957–967.

Kantor, D., & Lehr, W. (1975). *Inside the family*. New York: Harper & Row.

Kawai, M. (1965). Newly acquired pre-cultural behavior of the natural troop of Japanese monkeys on Koshima Islet. *Primates*, *1*, 1–30.

Kelley, H, Berscheid, E., Christensen, A., Harvey, J. H., Huston, T. L., Levinger, G., McClintock, E., Peplau, L. A., & Peterson, D. R. (1983). *Close relationships*. New York: Freeman.

Kelley, H., & Thibaut, J. (1978). *Interpersonal relationships*. New York: John Wiley & Sons.

Kendon, A. (1977). *Studies in the behavior of social interaction*. Bloomington: Indiana University Press.

Kendon, A. (1978). Differential perception and attentional frame in face-to-face interaction: Two problems for investigation. *Semiotica*, *24*, 305–315.

Kendon, A. (1982). The organization of behavior in face-to-face interaction: Observation on the development of a methodology. In K. Scherer & P. Ekman (Eds.), *Handbook of methods in nonverbal behavior research* (pp. 440–505). Cambridge: Cambridge University Press.

Kendon, A. (1990). *Conducting interaction: Patterns of behavior in focused encounters*. Cambridge: Cambridge University Press.

Kendon, A., & Ferber, A. (1973). A description of some human greetings. In R. P. Michael & J. H. Crook (Eds.), *Comparative ecology and behavior of primates* (pp. 591–668). London: Academic Press.

Kendon, A., & Sigman, S. J. (1996). Ray L. Birdwhistell (1918–1994). *Semiotica, 112*, 231–261.

Kenny, D. A. (1988). Interpersonal perception: A social relations analysis. *Journal of Social and Personal Relationships, 5*, 247–261.

Kenny, D. A. (1994a). *Interpersonal perception: A social relations analysis*. New York: Guilford.

Kenny, D. A. (1994b). Using the social relations model to understand relationships. In R. Erber & R. Gilmour (Eds.), *Theoretical frameworks for personal relationships* (pp. 111–127). Hillsdale, NJ: Lawrence Erlbaum.

Kenny, D. A. (1996). Models of non-independence in dyadic research. *Journal of Social and Personal Relationships, 13*, 279–294.

Kenny, D. A., & Judd, C. M. (1986). Consequences of violating the independence assumption in analysis of variance. *Psychological Bulletin, 99*, 422–431.

Kenny, D. A., & Kashy, D. A. (1991). Analyzing interdependence in dyads. In B. M. Montgomery & S. Duck (Eds.), *Studying interpersonal interaction* (pp. 275–285). New York: Guilford.

Kerferd, G. B. (1981). *The sophistic movement*. Cambridge: Cambridge University Press.

Kligman, G. (1988). *The wedding of the dead: Ritual, poetics, and popular culture*. Berkeley: University of California Press.

Knapp, M. L., & Miller, G. R. (1985). Introduction. In M. L. Knapp and G. R. Miller (Eds.), *Handbook of interpersonal communication* (pp. 7–24). Beverly Hills, CA: Sage.

Knapp, M. L., & Vangelisti, A. L. (1992). *Interpersonal communication and human relationships*. Boston, MA: Allyn and Bacon.

Kotlowitz, A. (1991). *There are no children here*. New York: Doubleday.

Kougl, K. M. (1983). Novels as a source for heuristics about interpersonal communication. *Communication Quarterly, 31*, 282–289.

Krebs, J. R., & Davies, N. B. (1982). *An introduction to behavioral ecology*. Sunderland, MA: Sinauer Associates.

LaRossa, R. (1995). Stories and relationships. *Journal of Social and Personal Relationships, 12*, 553–556.

Lederer, W. J., & Jackson, D. D. (1968). *The mirages of marriage*. New York: Norton.

Leeds-Hurwitz, W. (1989). *Communication and everyday life*. Norwood, NJ: Ablex.

Leeds-Hurwitz, W. (1992). Forum introduction: Social approaches to interpersonal communication. *Communication Theory, 2,* 131–139.

Leeds-Hurwitz, W. (1995). Introducing social approaches. In W. Leeds-Hurwitz (Ed.), *Social approaches to communication* (pp. 3–20). New York: Guilford Press.

Leeds-Hurwitz, W., Sigman, S. J., with Sullivan, S. J. (1995). Social communication theory: Communication structures and performed invocations, a revision of Scheflen's notion of programs. In S. J. Sigman (Ed.), *The consequentiality of communication* (pp. 163–204). Hillsdale, NJ: Lawrence Erlbaum.

Levenson, R. W., & Gottman, J. M. (1983). Marital interaction: Physiological linkage and affective exchange. *Journal of Personality and Social Psychology, 45,* 587–597.

Levine, J., & Snyder, H. (1980). *Social perception among five and six year olds.* Unpublished data set, University of Pittsburgh.

Levinger, G. (1994). Figure versus ground: Micro- and macroperspectives on the social psychology of personal relationships. In R. Erber & R. Gilmour (Eds.), *Theoretical frameworks for personal relationships* (pp. 1–28). Hillsdale, NJ: Lawrence Erlbaum.

Levinger, G., & Snoek, J. D. (1972). *Attraction in relationship: A new look at interpersonal attraction.* Morristown, NJ: General Learning Press.

Levi-Strauss, C. (1963). The structural study of myth. In *Structural Anthropology* (C. Jacobson & B. G. Schoepf, Trans.) (pp. 206–231). New York: Basic Books.

Lindbergh, A. (1955). *Gift from the sea.* New York: Random House.

Liska, J. (1986). Symbols: The missing link? In J. G. Else & P. C. Lee (Eds.), *Ontogeny: Cognition and social behavior of primates* (pp. 169–178). Cambridge: Cambridge University Press.

Liska, J. (1993a). Bee dances, bird songs, monkey calls, and cetacean sonar: Is speech unique? *Western Journal of Communication, 57,* 1–26.

Liska, J. (1993b). Signs of the apes, songs of the whales: Comparing signs across species. *European Journal of Cognitive Systems, 3–4,* 381–397.

Liska, J. (1994a). Sign arbitrariness as an index of semiogenesis. In J. Wind, A. Jonker, R. Allot, & L. Rolfe (Eds.), *Studies in language origins* (Vol. 3, pp. 161–177). Amsterdam: John Benjamins Publishing.

Liska, J. (1994b). The foundation of symbolic communication. In D. Quiatt & J. Itani (Eds.), *Hominid culture in primate perspective* (pp. 233–251). Boulder: University of Colorado Press.

Liska, J., & Cronkhite, G. (1995). On the death, dismemberment, or disestablishment of the dominant paradigms. *Western Journal of Communication, 58,* 58–65.

Lyotard, J-F. (1988). *The differend*. Minneapolis: University of Minnesota Press.

MacIntyre, A. (1984). *After virtue*. 2d ed. Notre Dame, IN: University of Notre Dame Press.

Maltz, D. N., & Borker, R. A. (1982). A cultural approach to male-female miscommunication. In J. Gumperz (Ed.), *Language and social identity* (pp. 196–216). Cambridge: Cambridge University Press.

Markman, H. J., & Notarius, C. I. (1987). Coding marital and family interaction: Current status. In T. Jacob (Ed.), *Family interaction and psychopathology: Theories, methods, and findings* (pp. 329–390). New York: Plenum.

Masheter, C. (1994). Dialogues between ex-spouses: Evidence of dialectic relationship development. In R. L. Conville (Ed.), *Uses of "structure" in communication studies* (pp. 83–101). Westport, CT: Praeger.

Matoesian, G. M. (1993). *Reproducing rape: Domination through talk in the courtroom*. Chicago, IL: University of Chicago Press.

McCall, G. (1970). The social organization of relationships. In G. McCall (Ed.), *Social relationships* (pp. 3–34). Chicago, IL: Aldine.

McCall, G. (1987). The self-concept and interpersonal communication. In M. Roloff & G. McCall (Eds.), *Interpersonal processes* (pp. 63–76). Newbury Park, CA: Sage.

McCall, G. (1988). The organizational life cycle of relationships. In S. Duck (Ed.), *Handbook of personal relationships* (pp. 467–484). New York: John Wiley & Sons.

McCall, G., & Simmons, J. (1991). Levels of analysis: The individual, the dyad, and the larger social group. In B. Montgomery & S. Duck (Eds.), *Studying interpersonal interaction* (pp. 56–81). New York: Guilford.

McCall, G. J., & Simmons, J. L. (1978). *Identities and interactions*. New York: Free Press.

McCarthy, T. (1987). General introduction. In K. Baynes, J. Bohman, & T. McCarthy (Eds.), *After philosophy: End or transformation?* (pp. 1–18). Cambridge, MA: MIT Press.

McPhee, R. (1989). Structure, agency, and communication: Linking macro- to micro-analysis. Unpublished paper presented at the International Communication Association Convention, San Francisco.

McPhee, R. D., & Poole, M. S. (1980). A theory of structuration: The perspective of Anthony Giddens and its relevance for contemporary communication research. Unpublished paper presented at the Speech Communication Association Convention, New York.

Metts, S. (1997). Face and facework: Implications for the study of personal relationships. In S. Duck (Ed.), *Handbook of personal relationships: Theory, research and interventions* (2d ed.). Chichester: John Wiley & Sons.

Metts, S., & Cupach, W. R. (1995). Postdivorce relations. In M. A. Fitzpatrick & A. L. Vangelisti (Eds.), *Explaining family interactions* (pp. 232–251). Thousand Oaks, CA: Sage.

Metts, S., Sprecher, S., & Cupach, W. R. (1991). Retrospective self-reports. In B.

M. Montgomery & S. Duck (Eds.), *Studying interpersonal interaction* (pp. 162–178). New York: Guilford.

Miell, D. (1987). Remembering relationship development: Constructing a context for interaction. In R. Burnett, P. McGhee, & D. Clarke (Eds.), *Accounting for relationships: Explanation, representation and knowledge* (pp. 3–21). London: Methuen.

Millar, F. E., & Rogers, L. E. (1976). The relational approach to interpersonal communication. In G. R. Miller (Ed.), *Explorations in interpersonal communication* (pp. 87–103). Newbury Park, CA: Sage.

Millar, F. E., & Rogers, L. E. (1987). Relational dimensions of interpersonal dynamics. In M. Roloff & G. R. Miller (Eds.), *Explorations in interpersonal processes: New directions in communication research* (pp. 117–139). Newbury Park, CA: Sage.

Miller, J. (1978). *Living systems.* New York: McGraw-Hill.

Miller, L. C., & Read, S. J. (1991). On the coherence of mental models of persons and relationships: A knowledge structure approach. In G.J.O. Fletcher & F. D. Fincham (Eds.), *Cognition in close relationships* (pp. 69–100). Hillsdale, NJ: Lawrence Erlbaum.

Mitchell, R. W., & Thompson, N. S. (Eds.). (1986). *Deception: Perspectives on human and nonhuman deceit.* Albany: State University of New York Press.

Montgomery, B. M. (1988). Quality communication in personal relationships. In S. W. Duck, D. F. Hay, S. E. Hobfoll, W. Ickes, & B. M. Montgomery (Eds.), *Handbook of personal relationships: Theory, research and interventions* (pp. 343–359). Chichester: John Wiley & Sons.

Montgomery, B. M. (1993). Relationship maintenance versus relationship change: A dialectical dilemma. *Journal of Social and Personal Relationships, 10,* 205–224.

Moss, C. (1988). *Elephant memories.* New York: Ivy Books.

Noller, P., & Fitzpatrick, M. A. (1993). *Communication in family relationships.* Englewood Cliffs, NJ: Prentice Hall.

Noller, P., & Ruzzene, M. (1991). Communication in marriage: The influence of affect and cognition. In G.J.O. Fletcher & F. D. Fincham (Eds.), *Cognition in close relationships* (pp. 203–234). Hillsdale, NJ: Lawrence Erlbaum.

Notarius, C. I., & Johnson, J. S. (1982). Emotional expression in husbands and wives. *Journal of Marriage and the Family, 44,* 483–489.

Ogden, C. K., & Richards, I. A. (1923). *The meaning of meaning.* New York: Harcourt, Brace.

Onions, C. T. (1966). *The Oxford dictionary of English etymology.* New York: Oxford University Press.

Osgood, C. (1963). On understanding and creating sentences. *American Psychologist, 18,* 735–751.

Osolsobe, I. (1986). Two extremes of iconicity. In P. Bouissac, M. Herzfeld, & R. Posner (Eds.), *Iconicity: Essays on the nature of culture* (pp. 95–117).

Tubingen: Stauffenburg-Verlag.

Owen, W. F. (1987). Mutual interaction of discourse structures and relational pragmatics in conversational influence attempts. *Southern Speech Communication Journal*, *52*, 103–127.

Park, R. E. (1927). Human nature and collective behavior. *American Journal of Sociology*, *32*, 733–741.

Parsons, T. (1954). The kinship system of the contemporary United States. In *Essays in sociological theory* (rev. ed.) (pp. 177–196). New York: Free Press.

Payne, K. B. (1991). A change of tune. *Natural History*, *3*, 45–46.

Pearce, W. B. (1989). *Communication and the human condition*. Carbondale: Southern Illinois University Press.

Pearce, W. B., & Foss, K. A. (1987). The future of interpersonal communication. *ACA Bulletin*, *61*, 93–105.

Pfenning, D. W., & Sherman, P. W. (1995). Kin recognition. *Scientific American*, *272*(6), 98–103.

Pinker, S. (1994, September 25). Is there a gene for compassion? *New York Times Book Review*, p. 3.

Pittenger, R. E., Hockett, C. F., Danehy, J. J. (1960). *The first five minutes: A sample of microscopic interview analysis*. Ithaca, NY: Paul Martineau.

Planalp, S. (1987). Interplay between relational knowledge and events. In R. Burnett, P. McGhee, & D. Clarke (Eds.), *Accounting for relationships: Explanation, representation and knowledge* (pp. 175–191). London: Methuen.

Planalp, S., & Benson, A. (1992). Friends' and acquaintances' conversations: 1. Perceived differences. *Journal of Social and Personal Relationships*, *9*, 483–506.

Planalp, S., & Rivers, M. (1996). Changes in knowledge of personal relationships. In G.J.O. Fletcher & J. Fitness (Eds.), *Knowledge structures in close relationships: A social psychological approach* (pp. 299–324). Mahwah, NJ: Lawrence Erlbaum.

Poole, J. H. (1987). Elephants in musth, lust. *Natural History*, *11*, 46–53.

Poole, M., Seibold, D., & McPhee, R. (1985). Group decision-making as a structurational process. *Quarterly Journal of Speech*, *71*, 74–102.

Poulakos, J. (1995). *Sophistical rhetoric in classical Greece*. Columbia: University of South Carolina Press.

Putnam, L. (1992). Bargaining teams and micro-macro issues of negotiation. Paper presented at the annual convention of the Speech Communication Association, Chicago.

Quiatt, D., & Reynolds, V. (1993). *Primate behavior*. Cambridge: Cambridge University Press.

Ragan, S. L., & Hopper, R. (1984). Ways to leave your lover: A conversational analysis of literature. *Communication Quarterly*, *32*, 310–317.

Rawlins, W. K. (1983). Negotiating close friendships: The dialectic of conjunctive freedoms. *Human Communication Research, 9*, 255–266.

Rawlins, W. K. (1989). A dialectical analysis of the tensions, functions and strategic challenges of communication in young adult friendships. In J. A. Anderson (Ed.), *Communication yearbook 12* (pp. 157–189). Newbury Park, CA: Sage.

Rawlins, W. K. (1992). *Friendship matters: Communication, dialectics, and the life course.* Hawthorne, NY: Aldine de Gruyter.

Rawlins, W. K. (1994). Being there and growing apart: Sustaining friendships during adulthood. In D. J. Canary & L. Stafford (Eds.), *Communication and relational maintenance* (pp. 275–294). San Diego, CA: Academic Press.

Rawlins, W. K., & Holl, M. (1987). The communicative achievement of friendship during adolescence: Predicaments of trust and violation. *Western Journal of Speech Communication, 51*, 345–363.

Reddy, M. J. (1979). The conduit metaphor: A case of frame conflict in our language about language. In A. Ortony (Ed.), *Metaphor and thought* (pp. 284–324). Cambridge: Cambridge University Press.

Reis, H. T. (1994). Domains of experience: Investigating relationship processes from three perspectives. In R. Erber & R. Gilmour (Eds.), *Theoretical frameworks for personal relationships* (pp. 87–110). Hillsdale, NJ: Lawrence Erlbaum.

Reynolds, V. (1994). Kinship in nonhuman and human primates. In D. Quiatt & J. Itani (Eds.), *Hominid culture in primate perspective* (pp. 137–165). Boulder: University of Colorado Press.

Ricoeur, P. (1971). The model of the text: Meaningful action considered as a text. *Social Research, 38*, 529–562.

Ristau, C. A. (1991). Aspects of the cognitive ethology of an injury-feigning bird, the piping plover. In C. A. Ristau (Ed.), *Cognitive ethology: The minds of other animals* (pp. 91–126). Hillsdale, NJ: Lawrence Erlbaum.

Robins, E. (1990). The study of interdependence in marriage. In F. D. Fincham & T. N. Bradbury (Eds.), *The psychology of marriage: Basic issues and applications* (pp. 59–86). New York: Guilford.

Robinson, E. A., & Price, M. G. (1980). Pleasurable behavior in marital interaction. *Journal of Consulting and Clinical Psychology, 48*, 117–118.

Rusbult, C. E., & Buunk, B. P. (1993). Commitment processes in close relationships: An interdependence analysis. *Journal of Social and Personal Relationships, 10*, 175–204.

Rusbult, C. E., Johnson, D. J., & Morrow, G. D. (1986). Determinants and consequences of exit, voice, loyalty, and neglect: Responses to dissatisfaction in adult romantic involvements. *Human Relations, 39*, 45–63.

Rusbult, C. E., Yovetich, N. A., & Verette, J. (1996). An interdependence analysis of accommodation processes. In G.J.O. Fletcher & J. Fitness (Eds.),

Knowledge structures in close relationships: A social psychological approach (pp. 63–90). Mahwah, NJ: Lawrence Erlbaum.

Rychlak, J. F. (1984). Relationship theory: An historical development in psychology leading to a teleological image of humanity. *Journal of Social and Personal Relationships, 1,* 363–386.

Sanders, R. E. (1995). A neo-rhetorical perspective: The enactment of role-identities as interactive and strategic. In S. J. Sigman (Ed.), *The consequentiality of communication* (pp. 67–120). Hillsdale, NJ: Lawrence Erlbaum.

Sapir, E. (1949). *Selected writings of Edward Sapir in language, culture and personality* (D. Mandelbaum, Ed.). Berkeley: University of California Press.

Schefflen, A. E. (1973). *Communication structure: Analysis of a psychotherapy transaction.* Bloomington: Indiana University Press.

Schegloff, E. A. (1995). Discourse as an interactional achievement: 3. The omnirelevance of action. *Research on Language and Social Interaction, 28,* 185–211.

Schrag, C. O. (1992). *The resources of rationality: A response to the postmodern challenge.* Bloomington: Indiana University Press.

Shaver, P. R., Collins, N., & Clark, C. L. (1996). Attachment styles and internal working models of self and relationships partners. In G.J.O. Fletcher & J. Fitness (Eds.), *Knowledge structures in close relationships: A social psychological approach* (pp. 25–61). Mahwah, NJ: Lawrence Erlbaum.

Shotter, J. (1993). *Conversational realities: Constructing life through language.* London: Sage.

Shotter, J., & Gergen, K. J. (Eds.). (1989). *Texts of identity.* London: Sage.

Sigman, S. J. (1987). *A perspective on social communication.* Lexington, MA: Lexington Books.

Sigman, S. J. (1991). Handling the discontinuous aspects of continuous social relationships: Toward research on the persistence of social forms. *Communication Theory, 1,* 106–127.

Sigman, S. J. (1992a). Do social approaches to interpersonal communication constitute a contribution to communication theory? *Communication Theory, 2,* 347–356.

Sigman, S. J. (1995a). Introduction: Toward study of the consequentiality (not consequences) of communication. In S. J. Sigman (Ed.), *The consequentiality of communication* (pp. 1–14). Hillsdale, NJ: Lawrence Erlbaum.

Sigman, S. J. (1995b). Question: Evidence of what? Answer: Communication. *Western Journal of Communication, 59,* 79–84.

Sigman, S. J. (Ed.). (1992b). *Introduction to human communication: Behavior codes and social action.* Needham, MA: Ginn Press.

Sillars, A. L., Folwell, A. L., Hill, K. C., Maki, B. K., Hurst, A. P., & Casano, R. A. (1994). Marital communication and the persistence of misunderstanding. *Journal of Social and Personal Relationships, 11,* 611–617.

Sillars, A. L., & Scott, M. D. (1983). Interpersonal perception between intimates: An integrative review. *Human Communication Research, 10,* 153–176.

Silverman, H. J. (Ed.). (1990). Introduction: The philosophy of postmodernism. In *Postmodernism: Philosophy and the arts.* New York: Routledge.

Simmel, G. (1950). *The sociology of Georg Simmel* (K. H. Wolff, Trans.). New York: Free Press.

Simpson, J. A., & Weiner, E.S.C. (1989). *The Oxford English dictionary,* 2d ed. Oxford: Clarendon Press.

Slater, P. E. (1963). On social regression. *American Sociological Review, 28,* 339–364.

Small, M. (1995). Rethinking human nature (again). *Natural History, 9,* 8–22.

Smuts, B. B. (1985). *Sex and friendship in baboons.* New York: Aldine.

Spencer-Brown, G. (1973). *Laws of form.* New York: Bantam.

Spitzberg, B. H. (1993). The dialectics of (in)competence. *Journal of Social and Personal Relationships, 10,* 137–158.

Stewart, J. (1995). *Language as articulate contact: Toward a post-semiotic philosophy of communication.* Albany: State University of New York Press.

Stewart, J., & Philipsen, G. P. (1984). Communication as situated accomplishment: The cases of hermeneutics and ethnography. In B. Dervin & M. J. Voigt (Eds.), *Progress in communication sciences, 5* (pp. 177–218). Norwood, NJ: Ablex.

Stott, W. (1986). *Documentary expression and thirties America.* Chicago, IL: University of Chicago Press.

Strum, S. (1987). *Almost human.* New York: Random House.

Sullaway, M., & Christensen, A. (1983). Couples and families as participant observers of their interaction. In J. P. Vincent (Ed.), *Advances in family intervention, assessment, and theory* (Vol. 3, pp. 119–160). Greenwich, CT: JAI Press.

Surra, C. A., Batchelder, M. L., & Hughes, D. K (1995). Accounts and the demystification of courtship. In M. A. Fitzpatrick & A. L. Vangelisti (Eds.), *Explaining family interactions* (pp. 112–141). Thousand Oaks, CA: Sage.

Surra, C. A., & Bohman, T. (1991). The development of close relationships: A cognitive perspective. In G.J.O. Fletcher & F. D. Fincham (Eds.), *Cognition in close relationships* (pp. 281–305). Hillsdale, NJ: Lawrence Erlbaum.

Surra, C. A., & Ridley, C. A. (1991). Multiple perspectives on interaction: Participants, peers, and observers. In B. M. Montgomery & S. Duck (Eds.), *Studying interpersonal interaction* (pp. 35–55). New York: Guilford.

Symons, D. (1979). *The evolution of human sexuality.* New York: Oxford University Press.

Tanner, N. M. (1981). *On becoming human*. Cambridge: Cambridge University Press.

Tanner, N. M., & Zihlman, A. (1976). The evolution of human communication: What can primates tell us? In S. R. Harnad, H. D. Steklis, & J. Lancaster (Eds.), *Origins and evolution of language and speech* (pp. 467–480). New York: New York Academy of Sciences.

Taylor, C. (1985). *Philosophy and the human sciences, 2*. Cambridge: Cambridge University Press.

Thayer, L. (1989). Communication: The human context. In W. Leeds-Hurwitz (Ed.), *Communication and everyday life: A social interpretation* (pp. ix–x). Norwood, NJ: Ablex.

Thayer, L. (1994). Diligently seeking structure. In R. L. Conville (Ed.), *The uses of "structure" in communication studies* (pp. 1–10). Westport, CT: Praeger.

Theunissen, M. (1984). *The other: Studies in the social ontology of Husserl, Heidegger, Sartre, and Buber* (C. Macann, Trans.). Cambridge, MA: MIT Press.

Thomas, S. (1980). Some problems of the paradigm in communication theory. *Journal for the Philosophy of the Social Sciences, 10*, 427–444.

Thompson, J.A.M. (1994). Cultural diversity in the behavior of pan. In D. Quiatt & J. Itani (Eds.), *Hominid culture in primate perspective* (pp. 95–115). Boulder: University of Colorado Press.

Thorpe, W. H. (1972). *Duetting and antiphonal song in birds: Its extent and significance*. Leiden: E. J. Brill.

Titunik, I. R. (1984). Bakhtin &/or Volosinov &/or Medvedev: Dialogue &/or doubletalk? In B. A. Stolz, I. R. Titunik, & L. Dolezel (Eds.), *Language and literary theory* (pp. 99–128). Ann Arbor: University of Michigan, Department of Slavik Languages and Literatures.

Tobach, E., & Greenberg, G. (1984). The significance of T. C. Schneirla's contribution to the concept of levels of integration. In G. Greenberg & E. Tobach (Eds.), *Behavioral evolution and integrative levels* (pp. 1–7). Hillsdale, NJ: Lawrence Erlbaum.

Todorov, T. (1984). *Mikhail Bakhtin: The dialogical principle*. Minneapolis: University of Minnesota Press.

Topoff, H. (1994). The ant who would be queen. *Natural History, 8*, 41–46.

Tyack, P. (1991). If you need me, whistle. *Natural History, 8*, 60.

Ulrich, W. (1986). The uses of fiction as a source of information about interpersonal communication: A critical view. *Communication Quarterly, 34*, 143–153.

Vanzetti, N., & Duck, S. (1996). *A lifetime of relationships*. Pacific Grove, CA: Brooks/Cole.

Vickers, B. (1988). *In defence of rhetoric*. Oxford: Clarendon Press.

Volosinov, V. N. (1973). *Marxism and the philosophy of language* (L. Matejka & I. R. Titunik, Trans.). Cambridge, MA: Harvard University Press.

Watzlawick, P. (1977). *How real is real?* New York: Vintage Books.

Watzlawick, P., Beavin, J. H., & Jackson, D. D. (1967). *Pragmatics of human communication.* New York: W. W. Norton.

Weber, M. (1947). *The theory of social and economic organization* (A. Henderson & T. Parsons, Trans.). Glencoe, IL: Free Press.

Webster, N. (1828). *An American dictionary of the English language,* Vol. 2. New York: S. Converse (New York: Johnson Reprint Corporation, 1970).

Weiss, R. L., & Heyman, R. E. (1990). Observation of marital interaction. In F. D. Fincham & T. N. Bradbury (Eds.), *The psychology of marriage: Basic issues and applications* (pp. 87–117). New York: Guilford.

Weiss, R. L., & Summers, K. J. (1983). Marital interaction coding system-III. In E. E. Filsinger (Ed.), *A sourcebook of marriage and family assessment* (pp. 85–115). Beverly Hills, CA: Sage.

Wells, R. S. (1991). Bringing up baby. *Natural History, 8,* 56–62.

Whiten, A., & Byrne, R. W. (1988). The manipulation of attention in primate tactical deception. In R. Byrne & A. Whiten (Eds.), *Machiavellian intelligence* (pp. 211–223). Oxford: Clarendon Press.

Wilder, C. (1982). Rigor and imagination. In C. Wilder & J. Weakland (Eds.), *Rigor and imagination* (pp. 5–42). New York: Praeger Publishers.

Wiley, N. (1988). The micro-macro problem in social theory. *Sociological Theory, 6,* 254–261.

Williams, W. C. (1984). *Doctor stories* (R. Coles, Compiler). New York: New Directions.

Wilmot, W. W. (1987). *Dyadic communication.* New York: Random House.

Wilmot, W. W. (1995). *Relational communication.* New York: McGraw-Hill.

Wilmot, W. W., & Shellen, W. N. (1991). Language in friendships. In H. Giles & W. P. Robinson (Eds.), *Handbook of language and social psychology* (pp. 413–432). New York: John Wiley & Sons.

Wilson, E. O. (1971). *The insect societies.* Cambridge, MA: Belknap Press of Harvard University Press.

Wilson, E. O. (1992). *The diversity of life.* Cambridge, MA: Belknap Press of Harvard University Press.

Winkin, Y. (Ed.). (1981). *La nouvelle communication.* Paris: Editions du Seuil.

Wold, A. H. (Ed.). (1992). *The dialogical alternative: Towards a theory of language and mind.* London: Scandinavian University Press.

Yang, M. C. (1945). *A Chinese village.* New York: Columbia University Press.

Index

Abstractness dimension: in macro-micro problem, 86; in social systems, 89–90

Abstract objectivism, vs. relational view of language, 40

Acceptance-judgment dialectic, 167

Accommodation, 119

Accommodation model, 123

Adaptation, and symbolic representations, 2

Agency: development of, 103–4; and social system, tie between, 91–92; stratification model of, 88, 100, 104; vs. structure, 85

Ants, signs of social networks, 13–15

Arbitrariness continuum: defined, 1–2; humans' place on, 21; for semiotic behavior, 2, 22n.1

Aristotle, and difference-identity dispute, 25–26, 29–30

Assimilation, 119

Autonomy: in modernity theory, 98; in structuration theory, 91, 92

Avian song learning, 19

Baboons, signs of kinship, 9–10

Bank swallows, signs of kinship, 9

Bateson, G., epistemology of form theory, 77–79

Behavioral perspective on relationships: implications, 114–16; research practices, 111–14

"Between": in Bateson's writings, 77; in Buber's writings, 31–38, 43; in relational communication perspective, 71, 77

Birds, signs of culture, 19

Bonobos: signs of culture, 20; signs of sexual relationships, 11–12

Bottle-nosed dolphins, signs of kinship, 8

Buber, M., relational perspectives of, 31–38

Burgess, E.W., approach to relationship, 73

Chapple, E.D., approach to relationship, 75

Chicago School, 73

Chimpanzees: semblamatic relationships, 16; signs of culture, 19–20;
  signs of family relationships,
  10–11; tool use and manufacture,
  15–16
Circumstances, sophistic view of, 28
Clapping, cultural transmission of, 20
Closed-open dialectic, 144, 145–47
Close friends: dialectical tensions
  between, 156, 167; making meanings with, 149–69
Codependency, pure relationships vs.,
  100
Coding procedures, 113
Cognitive perspective on relationships: implications, 120; research
  practices, 116–20
Cognitive structures: characterization
  of, 116; prototypes as, 116–17;
  relationship schemata as, 117–19
Coherence, in relationship schemata,
  119
Commitment: in communication
  consequentiality theory, 61–62;
  prototype attribute studies, 116–17;
  relational implications of, 63–65,
  102–3, 104
Common fate effects, 127
Common method variance, 109–10
Communication: conceptual models
  in, 84–85; consequentiality of (see
  Consequentiality of communication); message meaning as unit of
  analysis in, 49–50; ontological
  focus in, 23–25; products of,
  50–54; relational approaches to
  (see Relational communication
  perspective); research questions in,
  43–44; social approach to (see
  Social communication theory); in
  structuration theory, 87–88; system
  thinking in, 76, 77–78. See also
  specific type of communication
  perspective

Comparative perspective on relation-
  ships, 1–22; assumptions of, 6; on
  semblamatic relationships, 15–18;
  on signs of culture, 18–20; on signs
  of relationship, 6–15; on symbolicity, 21; system for, 3–6, 22n.3
Compelled-volunteered dialectic, 144,
  145–47
Competition, sophistic view of, 28
Complementarity, 78
Compositional effects, 127
Conceptual symbols, 5
Conflict: and relationship schemata,
  120; research on, 113
Confluent love, 97
Confluent relationships, 97, 98
Consequentiality of communication,
  48, 51, 60–63; and relationship
  continuity, 63–65; strong view of,
  51–52, 61–62; weak view of, 51,
  61
The Constitution of Society (Giddens),
  91–94
Contextual model of marital interac-
  tion, interdependence in, 122
Continuity of relationships, 48, 57–58,
  63–65, 74
Contradictions: in dialectical relationships, 140–41; in pure relationships, 99; in social systems, 90
Control: conversational patterns of,
  113; in relational communication
  model, 80
Conventional-indigenous dialectic,
  147, 148
Conversation. See Dialogue
Cultural institutions, as products of
  communication process, 51
Cultural-level relationship schemata,
  114
Culture: defined, 18; and language,
  18, 21; role of teaching and learning, 18–19; signs of, 18–20; and

symbols, 17–18, 21. *See also* Social-cultural repertoire

Dance metaphor, in relational communication perspective, 70, 82
Deception: and long-term relationships, 17; in nonhuman primates, 16–17; and symbols, 17; typology of, 22n.4
Democracy: dialogic, 98; in modernity theory, 98
Dependent-independent dialectic, 156, 167
Dialectic: acceptance-judgment, 167; closed-open, 144, 145–47; compelled-volunteered, 144, 145–47; conventional-indigenous, 147, 148; dependent-independent, 156, 167; dominant-submissive, 144, 145–47; Plato's view of, 29
Dialectical-dialogic theorizing, vs. modernity theory, 101–2
Dialectical relationships: contradiction and process in, 140–41; dimensions of, 138, 140, 144–47
Dialectical stasis, 146, 148
Dialectical tensions: between close friends, 156, 167; in communication consequentiality theory, 48; structural analysis of, 140–41, 144
Dialectics of relational transition, 138, 140–45
Dialects, cultural transmission of, 19
Dialogic democracy, 98
Dialogic perspective on relationships: dialectical and, 101–2; on ontologic priority of the "between," 31–32; in Volosinov's writings, 38, 41, 45n.5
Dialogue: between close friends, excerpts of, 151–65; control patterns in, 113; and laughter, 152, 166; musicality of, 163, 168; as reality of language, 39–42; in structuration theory, 92; world-defining

function of, 33–38. *See also* Discourse; Speech
Difference, interrelatedness of, 70, 77–78
Difference-identity dispute, 25–26, 29–31
Discourse: basic traits of, 134; dialectical-narrative-structural analysis of, 138, 140–45; and human action, analogy between, 133–36; relationships in, 136–40; spoken vs. written, 135–36. *See also* Dialogue; Speech
Disembedding of social systems, 95
Dissatisfaction in relationships, response strategies, 123
Dissoi logoi construct, 27–29
Distance regulation, in relational communication model, 80
Divorce, relational continuity after, 74
Documentary writing, relationship stories in, 138–40
Dolphins, signs of kinship, 8–9
Dominant-submissive dialectic, 144, 145–47
Double description, 78. *See also* Interrelatedness of difference
Duality: of interconnecting principle, 77–78; of message meaning, 78; of structuration theory, 87, 88
Duration of relationships, 48, 57–58, 63–65, 74
Dyadic interdependence, 126

Elephants, signs of family relationships, 10, 11
Epistemology of form, 77–79; complementarity in, 78; fusion of patterns in, 79; symmetry in, 78–79; system thinking in, 77–78; temporal aspects, 70–71, 72, 74
Error variance, 110, 128
Exclusivity, of social vs. interactional relationships, 59

Experience, sequestration of, 96

Face-to-face interactions: rules for, 55–57; semantic and syntactic features of, 57–60; vs. social relationships, 56–57
Family relationships, signs of, 10–11
Family therapy perspective, influence on communication research, 76
Females: acclimation to pure relationships, 98–99; sexual selection by, 13
Fixated relationships, 100
Forms of sociation, 73–74
Friends: dialectical tensions between, 156, 167; making meanings with, 149–69

Gender differences, in acclimation to pure relationships, 98–99
General relationship schemata, 117–18, 119
Giddens, A.: approach to relationship, 83–106; individual-society problematic, 84–86. *See also* Modernity theory; Structuration theory
Goffman, E., approach to relationship, 73
Gorillas, signs of family relationships, 11
Gottman, J.M., approach to relationship, 70–71
Grammar, universal, 40
Greeting behavior, rules for, 55

Hinde, R.A., approach to relationship, 74–75, 121
Holistic thinking. *See* System perspective on relationships
Human action, traits of discourse in, 133–36
Human relationships: as measure of all things, 27, 28; semblamatic, 16; separation between sex and repro-

duction in, 12; sexual dimorphism in, 13; signs of kinship in, 10; symbolicity in, 21; uniqueness of, 2–3, 21

I and Thou (Buber), 32–34
Iconic semblances, 4–5, 17
Identity: consequential view of, 51–52; in modernity theory, 95–96
Identity-difference dispute, 25–26, 29–30
Identity equations, 30–31
Independent-dependent dialectic, 156, 167
Indigenous-conventional dialectic, 147, 148
Individualistic subjectivism, vs. relational view of language, 39–40
Individual-society model, 84–86
Influence attempts, conversational vs. relational, 56
Initiation, in structuration theory, 91
Insects: signs of culture, 19; signs of social networks, 13–15
Institutional differentiation of society, 87–88
Institutional reflexivity, 95
Institutions: as products of communication process, 51; spatial-temporal spread of, 89–90
Integrity, in modernity theory, 96
Interaction, constitutive nature of, 105
Interactional episodes. *See* Face-to-face interactions
Interaction order: behavioral rules of, 54–57; in structuration theory, 87
Interaction patterns: analogy to jazz music, 70–71; behavioral research on, 114–16; complementarity in, 78; fusion of, 79; interdependence in, 121–22; in relational communication perspective, 77–79, 82; relationship categories based on, 114–16; in structuration theory,

90–94; symmetry in, 78–79; vs. individual contributions, 71, 125

Interactive dimensions of relationships, 74

Interactive praxis, in structuration theory, 87–88, 101, 105, 106n.2

Interconnecting principle, in relational communication perspective, 70–71, 77–78

Interdependence: between-dyad, 126; levels of, 121–22; reciprocal, 127; in relational communication perspective, 70–71; in social relations model, 125–27; unilateral, 127; within-dyad, 126. *See also* System perspective on relationships

Interpersonal communication: history of research, 76; relational focus, vii. *See also specific type of communication perspective*

Interrelatedness of difference, 70–71, 77–78

Interruptability, of social vs. interactional relationships, 58

Intimacy: in modernity theory, 97–98; in relational communication model, 81

Japanese macaques, signs of culture, 20

Jazz music metaphor, in relational communication perspective, 70–71

Judgment-acceptance dialectic, 167

Kelley, H., approach to relationship, 75

Kendon, A., approach to relationship, 75

Kinship relationships, signs of, 7–10

Knowledgeability, in structuration theory, 88, 93, 95

Language: comparative perspective on, 5, 21; constitutive view of, 33–38; and culture, 18, 21; identity equations in, 30–31; pidgin, 22n.5; relationality of, 25, 33–42, 43; Volosinov's philosophy of, 38–42; vs. speech communication, 42

Language-speech, 42

Laughter, and dialogue, 152, 166

Let Us Now Praise Famous Men, 139–40, 141–45

Linguistics, weaknesses of, 41

Logos, in sophistic thinking, 27

Love: confluent, 97; prototype attribute studies, 116–17

Macro-micro problem, 85–86, 90, 105–6

Males, acclimation to pure relationships, 98–99

Mammals, semblamatic relationships, 16

Marriage: interdependence in, 122; as pure relationship, 97; and relationship-specific schemata, 118

Marxism and the Philosophy of Language (Volosinov), 38–42, 45n.5

McCall, G., approach to relationship, 73

Meaning: identities and relationships as categories of, 51–52; persons as organized clusters of, 50; as unit of analysis, 49–50

Meaning-making processes of relationship, 149–69; excerpts from dialogue between friends, 151–65; reflections on meanings made, 165–69

Measures of association, common method variance in, 109–10

Message behaviors, in relational communication perspective, 82

Message meaning: duality of, 78; as unit of analysis, 49–50

Metatheory, Giddens'. *See*
Structuration theory
Modernity theory: individual-society
model in, 84–85; institutional
dimensions of, 94–96; in interpersonal realm, 96–103; and lifestyle
politics, 96; nature of, 86, 94–96;
and self-identity, 95–96; theoretical
promise of, 100–101; and theory of
structuration, 86, 87–90; and trust,
95; vs. dialectical-dialogic theorizing, 101–2
Monologic utterance, as abstraction,
41
Mother-child relationships: behavioral
research on, 115; comparative
perspective on, 7–8; Giddens's
treatment of, 103
Music: as communication metaphor,
70–71; in dialogue, 163, 168
Mutual dependency. *See*
Interdependence

Narrative-dialectical-structural analy-
sis of relationships, 138, 140–45
Networks: signs of, 13–15; size and
complexity of, 86, 105–6
Norms, in structuration theory, 87–88
"Now," Aristotle's view of, 29–30

Objectivism: abstract, 40; vs. rela-
tivism, 26
Observational data, 113–14
Observer judgment procedures, 113,
114
On-behalfness, 59
On-callness, 58
Ontology of potentials, 86, 106n.1
Open-closed dialectic, 144, 145–47
Opportunity, sophistic view of, 28

Parallel pattern of patterns, 79
Parent-child relationships: behavioral
research on, 115; comparative

perspective on, 7–8; Giddens's
treatment of, 103
Park, R.E., approach to relationship,
73
Parmenidean equations, 30
Participant judgment procedures, 113
Partner effects, 128
Patterns of interaction. *See* Interaction
patterns
Persons: as products of communica-
tion, 50; and social-cultural reper-
toire, 50–51
Persuasion, in sophistic thinking, 27
Physical separations: and dependent-
independent dialectic, 156, 167;
relationship construction and, 56
Pidgin languages, 22n.5
Plato, and difference-identity dispute,
25–26, 29
Play behavior, 16
Playfulness, sophistic view of, 28
Plurivocity, 28, 29–30, 43
Positioning, in structuration theory,
93–94
Postmodernism: in Buber's philoso-
phy, 33; modernity theory vs., 94
Power, in structuration theory, 87–88
Pragmatic perspective. *See* Relational
communication perspective
*The Pragmatics of Human
Communication*, 76
Praxicality, 43
Praxis: described, 87; in structuration
theory, 87–88, 101, 106n.2
Primates: semblamatic relationships,
16–17; signs of kinship, 9–10
Problem-solving, 113
Process, in dialectical relationships,
140–41
Proper symbols, 5
Protagoras, 27, 28, 32
Prototype attribute studies, 116–17
Pure relationships: confluent love in,
97; contradictions in, 99; gender

differences in, 98–99; in modern era, 97–101; undersociality of theory, 102–3, 106; vs. codependency, 100; vs. romantic ideal, 97–98; vs. sexual addiction, 100

Rating procedures, 113

Rationalization, in structuration theory, 88

Reality: Buber's primal category of, 33–34, 37–38; in difference-identity dispute, 26, 29–31; of language, dialogue as, 39–42; nature of, 22n.2; from relational communication perspective, 24–25, 27, 31; symbols in creation of, 17–18

Reciprocal effects, in social relations model, 128–29

Reciprocity, social vs. system, 89

Reflexion, vs. turning toward, 37

Reflexive monitoring, 88, 90, 91

Reflexivity, institutional, 95

Relation, origin of term, viii

Relational communication perspective, 23–46; in Buber's "between," 31–38; and control, 80; dance metaphor in, 70, 82; definition of relationship, 79; developmental backdrop, 76; in interpersonal communication research, vii–viii; intimacy in, 80–81; meaning of relationship, 77–79; model of relationship, 79–81; recent criticisms of, 26–27; research techniques, 113; social construction of reality metaphor in, 24–25; in sophistic thinking, 25–31; and trust, 80; in Volosinov's philosophy of language, 38–42

Relational transition, dialectics of, 138, 140–45

Relationship categories, background understandings and rules of, 54–57

Relationship effects, in social relations model, 128–29

Relationship research: analytical framework for (see Social relations model); behavioral perspective, 111–16; cognitive perspective, 116–20; individual-level data in, 109–10; methodological issues in, 107–11; system perspective, 120–25

Relationship(s): close vs. distant, 75; community criteria for, 53; comparative perspective on, 1–22; consequential view of, 48, 51–52, 61–63; definitions of, viii–ix, 52, 72–76, 79; dialectical dimensions of, 138, 144–47; dimensions of, xii, 74–75, 80–81; dissatisfaction in, 123; historical use of term, viii–ix; interpersonal emphasis on, vii; in modernity theory, 96–103; multiparticipant organization of, 53–54; ontological meaning of, 23–24; as product of community and communication, 52–54; semantic and syntactic features of, 57–60; signs of, 6–15 (see also Semiotic distinctions); social communication view of, 47, 52–60; social realist view of, 48; social rules for, 55–57; structural analysis of, 140, 141–45; underdeveloped conceptual treatment of, ix, 76, 102–3, 106; vs. face-to-face interactions, 56–57

Relationship schemata, 117–19

Relationship stories, 136–40

Relativism, vs. objectivism, 26

Repertoire. See Social-cultural repertoire

"Replies to My Critics" (Buber), 34–35

Research techniques: behavioral, 111–14; cognitive, 116–20; holistic, 122–24

Reticular context, in macro-micro problem, 86, 105–6

Rhetoric: philosopher's view of, 29–30; sophistic view of, 28–29

Ricoeur, P., analogy between discourse and human action, 133–36

Ritualization, 4, 15

Ritual semblances, 4, 15–16

Romantic ideal, 97–98

Routines, in structuration theory, 92

Sarasota dolphins, signs of kinship, 8–9

Satisfaction in relationships, response strategies, 123

Schemata, relationship, 117–19

Self-actualization, 95–96

Self-report data, 111–12

Semblances, 4–5, 15–18; iconic, 4–5, 17; ritual, 4, 15–16

Semiotic distinctions: continuum of arbitrariness for, 2, 21, 22n.1; cultural, 18–20; between family members, 10–11; genetically-derived, 6, 15; between kin, 7–10; semblamatic, 4–5, 15–18; sexual, 11–13; within social networks, 13–15; symbolic, 5; symptomatic, 4; types of, 4–6

Semiotic order, behavioral rules of, 54–57

Separations: and dependent-independent dialectic, 156, 167; relationship construction and, 56

Sequestration of experience, 96

Sexual addiction, pure relationships vs., 100

Sexual dimorphism, 13

Sexual relationships, signs of, 11–13

Sexual selection, 12–13

Signs of relationship. See Semiotic distinctions

Simmel, G., approach to relationship, 73–74

Simulacrum, in dialectical-narrative-structural discourse analysis, 138, 144

Snake metaphor, 7

Social communication theory, 47–67; consequentiality in (see Consequentiality of communication); focus of, 47; principles of, 49–52; relationships in, 47–48, 52–60, 63–65

Social construction of reality metaphor, in relational perspectives, 24–25

Social-cultural repertoire: in communication consequentiality theory, 61–62; and personhood, 50–51; and relationships, 48, 63. See also Culture

Social differentiation, in macro-micro problem, 86

Social institutions, as products of communication process, 51

Social integration, 89

Social networks: signs of, 13–15; size and complexity of, 86, 105–6

Social ontology, 31–32

Social order: behavioral rules of, 54–57; in structuration theory, 87

Social realist view of relationships, 48

Social relationships: comparative perspective on, 1–22, 22n.3; in development of agency, 103–4; rules for, 55–57; semantic and syntactic features of, 57–60; in social communication theory, 47; in structuration theory, 93; under-developed conceptual treatment of, ix, 76, 102–3, 106; vs. face-to-face interactions, 56–57

Social relations model: components of, 127–29; implications of, 130–31; limitations of, 129–30; methodological issues addressed by, 107–11; nature of interdependence in, 125–27

Social systems: abstract features, 89–90; agency and, tie between, 91–92; disembedding of, 95

Sociation, forms of, 73–74

Society: institutional differentiation of, 87–88; spatial-temporal spread of, 89–90

Sociology: classic problems in, 85–86; individual-society model in, 84–85

Sophistic thinking: *dissoi logoi* in, 27–29; philosophers' response to, 27, 28, 29–30; relational perspectives in, 25–31

Spatiotemporal dimension. *See* Time-space dimension

Speech: constitutive view of, 33–38; living, 40; turning toward vs. reflexion in, 37; vs. language, 42; world-building vs. world-shattering, 37. *See also* Dialogue; Discourse

Stages, in social vs. interactional relationships, 59–60

Stories, and relationships, 136–40

Stratification model of agency, 88, 104

Structural-narrative-dialectical analysis of relationships, 138, 140–45

Structuration theory, 85, 86, 106n.1; agency in (*See* Agency); dimensions of, 87–88, 105; duality of, 87, 88; interaction and relationships in, 90–94; interactive praxis in, 87–88, 101, 105, 106n.2; proposed changes in, 104–6; unanswered questions in, 94

Subjective dimensions of relationships, 74–75

Subjectivism, individualistic, 39–40

Subject-object analysis: limitations of, 33; in social construction of reality metaphor, 24

Submissive-dominant dialectic, 144, 145–47

Symbols, 5; and adaptation, 2; characteristics of species using, 6; comparative perspective on use of, 21; conceptual, 5; in creation of reality, 17–18; and deception, 17; proper, 5; syntactic, 5

Symmetry, in epistemology of form, 78–79

Symptomatic relationships, 4

Syntactic symbols, 5

Systemic-functional complexity, in macro-micro problem, 86, 106

System integration, 89

System perspective on relationships, 120–25; in communication discipline, 76, 77–78; in epistemology of form, 77–78; implications, 124–25; interdependence in, 121–22; research practices, 122–24. *See also* Interdependence

Tactile communication, in elephants, 10

Target effects, 128

Tensionality: in Buber's philosophy, 33, 37, 43; between close friends, 156, 167; in communication consequentiality theory, 48; sophistic view of, 28–29; structural analysis of, 140–41, 144

Threat displays, 16

Time-space dimension: changes in, relational implications of, 102; in macro-micro problem, 86; in modernity theory, 94–95; in relational communication perspective, 70–71, 72, 74; in structuration theory, 88–90, 93–94

Tool use and manufacture: in chimpanzees, 15–16; cultural transmission of, 19–20

The Transformation of Intimacy
(Giddens), 96–97
Translinguistic perspective on relationships, 38, 41, 45n.5
Trust: in modernity theory, 95; in relational communication model, 80; in structuration theory, 91
Two-headed snake metaphor, 7

Utterances, dialogic vs. monologic, 41–42

Variance: error, 110, 128; partitioning of, 128

Vervet monkeys, signs of kinship, 9
Vocalizations, in elephants, 10
Voles, signs of sexual relationships, 12
Volosinov, V.N.: dispute over authorship, 45n.5; relational perspectives of, 38–42
Volunteered-compelled dialectic, 144, 145–47

Weber, M., approach to relationship, 72–73
Written discourse, traits of, 135–36

About the Contributors

Richard L. Conville is Professor of speech communication at the University of Southern Mississippi where he teaches interpersonal communication and qualitative methods. His work has appeared in such journals as the *Journal of Social and Personal Relationships* and *Communication Monographs*. Books include *Relational Transitions* and *Uses of "Structure" in Communication Studies*.

Jo Liska holds a research appointment in the department of anthropology at the University of Colorado, Denver. Her research interests include primate communication systems and media representations of wildlife and their effects on public opinion. Her research has appeared in such journals as *Animal Behavior* and *Human Evolution*. She recently co-authored *An Ecological Perspective on Human Communication Theory*.

Robert D. McPhee is Associate Professor and Chair of the department of communication at the University of Wisconsin–Milwaukee. His focal interests include organizational communication, and communication and social theory.

Sandra Metts is Professor of communication at Illinois State University where she teaches interpersonal communication and language. Her research focuses on the management of problematic communication episodes and has appeared in such journals as *Communication Monographs* and the *Journal of Social and Personal Relationships*. Co-authored books include *Self-disclosure* and *Facework*.

William K. Rawlins is Professor and Director of Graduate Studies in the department of communication at Purdue University, where he teaches courses in interpersonal and relational communication, communication theory, and qualitative-interpretive research methods. He is the author of *Friendship Matters: Communication, Dialectics, and the Life Course*, and many of his journal articles have dealt with the challenges and dialectical tensions of communicating in friendships.

L. Edna Rogers is Professor of communication at the University of Utah. Her research interests focus on the study of interpersonal relationships, family communication systems, and social interaction analysis.

Stuart J. Sigman is Associate Professor of communication at the State University of New York, Albany. Previous publications focus on social communication theory, qualitative research, and problems of micro-macro levels of analysis. He is the author of *A Perspective on Social Communication*, editor of *The Consequentiality of Communication*, and editor of the Erlbaum series, *Everyday Communication: Case Studies of Behavior in Context*.

John Stewart is Professor of speech communication at the University of Washington. He teaches interpersonal communication and philosophy of communication to undergraduates and graduates. Recent publications include *Language as Articulate Contact: Toward a Post-Semiotic Philosophy of Communication* and "Social Theory and Dialogue" in *Communication: Views from the Helm for the Twenty-First Century*.

ISBN 0-275-95211-8

9 780275 952112

HARDCOVER BAR CODE